Artificial Intelligence and Neuroenhancement in Sport

This book is the first to take a close look at artificial intelligence and neuroenhancement in the context of sport and at the potential of these new technologies to act as enablers of neurodoping. It considers the interesting possibilities that these technologies raise for enhancing athletic performance and explores their implications for the ethics, integrity and governance of sport.

Featuring the work of leading researchers in sports ethics, bioethics, digital ethics and biotechnology, the book draws on multidisciplinary perspectives from philosophy, education, biology, neuroscience and more to shine light on a technological development that is not yet listed as a prohibited method in the WADA anti-doping code. Exploring fascinating topics including neurostimulation, brainchips, cyborgization and the importance of establishing sound ethical regulations, the book takes a positive ethical view, seeing the lack of previous work in this area as an opportunity to embed ethics in sports technology and promote AI for good in sport.

This book is important reading for any advanced student, researcher, administrator or policy-maker with an interest in the ethics of sport, sport technology, sport governance or artificial intelligence.

Alberto Carrio is Senior Lecturer, Director of Research Programs at the Barcelona School of Management of the Pompeu Fabra University, Spain. Alberto is also Associate Professor of Legal Philosophy at the Law Department of Pompeu Fabra University. He is the lead researcher of two research programs on the ethics of artificial intelligence in sport funded by the Fundacion BBVA and the Olympic Studies Center, respectively, and he is currently Deputy Director of *Fair Play, Journal of Philosophy, Ethics and Sports Law*.

Ethics and Sport

Series editors
Mike McNamee, *University of Wales Swansea*
Jim Parry, *Charles University, Prague, Czech Republic*

The *Ethics and Sport* series aims to encourage critical reflection on the practice of sport, and to stimulate professional evaluation and development. Each volume explores new work relating to philosophical ethics and the social and cultural study of ethical issues. Each is different in scope, appeal, focus and treatment but a balance is sought between local and international focus, perennial and contemporary issues, level of audience, teaching and research application, and variety of practical concerns.

Titles in the series:

Coaching, Sport and the Law
A Duty of Care
Neil Partington

The Philosophy of Mixed Martial Arts
Squaring the Octagon
Edited by Jason Holt and Marc Ramsay

Philosophy, Sport and the Pandemic
Edited by Jeffrey P. Fry and Andrew Edgar

Return of the Grasshopper
Games, Leisure and the Good Life in the Third Millennium
Bernard Suits, edited by Christopher C. Yorke and Francisco Javier López Frías

Political Expression in Sport
Transnational Challenges, Moral Defences
Cem Abanazir

Vicarious Liability in the Sports Industry
James Brown

Artificial Intelligence and Neuroenhancement in Sport
Edited by Alberto Carrio

For more information about this series, please visit: https://www.routledge.com/Ethics-and-Sport/book-series/EANDS

Artificial Intelligence and Neuroenhancement in Sport

Edited by Alberto Carrio

Routledge
Taylor & Francis Group
LONDON AND NEW YORK

First published 2026
by Routledge
4 Park Square, Milton Park, Abingdon, Oxon OX14 4RN

and by Routledge
605 Third Avenue, New York, NY 10158

Routledge is an imprint of the Taylor & Francis Group, an informa business

British Library Cataloguing-in-Publication Data
A catalogue record for this book is available from the British Library

ISBN: 9781032858814 (hbk)
ISBN: 9781032858821 (pbk)
ISBN: 9781003520290 (ebk)

DOI: 10.4324/9781003520290

Typeset in Optima
by Deanta Global Publishing Services, Chennai, India

Contents

Introduction

Alberto Carrio

This book is about sport and technology – specifically, the impact of new AI-driven neurotechnologies on sport. However, sport can be understood in several ways, and depending on how it is defined, the impact of technology has different implications too. That is why this book provides a multidisciplinary reflection on the tidal relationship between sport and technology, and how the latter has shaped the former. Consider, for example, the importance of technology in the design of sports equipment (balls, pitches, clothes and so on) and how that has contributed to the improvement of performance and endurance and to the setting of new records, but also to making sport more inclusive. All of this could be overtaken in the coming years by the introduction of new AI-driven technologies, which are already making rapid inroads into sport.

But sport is not only about displaying skills and competition. Since ancient times sport has been an important social and cultural tool, as is currently stated at the forefront of the European Sports Charter.[1] Many years ago, Aristotle had already highlighted the values of sport through the use of sporting contests as an example of virtue in practice (Aristotle, 1999). Certainly, sports contests have both autotelic and instrumental values symbolising discipline, respect for the rules and moral excellence or *areté* (Reid, 2019; Mareš, 2021). Displaying *areté* in public and private life is the ideal criterion of the good citizen (Aristotle, 1999). It is not by chance that these values have transcended time and borders to become the hallmark of sport. In fact, both the internal values and the instrumentality of sport for achieving the highest goals for society around the world are at the basis of the understanding of Olympism as a philosophy of life, as stated by Principle I of the Olympic Charter.[2]

Nowadays sport is also a growing industry. In the last few decades, the increasing professionalisation of leagues, the globalisation of fanbases and the monetisation of media rights have transformed sport into a vast industry, representing around 2.12% of the European Union Gross Domestic Product (EU, 2018). Macro sports events such as the Olympic Games and the World

DOI: 10.4324/9781003520290-1

Cup are becoming more and more popular and attracting the interest of new partners. Having a voice in this industry is sometimes beyond economic benefits as is currently happening with the rising investments of Gulf States in sports. The growing economic and political impact of professional sport has increased competition among athletes and organisations, creating an urgent need for innovative tools to optimise performance, endurance and strategy. In some cases, even to the point of challenging established organisations and policies, such as those of the World Anti-Doping Agency, as is currently taking place with the so-called Enhanced Games,[3] whose main declared aim is to reinvent sport and push athletes to their limits with the help of science and technology.

There is no doubt that the integration of science and technology into sport has played a key role in meeting the demands of a growing industry. From the invention of standardised equipment to the development of sophisticated tracking systems, the tidal relationship between sport and technology is almost symbiotic. In this sense, technology has always raised the standards of athletic performance, while sport provides a dynamic testing ground for technological advances. As I have argued elsewhere (Carrio, 2024), sport has always been a testing ground for technology, with athletes in most cases serving as guinea pigs for technological and scientific development. Current modern innovations such as wearable devices, advanced analytics and artificial intelligence have redefined how athletes train, compete and recover. By providing actionable insights and facilitating real-time adjustments, these tools are bridging the gap between raw human potential and optimal performance. In addition, the use of AI has transformed coaching methods, enabled referees to make more accurate decisions and allowed athletes to monitor their physical and mental states with unprecedented accuracy. This synergy underscores a shared path: technology enhances the essence of sport, while sport drives the practical application of cutting-edge technologies. At the forefront of these technological and scientific advances is the revolutionary field of AI-driven neurotechnologies, which are leading to a new era in sport. The combination of artificial intelligence and neuroscience is pushing the boundaries of human performance. Brain-computer interfaces, for example, allow athletes to improve their concentration and reaction times by interacting directly with neural signals. Neurofeedback systems help manage stress and mental fatigue, enabling athletes to maintain peak cognitive states during high-pressure scenarios. Real-time cognitive monitoring can track decision-making efficiency, resilience and even emotional states, offering personalised strategies to improve both mental and physical performance.

Beyond enhancing individual skills, AI-driven neurotechnologies are introducing new ways of playing and understanding sports, where mental acuity and neural adaptability are as critical as physical strength, if they can be distinguished at all. However, these advances are not without challenges. They raise important questions for the governance of sport, particularly in areas such as anti-doping policy, ethical use and equity of access. How should governing bodies define the boundaries between fair competition and technological enhancement? Should these boundaries be erased altogether, as proponents of the Enhanced Games advocate? Would athletes then become mere instruments at the service of technological enhancements, to be replaced like spare parts? More importantly, does this call into question the essential nature of sport as a human activity? It seems that the governance of sport is at a critical juncture. At this crucial moment, sports governing bodies cannot shirk their responsibilities. New safeguards must be put in place to ensure the autonomy and well-being of athletes and the safe and ethical use of these tools. Ultimately, the question is whether we want to preserve the human essence of sport, while allowing it to benefit from technological and scientific advances in an era of machine augmentation, or whether we want to completely transform the nature of sport and embark on a new era.

This book examines the profound impact of AI-driven neurotechnologies on the present and future of sport. By exploring their applications, potential benefits and ethical dilemmas from a multidisciplinary approach, the book seeks to illuminate how these innovations are not only transforming athletic performance but also reshaping the governance of sport and even the cultural, ethical and humanistic foundations of sport itself.

The book is divided into three parts, each of which navigates through different chapters and several aspects of AI-driven neurotechnologies in sport, such as the potential and impact of neuroenhancement, the foreseeable future of sport in which the cyborgisation of athletes is a reality and the importance of education and preserving the values of sport in the age of changing game technologies.

The first part is divided into four chapters covering different aspects of neurostimulation technologies in sport, such as their potential to enhance performance, their impact on the concepts of fairness and equality in sport and their compatibility with the internal values and essential human nature of sport itself.

In Chapter 1, Oskar MacGregor, Senior Lecturer in Informatics at the University of Skövde, focuses on the enhancement potential of different neurotechnologies. MacGregor argues that because their potential is easily exaggerated by those unfamiliar with the inherent limitations and constraints of the technologies, it is important to present these in order to confine the ethical debate to what is currently (or conceivably) feasible. In his 'primer' chapter on the most commonly used neurotechnologies, MacGregor provides a brief overview not only of their respective strengths and weaknesses but also of their potential uses for athletic performance enhancement. He argues that this knowledge limits (without thereby determining) the ensuing ethical debate, but also notes that knowledge of the technologies' nature provides *prima facie* reasons to think they are less ethically problematic than typically acknowledged – more *neuro-training* than *neuro-doping*.

Chapter 2 is authored by Jonathan Pugh, from the Uehiro Centre for Practical Ethics, Oxford University. Pugh takes transcranial direct current stimulation (tDCS) as a case study of a neurostimulation technique that is already being employed as a performance-enhancing intervention by elite athletes. Pugh provides an updated overview of the empirical evidence of the potential performance-enhancing effects of tDCS in sport, noting that, whilst some of this evidence is promising, there remains substantial disagreement about tDCS's potential to enhance athletic performance. Moreover, he notes that even assuming that it can enhance athletic performance, there is little consensus about the mechanism of action via which tDCS evinces such effects. With that in mind, Pugh considers two key arguments that have been raised in the neuroethical debate around neuro-doping. The first, which he terms 'the argument from effort', claims that tDCS undermines the possibility of praiseworthy sporting achievements because it significantly diminishes the need for hard work in sporting performance. Pugh counters this argument in two ways – first, he raises doubts about the claim that hard work is necessary for the possibility of praiseworthy sporting achievement. Second, he also explains that it remains unclear whether tDCS would in fact significantly diminish the need for hard work in sporting performance. The second argument that Pugh considers is what he terms 'the argument from fairness'. Although there are many permutations of fairness-based arguments against the use of performance-enhancing interventions, Pugh focuses on the idea that neuro-doping might create inequality in opportunities to win. Here, he draws on Petersen and Lippert-Rasmussen's previous sceptical treatment of this argument with respect to neuro-doping, noting that strong interpretations of this argument would have highly revisionary implications for conventional forms of performance enhancement in sport, such as nutrition and training programs. In their work, Petersen and Lippert-Rasmussen suggest that sport is governed by a conventional approach to fairness rather than a principled philosophical understanding, and that the use of neuro-doping is less likely to be incompatible with the former. Whilst Pugh is sympathetic to this conventionalist understanding of fairness, he concludes his discussion by noting that our conventional understanding of fairness in sport is currently under some degree of revisionary pressure due to ongoing debates about the classification of certain athletes.

Chapter 3 is authored by Alberto Carrio, Senior Lecturer at the Barcelona School of Management and Associate Professor at the Law Department of Pompeu Fabra University. Carrio begins his chapter with a broad overview of neurostimulation in sport, from natural and chemical substances to modern AI-driven technologies. Carrio then examines the increasing use of high technology in sport in the light of WADA's current anti-doping policy and critically examines the rationale behind the WADA Code and Prohibited List. The author then considers the viability of AI-driven neurotechnologies in sport by presenting and discussing two arguments, one for and one against the consideration of AI-driven neurostimulation as a prohibited method under the rationale of the WADA Code. Carrio concludes by suggesting an exploratory way for WADA to monitor the enhancing effect and safe use of these devices in elite sport, focusing on the protection of athletes' rights and well-being.

Chapter 4 is authored by Sigmund Loland and Niko Vuorinen, Professor and PhD candidate, respectively, of the Institute for Sport and Social Sciences at the Norwegian University of Sport Sciences. The chapter addresses the limits of acceptability to enhance sports performance with artificial intelligence in the context of agency. AI systems can be seen as displacing aspects of agency from the athlete to the system. Typically, sports performance is seen as being about the natural talent and capabilities of the athlete. Natural talent also includes the performance-related decision-making processes, an integral part of agency. The use of an AI system interferes with the decision-making processes that are normally governed by the athlete, causing a tension: when should the performance be agentially attributable to the athlete? As AI systems come in many forms and advance rapidly, a need for a general evaluation framework is apparent. The framework should be able to remain useful not just with the current existing systems but also with potential future ones. The chapter provides such a framework, utilising a functionalist machinery to connect agency displacement with performance enhancement. A modified version of Donald Davidson's causal agency model is developed to provide a four-part classification to identify different types of agency displacement. Performance fundamentals, or sport-specific properties crucial for success, are introduced to provide a mapping from the AI system outputs to sporting performance enhancement. A contractualist theory of sport and the existence of the ethos of sport are assumed to establish the normative component for acceptability analysis. To provide an example of practical application for existing and potential AI technologies, the framework is tested against two EEG-based brain-computer interface technologies: a neurofeedback training system and a hypothetical closed-loop transcranial direct current stimulation system to reduce mental fatigue and increase concentration during sporting performance. The practical examples focus on épée fencing, where mental capabilities and tactical decision-making play a major role in a successful performance. The analysis demonstrates how the framework can guide decisions about AI adoption in competitive sports.

The second part of the book consists of three chapters that explore the present and future possibilities of brain-computer interfaces and neural implants in sport, welcoming an imminent future of increasing human-technology merging in sport, while not forgetting its risks.

In Chapter 5, Mirko Daniel Garasic, Assistant Professor in Moral Philosophy at the Department of Education Science, Roma Tre University, affirms that while the integration of technology in sport has always been a topic of intense debate, the emergence of neural implants that interface directly with the nervous system to enhance cognitive and physical abilities marks a significant shift with far-reaching consequences for the future of sport. In line with these considerations, Garasic's chapter explores the ethical dilemmas posed by brain chips and their potential to undermine the essence of sportsmanship. Specifically, Garasic wants us to look into the challenges that brain-computer interfaces, like Neuralink, could bring to the concept of doping in sport. To do so, the chapter begins with a brief overview of what brain chips are and their capabilities, before examining their implications in the context of sport. It then delves into the concepts of doping and the spirit of sport, emphasising the complications these performance enhancements present in maintaining fair competition. To deepen the analysis, Garasic brings Clark and Chalmers' Extended Mind Thesis into the discussion to question the boundaries of our technological identities. Finally, the chapter builds on recent literature to engage with the Right to Mental Integrity and how this recent development in neuroethical research should be understood in the context of sport, underscoring the pressing need for clear regulations governing the use of neural implants in such a domain.

Chapter 6 is co-authored by Francesca Minerva, Associate Professor of Moral Philosophy at the University of Milan, and Vittorio Grasso, MA student of Philosophical Sciences at the University of Padua. This chapter examines the ethical implications of the integration of brain-computer interfaces (BCI), computer-brain interfaces (CBI) and brain-brain interfaces (BBI) into athletic performance. The authors explore how these new and emerging technologies could be used in athletic training and competition. Such technologies have the potential to bolster key features of sports performance, such as team coordination, endurance, cognitive abilities and recovery by combining cognitive enhancement and real-time neural feedback. Athletes using BCI, CBI and BBI may acquire an unprecedented competitive edge. Thus, different ethical issues are considered, such as fairness, autonomy and privacy. Bodily autonomy and moral responsibility are especially relevant issues in a context where these technologies are used to alter decision-making processes. The potential loss of athlete autonomy due to external control over bodily movements poses the challenge of attributing moral responsibility for actions performed under such influence. Safety concerns, particularly related to privacy breaches or unwanted exposure, even to other team members, and long-term physical or psychological effects are also examined. The chapter highlights how these technologies could potentially alter the fundamental nature of sports, where athletes' moral responsibility and agency prove crucial. It is also argued that blending them with human-machine interaction could challenge traditional notions of self-proprioception and athletic independence.

Chapter 7 is also a co-authored work by Francesco Bianchini, Associate Professor of Logic and Philosophy of Science, Department of Philosophy and Communication Studies at the University of Bologna, and Silvia Camporesi, from the Centre for Biomedical Ethics and Law, Department of Public Health and Primary Care, KU Leuven University. In their chapter, the authors argue that regulatory bodies consistently prioritise the protection of the integrity of sport over the inclusion of athletes with disabilities, using containment strategies that impose restrictions on bodies that deviate from the accepted able-bodied norm. As a result, the abilities of athletes who use assistive technology are generally unchallenged unless their performance begins to approach the existing and necessarily contingent upper human limit, which is determined based on the performance of an athlete without assistive technology. Concerns about unfair advantage from assistive technologies are addressed by sports governing bodies by comparing the performance of athletes to existing able-bodied human capabilities. This approach, which they term a 'strategy of containment', reflects widespread ableist assumptions in sport. It is a tactic designed to exclude athletes who are perceived as challenging the dominant status of able-bodied competitors.

The integration of AI with assistive technologies could drive an evolution of sport beyond the binary categorisation of able-bodied events and para-events. To this end, the authors first discuss Cybathlon, which offers the possibility of experimenting with radically new functionalities of the body that go beyond simply restoring previous functions or augmenting existing ones. The authors also discuss brain-computer interfaces (BCI), which could in the near future lead to forms of compensation and standardisation based on a minimum set of standard characteristics required for a given discipline. In this sense, the authors argue that an approach to sport that integrates AI with assistive technologies could focus not only on the idea of 'levelling the playing field' using the able-bodied human norm as a standard, but rather on comparing athletic aspects and performance elements of AI-integrated assistive technologies using the 'cyborg' as a new benchmark for human performance. Ultimately, this could allow able-bodied athletes and those who require assistive technologies to compete together in a new category of human athletes for whom the technology can be read on multiple levels as assistive, optimising or enhancing.

The third and final part of the book consists of three chapters on new perspectives on the use of AI-driven neurostimulation in sport, from education to the problem of seeking perfection in sport, including a discussion on the pros and cons of using ethical guidelines to regulate the use of AI-driven neurotechnologies.

Chapter 8, co-authored by Barbora Baďurová and Daniela Kováčová, researchers at Matej Bel University, addresses the debate on the ethics of neuro-doping in a practical, educational dimension, as the authors approach the issue from the point of view of virtue ethics. As is well known to experts in the field, this type of doping is particularly difficult to detect, so the demand for fair detection and punishment is not entirely sufficient. The authors emphasise the ethical-educational dimension of the issue, suggesting that education on the ethical aspects of neuro-doping could strengthen individual responsibility and promote sound moral judgement. The moral evaluation of neuro-doping, as discussed throughout the book, is multidimensional. The diversity of sports and the different forms of neuro-doping contribute to a range of situations that need to be addressed and a variety of guidelines for numerous potential applications. The negative health effects may be more easily recognised as unethical, but the other effects may be more difficult to morally assess. In addition, the issue is evolving with ongoing discussions about the best solutions. This raises doubts as to whether simply teaching legal rules and regulations would be sufficient, and therefore, the promotion of virtues and critical thinking is desirable. Virtue ethics education in relation to neuro-doping ideally takes into account cognitive, emotional and motivational aspects. This approach not only considers outcomes and reasoning but also the emotional dimension of actions, since a truly virtuous individual acts for the right reasons and experiences the appropriate emotions. Actions that mimic virtuous behaviour on the basis of consequences alone are not truly virtuous if they lack the right intentions and emotions. By developing qualities such as courage, wisdom, justice and temperance, we can enhance moral and ethical integrity on a personal level, emphasising the authenticity of individual actions. Thus, the authors insist on the importance of neuro-doping ethics education based on virtues as one of the key tools for dealing with the complex ethical issues surrounding neuro-doping.

In Chapter 9, Thomas Søbirk Petersen, Professor of Ethics at Roskilde University, presents and critically discusses the pros and cons of using ethical guidelines when using AI to increase the detection rate of (neuro)doping fraud. A key advantage of focusing our attention on such guidelines is that we can be equipped with ammunition for the critical reasoning necessary for the moral evaluation of the use of AI. Consulting such guidelines and trying to assess the extent to which a particular use of AI conforms to them can make us stop, think and discuss whether that use is morally acceptable, morally unacceptable or morally obligatory. However, the main part of the chapter is devoted to a critical discussion of four different strategies that can be used to deal with an obvious challenge to the use of ethical guidelines. Namely, the problem that different values can be in conflict and therefore provide inconsistent guidance. The four strategies that Petersen presents and critically discusses are metaethical cognitivism, the ranking view, value monism, and the 'acceptance of conflict view'. Petersen criticises the first three strategies and argues that the last strategy is the least bad 'solution' to value conflicts.

Finally, in Chapter 10, Andrea Lavazza, senior research fellow at the Centro Universitario Internazionale, Arezzo, Italy, and Adjunct Professor of Neuroethics at the University of Milan and the University of Pavia, examines the profound ethical implications of emerging neurotechnologies in sport, focusing on the tension between human imperfection and the pursuit of perfection. Sport has long played a unique cultural role, celebrating both individual excellence and the unpredictability that makes competition compelling.

However, the relentless pursuit of excellence has opened up a new frontier: the integration of cutting-edge technology into sporting performance. Among the most intriguing and controversial developments is neuroenhancement, which involves interventions directly targeting the brain to optimise motor skills, endurance and concentration. This chapter explores the implications of such advances, focusing on technologies such as transcranial direct current stimulation (tDCS). This non-invasive tool alters brain activity to enable faster reaction times, greater precision and prolonged effort, and promises to revolutionise professional athletics.

To explore these dilemmas, Lavazza draws on speculative fiction, in particular Dave Eggers's *The Every*, which imagines a world of precision thanks to technologies such as 'Muscle Precision Optimisation' (MPO). This hypothetical neurotechnology perfects coordination, allowing athletes to achieve a near-flawless performance. Eggers's narrative serves as a thought experiment, exploring the implications of perfection in sport. While such enhancements could take performance to unprecedented levels, they risk undermining the essence of competition by removing the unpredictability and fallibility that make sport meaningful.

Lavazza argues that the imperfections of sport are essential to its cultural and ethical significance. These imperfections foster resilience, creativity and growth, while ensuring the integrity of competition. Neuroenhancement technologies, while appealing for their potential to optimise human capabilities, may ultimately clash with the spirit of sport, reducing it to a mere exhibition of mechanical precision. By embracing technologies such as MPO, sport risks losing its humanistic core: a shared experience of effort, vulnerability and triumph against the odds.

By reflecting on these issues through literature and philosophy, the chapter provides a critical framework for understanding the evolving relationship between technology and sport. Lavazza advocates a careful balance: embracing advances that enhance safety and opportunity while preserving the unpredictability and fallibility that define the essence of competition. Ultimately, this discussion highlights the need to protect the cultural and ethical values that make sport not only a spectacle of physical excellence but also a profound celebration of the human spirit.

This is an exciting journey into the transformation of sports through the use of advanced neurotechnologies, seen from different angles. This will allow the reader to reflect on the nature of sport, the importance of preserving its humanity and the profound changes taking place in the field of sport, opening up a new era with unpredictable consequences.

Notes

1 Art. 1 of the European Sport Charter, available at https://rm.coe.int/recommendation-cm-rec-2021-5-on-the-revision-of-the-european-sport-cha/1680a43914.

2 https://stillmed.olympics.com/media/Documents/International-Olympic-Committee/IOC-Publications/EN-Olympic-Charter.pdf. Retrieved, 23 December 2024.
3 The information about aims and means can be checked at: https://www.enhanced.com/.

References

Aristotle. (1999). *Nicomachean Ethics* (Terence Irwin, Trans.). Hackett.

Carrio Sampedro, A. (2024). Artificial intelligence in sport: A revolutionary technology that must be handled with care. *Movimento, 30,* e30054. https://doi.org/10.22456/1982-8918.143278

European Union (2018). *Study on the Economic Impact of Sport through Sport Satellite Accounts,* ISBN: 978-92-79-76925-2 doi: 10.2766/156532.

Mareš, L. (2021). The role of sport in a good life: Aristotle and suits. *Sport, Ethics and Philosophy, 16*(4), 544–562. https://doi.org/10.1080/17511321.2021.2020441

Reid, H. (2019). Athletic virtue and aesthetic values in Aristotle's ethics. *Journal of the Philosophy of Sport, 47*(1), 63–74. https://doi.org/10.1080/00948705.2019.1691923

Chapter 1

Science Fiction vs. Science Fact

A Primer on Neurotechnology-Assisted Athletic Performance Enhancement

Oskar MacGregor

In a perfectly ordinary sense, a lot of training is already *neurotraining*. Whether snatching a heavy weight, kicking a ball into the precise upper left corner of a goal, or performing a perfect dismount off the balance beam, repeatedly rehearsing a specific sequence of movements is essential for strengthening the relevant synaptic connections in the motor cortex. As the tagline of neural (Hebbian) plasticity has it: neurons that fire together, wire together (Löwel & Singer, 1992). In this manner, repetition of a desired sequence of movements will, over time, help solidify the sequence's performance, so that an athlete can hope to pull it off perfectly when it really counts.

Likewise, in a perfectly ordinary sense, a lot of doping is already *neurodoping*. Whether an athlete takes a central nervous stimulant (such as ephedrine) to increase endurance, an opioid (such as oxycodone) to minimize pain, or a beta-blocker to reduce tremors, they all work by directly impacting the function of the central nervous system in some manner. In addition, they are all already on the World Anti-Doping Agency's (WADA's) *Prohibited List* (WADA, 2024).

But I'm not interested here in these perfectly ordinary senses. Instead, when I speak of neurotraining and neurodoping, the prefix "neuro" is meant to signify something beyond the ordinary, namely, *neurotechnology-assisted* athletic performance enhancement. This is, I take it, what most readers have in mind when picking up this volume: the informed application of some sort of neuroscientific knowledge that feels more akin to science fiction than the mundane day-to-day with which we're already familiar; more like experts in lab coats doing complicated brainwave readings than regular old training and prescription painkillers.

And, as many of the other chapters in this volume clearly demonstrate, this air of science fiction can also give rise to various concerns in the sports context, everything from electrical stimulation of the brain offering an unfair competitive advantage to the potential development of cyborg athletes who are incapable of making mistakes (see also the various contributions to the *Neuroethics* 2021 special issue on "Neuro-doping and Ethics"). Of course, that a technology holds this sort of science-fiction appeal doesn't delegitimize

DOI: 10.4324/9781003520290-2

such attendant concerns, but it does entail a need for extra caution. There is a well-established tendency for neuroscience in particular to easily give rise to *neurohype*, where speculation about what is possible now – or what may become possible in the "very near future" – can tend to run a little wild (cf. Beyerstein, 1990; Lilienfeld et al., 2017; Weisberg et al., 2008).

To this end, my aim in this chapter is to try to improve the reader's understanding of neuroscience, by providing a brief but reasonably exhaustive overview of the sorts of functional neurotechnologies that already – or might conceivably – come into play in the sports context.[6] Distinguishing (legitimate) neurotraining from (illegitimate) neurodoping requires this sort of grounded understanding of the nature of the technologies, to ensure that any ensuing philosophical and ethical discussion is constrained by the concrete realities of the topic. Only in this manner can we avoid falling into the neurohype trap.

1.1 A Basic Neuroscience Primer

Neuroscience aficionados can today explore a veritable jungle of available neurotechnologies, each with its own complicated name and attendant applications. However, to fully appreciate their inherent possibilities and limitations, a brief introduction to neural physiology – how the human brain works – is required first.[1]

Essentially, the brain takes in, transmits, and processes information through a vast network of interconnected neurons. This information-relaying capacity is facilitated by two basic electrophysiological processes: *action potentials* and *membrane* (or *graded*) *potentials*. Action potentials occur when a neuron "fires", a binary, all-or-nothing occurrence that happens as the result of the neuron becoming sufficiently primed (depolarized) to initiate the action potential, which is then propagated away from the neuron's cell body down its *axon* to *synapses* connecting it with other neurons.

Membrane potentials, on the other hand, refer to the small, graded changes in electric potential (voltage) that occur across a neuron's cell wall, at various locations, as a result of fluctuating concentrations of charged particles – ions – inside and outside the cell. These fluctuations happen due to the activities of various *channels*, *gates*, and *pumps* in the membrane, which are in turn activated by different proximate changes, such as nearby de- or hyperpolarization due to, e.g., some neurotransmitter being released across a synaptic cleft.

Both action and membrane potentials are extremely rapid, taking place on the level of milliseconds. They are also metabolically expensive, and so require an extensive cerebral vascular network to allow the blood to flexibly and adaptively transport oxygen and glucose to wherever it is most needed at the moment. In a simplified sense, this entails that increased neural activity in a particular region of the brain will typically be accompanied by an increased blood flow to the same region. Unlike the rapid neural activity itself, this blood-flow response is quite slow, on the order of several seconds.

All this activity takes place within the many nooks and crannies of the brain. Briefly, the brain's outermost layers are known as the *cerebral cortex*, most of which consists of six sub-layers, each with its own typical neuron types and functions. The cortex – with all its layers – makes up around 40% of the total mass of the human brain, with the remainder consisting mostly of bundles of myelinated axons (*white matter*) and various *subcortical structures*, such as the hippocampus, amygdala, thalamus, and basal ganglia, as well as the brainstem and cerebellum.

The cerebral cortex is further divided into various functional regions, where the overarching story of the past century of neuroscience might be summed up as that many, if not most, regions show significant functional diversity. In other words, their activity is not easily circumscribed to any one, isolated mental state or capacity, despite popular-science claims to the contrary (of the variety "Researchers have now discovered the *pastry-craving center* of the brain!"). In fact, as a story that is still very much being written, one of the main lessons of neuroscience so far has been that our commonsense mental concepts very rarely rhyme neatly with our actual functional neurophysiology.

This is a point of direct relevance to the discussion of neurodoping: it is currently inconceivably difficult to identify and activate the precise neural correlates of any one single, complex mental state or sequence of movements or similar, such as performing a perfect Fosbury flop. In practice, this means that *any* sports-relevant neural activation or stimulation is likely intermingled with an entire host of other, largely sports-*irrelevant* neural activity. Essentially, just as for medicines, we might summarize this as "no real effect without unintended side effects", with all the potential for performance deterioration that this entails.

I turn now, in the next several sections, to the various functional neurotechnologies that may be of potential interest to athletes. To start with, by far the most widely used such neurotechnologies within clinical and research contexts are what I'm here referring to as *passive*, namely those that attempt to track the brain's function, without modifying it in any manner. These technologies can be further divided into two sub-groups: passive technologies that track neural activity *directly*, and those that track it *indirectly* through some *biological proxy*, such as blood flow or glucose metabolism. I begin with the former.

1.2 Passive Direct Functional Neurotechnologies

Passive neurotechnologies that track neural activity directly include *electroencephalography* (EEG) and *magnetoencephalography* (MEG). Of these, EEG is the oldest, invented by German physiologist Hans Berger a century ago, in 1924, and first published five years later (Berger, 1929). Essentially, EEG works by picking up the aforementioned changes in membrane potentials. When a sufficient number of such changes occur in synchrony across many neurons, they aggregate together into a larger signal – called an *equivalent current dipole* – that may be picked up by *scalp electrodes*, small metal-alloy discs connected to a voltmeter.[2]

More specifically, EEG mostly picks up *excitatory postsynaptic membrane potentials* in specific (pyramidal) neurons in the outermost cortical layer or two. To generate a sufficiently large equivalent current dipole to be readable by the scalp electrodes, the same sort of excitation must occur around the same time in neural populations consisting of anything from some tens of thousands up to a few million neurons. In addition, unless the neurons are oriented in a relevant manner (mostly radial to the scalp), even large equivalent current dipoles won't be readable from the scalp electrodes.

In other words, EEG does not pick up action potentials, nor indeed any membrane potential activity that is inhibitory, below the outermost cortical layer(s), asynchronous, from a smaller neural population, or located or oriented in a way that prohibits its propagation to the scalp electrodes. In other words, even under ideal conditions, the neural activity picked up by EEG still represents only a minute portion of all the neural activity in the brain. In this sense, EEG is like trying to follow the ins and outs of a football game by listening to the crowds cheering from outside the stadium. It may well be possible to make some highly qualified educated guesses about what's actually going on, but a lot of (often crucial) detail will inevitably be unavailable.

In addition, the recorded EEG signal at the scalp is typically the result of an unknown number of underlying neural activity sources, mixed together. Mathematically, the question of which sources make up the EEG signal is *ill-posed*, meaning the signal at the scalp has an infinite number of possible sources. In EEG research, this is called the *inverse problem*, and can only be tentatively solved by making various assumptions to constrain the solution space, including assumptions based on convergent evidence from other neurotechnologies about, e.g., the number of neural sources involved in some specific neural process. Even when this is known, however, the inverse problem remains formidable, as the equivalent current dipoles from different neural sources are also distorted or "smeared out" by the biological tissue – the meninges, cerebrospinal fluid, skull, scalp, and hair – between the sources and the electrodes.

On top of this, the nature of EEG hardware also renders the equipment highly sensitive to various additional sources of noise, including noise from the experimental participants themselves (movement, blinks, swallowing, heartbeat, vocalization, etc.) as well as different environmental factors (power cables and outlets, computer screens and other electronics, nearby elevators or helicopters, etc.). In this sense, the recorded EEG signal is almost never a true representation of neural activity, but a more general summary overview of different equivalent current dipoles' ebb and flow, mixed with various extraneous signals in largely unknown proportions. To return to the previous metaphor, it is rather like trying to make sense of the game from outside the stadium by listening to the crowds cheering, but having to also contend with the sounds of passing pedestrians, city traffic, ads blared from loudspeakers, and a jet plane taking off from the nearby airport: difficult to extract the sounds of interest from the surrounding cacophony.

MEG improves somewhat on these signal-to-noise ratio issues, by relying on the magnetic counterparts of the electrophysiological signal, which are less prone to being "smeared out" by intermediary biological tissue. This provides some additional – and often convergent – support for our understanding of neural activity, but comes with a rather hefty price tag, both literally and figuratively. The magnetic perturbances caused by (superficial cortical, synchronous, correctly oriented, etc.) neural activity are namely so minuscule that tracking them requires some highly specific and rather extreme conditions to be met (Gross, 2019).

First, the recording must take place within a magnetically shielded room. The earth's magnetic field – the same field that moves compass needles to the north – is around 50 μT (0.00005 T) strong, while the magnetic fields from neural activity, picked up at the scalp by the MEG sensors, are closer to 50 fT (0.00000000000005 T), or around a billion times weaker. Without a magnetically shielded room to keep out noise such as the earth's magnetic field, hearing the magnetic whispers of the cortex would simply be impossible. Second, the only way to record such minuscule magnetic perturbances is by using so-called *super-conducting quantum interference devices* (SQUIDs) – extremely sensitive magnetometers that utilize quantum phenomena and require extremely cold temperatures, close to absolute zero, to function. This entails significant operating costs and technical requirements for running a MEG, which goes some way to explain why the technology is nowhere near as common as EEG in medical and research contexts (Hari & Puce, 2023). Third, even more than for EEG, the MEG signal is very sensitive to noise, meaning that, e.g., the slightest head movements are likely to cause artifactual distortion that may render the signal unusable. In practice, this means that MEG, like EEG, is not going to be useful in a sports context for much more than passive monitoring of, e.g., mental states (cf. Thompson et al., 2008). For athletes looking to enhance their performance, the most feasible possibility would therefore be to use the technologies for neurofeedback-related training to recognize specific, desired states.

One phenomenon that both EEG and MEG capture rather well is (superficial cortical, synchronous, correctly oriented, etc.) neural oscillations. It is well-established that the membrane potential activity of neural populations tends to oscillate at different frequencies during certain forms of mental activity. For instance, *alpha* waves (ca. 8–12 Hz) are more strongly correlated with drowsiness, while *beta* waves (ca. 12–30 Hz) are more strongly correlated with alertness (Bazanova & Vernon, 2014). As it is computationally trivial to calculate the power of specific frequency ranges within a complex signal, many EEG applications in *brain-computer interfaces* (BCIs) utilize this to provide neurofeedback (Marzbani et al., 2016). In a typical consumer BCI setting, a user connects a cordless EEG headband to a dedicated smartphone app and is tasked with some visually compelling scenario, such as keeping a balloon inflated, where their success at the task is determined by the relative power of different frequency ranges in the EEG signal. In this manner, the user may learn what it *feels like* to, e.g., have a higher proportion of beta waves in their EEG ("The balloon inflates!"), as a purported means of training their ability to maintain an intense mental focus (Vasiljevic et al., 2020).

Note that while these sorts of frequency-range-focused BCI applications are burgeoning in both research and consumer contexts – including being put to use for purposes of athletic performance enhancement (Jeunet et al., 2019) – they all suffer from numerous methodological shortcomings. For high-grade lab equipment, experiments with low statistical power and issues with high inter-individual variability stymie researchers' ability to reach much consensus on generalizable truths: which frequency ranges in which regions of the scalp correlate with which particular mental states (Donoghue et al., 2022). Lower-grade consumer equipment (e.g., EEG headbands with smartphone apps) suffer the same problems, as well as additional problems stemming from, e.g., electrode quality causing unacceptably high levels of noise, or a headband being limited to only one or two dry electrodes, which yields only an extremely limited EEG signal from which to attempt to calculate relevant frequency ranges (Rashid et al., 2020). To give an illustrative example: despite decades of BCI research, most systems for detecting fatigue (e.g., in truck drivers or pilots) still tend to rely more on, e.g., blinks and eye aspect ratios than on EEG signals (Sikander & Anwar, 2018).

Although similar use cases are perfectly *technically* feasible for MEG, and indeed could potentially overcome some of the limitations noted above, the complex and expensive nature of MEG means that it is not generally utilized or available for BCI purposes.

To sum up, as regards passive direct neurotechnologies in the sports context, the current availabilities are by their very nature essentially limited to athletes using them for neurofeedback-related training to recognize specific mental states. And even then, a lack of robust consensus in the research literature means we are nowhere near knowing what sort of reliable EEG or MEG signal, across numerous individual athletes, corresponds with a "winner's drive", or for that matter "choking" or having the "yips" or "twisties" or similar. At best, these technologies *may* help athletes practice a rudimentary form of mental focus, although arguably no more effectively than what can already be achieved through, e.g., standard mindfulness meditation (Tan et al., 2014).

1.3 Passive Indirect Functional Neurotechnologies

There are three different widely known passive *indirect* functional neurotechnologies, i.e., those that don't track neural activity directly, but some biological proxy of it. In order of their historical development, they are positron emission tomography (PET), functional magnetic resonance imaging (fMRI), and functional near-infrared spectroscopy (fNIRS).

PET leverages radioactive decay to track brain function. The technology relies on first creating a synthetic, radioactive variant of a chemical substance used by the body, such as glucose or water. After being injected into a person, the decaying isotopes emit positrons (antiparticles of electrons). When one of these collides with an electron, the two produce a pair of *annihilation photons* travelling outward in opposite directions from each other, which are then picked up by the PET scanner (Muehllehner & Karp, 2006). With sufficient annihilation photon pairs, different concentrations of the injected radioactive substance in different regions become clear.

A significant proportion of PET research has been devoted to identifying the most promising substances to make radioactive (Muehllehner & Karp, 2006). The substance most often used for functional neuroimaging is oxygen-15 (^{15}O), which follows the blood flow and has a half-life of around two minutes. In practice, this means that the isotope needs to be actively created in a medical cyclotron and continuously pumped into the experimental participant – its half-life is too short for anybody to realistically run the substance from a radiology department to a physically separate neuroscience department. Nevertheless, two minutes is still a long time to be engaged in a single mental task or state (if in doubt, try thinking only about, e.g., the specific moment of winning a race for two minutes straight). For this reason, neuroscientific use of PET is limited to so-called *block experimental designs*, where the same condition is repeated numerous times in an experimental block, to ensure sufficient concentrations of oxygen-15 in whichever brain region is recruited for that condition (Tashiro et al., 2008).

Given the injection of radioactive substances into the body, there are safety limits to the number of times a person can submit to a PET scan. This – together with the high complexity and cost of running (and, therefore, the relative scarcity of) PET scanners – makes it exceedingly unlikely to be utilized by athletes for any repeated, ongoing performance-enhancement purposes. Repeated use is, however, not a safety concern when it comes to fMRI. In addition, fMRI is much faster and generally with a higher spatial resolution than PET, and most sufficiently large universities and/or university hospitals in the world have a compatible MRI scanner, making it a much more practically feasible alternative for interested athletes.

Briefly, MRI works by bombarding the brain with extremely powerful magnetic fields – often at 3T, or around a hundred thousand times stronger than the earth's magnetic field.[3] Like MEG, this requires magnetically shielded rooms, but for the exact opposite reasons: the MRI's magnetic field is powerful enough to pull metal objects into the scanner bore at projectile speed, potentially injuring or even killing any person inside it. When activated, the MRI magnets oscillate at extremely high frequencies – several tens or hundreds of thousands of times per second – in order to create *resonance* in the brain's hydrogen protons, a form of heightened energy state. Then, when the oscillating magnets are switched off, this extra energy is released and picked up by the MRI's *receiving coil*. By combining various sequences of such oscillatory magnetic pulses (the various clunks and whirrs of the MRI machinery), the scanner can relatively quickly map out the entire three-dimensional brain.

To get from (structural) MRI to fMRI requires some additional considerations. As already noted above, the more neural activity there is in some brain region, the more the blood flow tends to increase to that area, in order to provide glucose and oxygen. The blood consists of – among other things – a mix of oxygenated and deoxygenated hemoglobin. When neural activity increases, the relative ratio of oxygenated-to-deoxygenated hemoglobin (called the *blood-oxygen-level-dependent*, or BOLD) increases as well. This may seem counterintuitive: more activity typically uses up more oxygen, so one might expect the BOLD to *decrease*. In fact, what happens instead is that the cerebral vasculature quickly provides more blood than is required, possibly as a form of biological buffer.

Regardless, deoxygenated hemoglobin is paramagnetic, meaning that in the MRI excitation-and-relaxation sequences, it distorts the resulting images ever so slightly. In this manner, fMRI is simply a quantification of the relative changes in image distortion, or signal loss, in different regions between experimental conditions. If, for instance, the motor cortex is activated when a person imagines performing some movement sequence, then this activation will show up in the fMRI as a reduced distortion (due to an increased BOLD signal) in the area.

There are many benefits with fMRI, such as its being able to pick up activity from the entire brain, including subcortical regions, with higher both temporal and spatial resolution (and fewer safety concerns) than PET. Nevertheless, it still has several limitations. For one, like most of the technologies discussed so far, it is highly sensitive to head movements – anything more than a millimeter or two will significantly distort the resulting image. This means that, like for EEG and MEG, fMRI is unlikely to be used by athletes for any purpose other than passive neurofeedback-related training, with the same sorts of considerations as already noted above. In addition, the naturally slow onset and offset of the BOLD response means that despite its excellent spatial resolution, fMRI does not pick up intricate sequences of neural events, such as the specific correlates of completing one perfect butterfly swim stroke in one's mental imagery. The fMRI signal might reveal which general parts of the brain are used in such a case (hint: the motor cortex), but only in a temporally diffuse manner, comparable to seeing an aggregation of lights from a distance at night: there's definitely something there, but it will be impossible to distinguish any of the detail.

Finally, the third passive indirect neurotechnology is fNIRS. Like fMRI, fNIRS tracks blood flow in the brain, but instead of bombarding the individual with extremely powerful magnetic fields, it utilizes a comparatively simple approach: emitting harmless, near-infrared light from diodes to detectors, both placed on the scalp. Near-infrared light easily traverses skin, tissue, and bone, but tends to be absorbed by blood, with the rate of absorption differing between oxygenated and deoxygenated hemoglobin. In this manner, fNIRS can yield an approximation of the fMRI BOLD signal (Pinti et al., 2020).[4]

Although fNIRS is both highly portable and reasonably tolerant of head and body movements, and therefore of much potential interest in the sports research context (Balardin et al., 2017), it is restricted by the same poor temporal resolution as fMRI – tracking only slow blood-flow changes. On top of this, the fNIRS diodes and detectors are positioned in such a manner that it is only possible to say more generally which larger regions of the brain are active in any given task, i.e., its spatial resolution is much poorer than fMRI, and more similar to EEG. In addition, due to the way the near-infrared light curves, fNIRS – like EEG and MEG – is limited to tracking activity only in the more superficial cortex (Pinti et al., 2020).

To sum up this section: from a sports-context perspective, PET is generally too unsafe and unavailable to use repeatedly, while both it and fMRI and fNIRS all suffer from poor temporal resolution, meaning they will only ever provide a diffuse blood-flow-based view of neural activity. Between the two latter technologies, fMRI has far better spatial resolution, while fNIRS is far more robust to movement artifacts, meaning that neither of them can provide all the possibilities a neurotraining-interested athlete might be after. Like for EEG and MEG, it is possible to utilize fMRI and fNIRS for neurofeedback-related training, but with the same sorts of limitations as already noted above.

1.4 Active Functional Neurotechnologies

While passive neurotechnologies are limited to tracking neural activity or some biological proxy of it, *active* neurotechnologies aim instead to modify brain function in some manner. They consist of a cluster of technologies, including transcranial electrical stimulation (TES) and transcranial magnetic stimulation (TMS). Of these, the most widely used technology is TES, which includes transcranial direct current stimulation (tDCS), transcranial alternating current stimulation (tACS), and transcranial random noise stimulation (tRNS). All these TES technologies function according to the same basic principles – running a gentle current, usually of around 1–2 mA, between two large scalp electrodes – and differ only in their stimulation protocols. While tDCS runs a (constant or pulsed) direct current, tACS runs a (constant or pulsed) alternating current at a chosen oscillation frequency, and tRNS runs an alternating current of random and constantly changing amplitude and frequency.

TES has been in broad use since around the turn of the millennium, and widely studied in both clinical and non-clinical – including athletic performance-enhancement – research (Edwards et al., 2017; Fertonani & Miniussi, 2017). (It is therefore also the first neurotechnology that tends to come to mind when one first encounters "neurodoping" research.) The current that is run between the two electrodes is small enough to not cause much or any discomfort or pain, yet large enough to still presumably penetrate the scalp and skull into the outermost layers of the cortex. In doing so, there is insufficient current to induce action potentials directly, but the effects of TES are believed to lie in its capacity to slightly de- or hyperpolarize neurons, leading to an increased or decreased chance, respectively, of subsequent action potentials (Chase et al., 2020). An additional possibility, with tACS specifically, is to engender neural oscillations at a chosen, biologically feasible frequency, a process referred to as *neuronal entrainment* (Lakatos et al., 2019).

TES treatment consists of a particular predetermined stimulation protocol, which dictates the precise number and frequency of sessions, current amplitude(s), direction of current in tDCS (i.e., which electrode serves as the cathode and which as the anode), oscillation frequency in tACS, stimulation length and/or pulse sequence(s), precise electrode locations, possible simultaneous activity by the participant, and so on. When conducting TES research, it is also crucial to include a relevant placebo or "sham" condition, in order to ensure that any resulting research findings are not mere placebo effects, given that the presence or absence of a current across the scalp is clearly felt by participants (Fonteneau et al., 2019).

In fact, some researchers have argued that most TES-related findings are likely mere placebo effects (cf. Liu et al., 2018; Vöröslakos et al., 2018), although the current consensus is that there does seem to be an actual effect of the technology in at least some therapeutic instances (Fregni et al., 2021). The exact nature of this effect is, however, difficult to determine, due to highly varying experimental protocols that undermine easy aggregations and comparisons of results from different studies, a problem that cuts across most neuropsychology, regardless of the specific technology used. In addition, however, there seems to be particularly high inter-individual variability in the effects of TES, suggesting that it may induce the expected effect in some individuals, and no – or even a contrary – effect in others (Hsu et al., 2016; Palm et al., 2018).

Regardless of how well it works, it is important to note that even in a "best-case scenario" where the effect of TES is taken as clearly established, its effects are limited to the cortical surface, and thus the limited sorts of neural processes that occur there (Vöröslakos et al., 2018). In addition, the electrodes are relatively large, and the way in which the current interacts with the underlying tissue leads to its impact being spatially quite diffuse. In other words, it is exceedingly unlikely that TES could be used for fine-grained targeting of specific neural events or sequences. It may provide some vaguely general effect, but given the aforementioned inter-individual variability, this seems just as likely to be either deleterious or enhancing for an athlete's performance.

TMS – as the name suggests – uses strong magnetic fields to perturb brain activity. Its magnetic field strengths are similar to those that occur within an MRI scanner, but as they are typically active for only a few milliseconds, and only extend a few centimeters from the electromagnetic coil, they don't entail any corresponding risk of fatal metal projectiles or similar, nor do they require magnetically shielded spaces. The exact impact of TMS on neural activity is somewhat poorly understood, but the technology is often used to disrupt specific neural events, in effect creating temporary and harmless brain lesions (Siebner et al., 2022). Because of its timing precision and focused magnetic field pulse, TMS is considered to have excellent both temporal and spatial resolutions, meaning it can be used to target specific steps in neural events and sequences far more precisely than any of the aforementioned technologies (Hallett, 2007). However, this benefit is of limited use in the sports context, as the nature of TMS mostly allows it to be used to interrupt the step or event in question, primarily as part of research aiming to map out the nature of the discrete process components of some neural event.

The magnetic perturbances of TMS can also be applied at a chosen frequency, as part of repetitive TMS (rTMS; Hallett, 2007). This – like tACS – has the potential to induce neuronal entrainment, which might be one of the most promising current avenues for genuine athletic performance-enhancing effects. Unfortunately, as already noted above, we have a limited current understanding of which precise combinations of frequencies in which precise regions have which sorts of effects, as well as how much variation to expect between individuals. It is not inconceivable that researchers painstakingly begin mapping out this knowledge space more consistently than they have managed to so far, but there is by any reasonable measure a long way to go before we have robust, reliable, actionable tACS or rTMS protocols to use for consistently performance-enhancing effects in professional athletes.

1.5 Invasive Functional Neurotechnologies

Finally, invasive technologies primarily concern those that involve opening the skull to directly access the brain, as in the surgical introduction of electrodes to, e.g., facilitate deep brain stimulation (DBS), placing electrode grids directly onto the brain's cortical surface (as in electrocorticography, or ECoG), or introducing optogenetically engineered viral vectors into specific neurons in order to control them with light (Krauss et al., 2021; Miller et al., 2020;

Shen et al., 2020). This could also conceivably include surgical resection of specific brain tissue to remove some undesired corresponding functionality. In addition, the notion of invasive neurotechnologies arguably covers some that do not require opening the skull at all, such as the possible use of drugs or electroconvulsive therapy (ECT) to create permanent brain lesions.[5]

Regardless of whether opening the skull is part of the invasive element of any such intervention, the significant risks inherent to all of them render their inclusion in a discussion of athletic performance enhancement a relatively moot point. Much like elite athletes are unlikely to selectively amputate their own legs in order to benefit from any supposed performance-enhancing effects of carbon-fiber prosthetic running blades, so they are also unlikely to permanently alter their neurophysiology through major brain surgery (or equivalent) in order to benefit from some supposed neuro-performance-enhancing effect. Realistically, the risks far outweigh any highly dubious potential benefits.

The same can be said for the most recent high-profile developments in invasive neurotechnology: Elon Musk's *Neuralink*. Musk is known for hyping his products, e.g., suggesting that technological telepathy and human memory backups are on the verge of being developed (Regalado, 2020; Rogers, 2020). Even in theory, this is unlikely. We know from all the aforementioned neurotechnologies that a large number of neural processes consist of, or incorporate, cascades of neural events across enormous neural populations. These are simply too large to be tracked by surgically implanted brain chips, meaning the chips will at best provide an incredibly limited view of the brain's neural activity, and a correlated limited capacity to stimulate proximate neural populations.

More crucially, these problems cannot be solved by making the chips larger, to cover more brain area, both because of the irreversible damage of the installation procedure and because even the current generation of chips yield enormous amounts of data, which in turn entails massive data-transfer requirements that are far beyond what is even currently technically feasible. In fact, Neuralink has just recently issued a "Compression Challenge" to the general public to try to circumvent this data-transfer bottleneck, which some experts have described as "impossible" (Pearson, 2024).

In reality, then, while brain chips might conceivably help a paraplegic individual to be a little more independent by, e.g., providing rudimentary movement of robotic limbs, it is not currently conceivable how they could help professional athletes level up their already extremely finely tuned sporting abilities. If any lesson is to be drawn from the entire foregoing discussion, it's that neuroscience is still very much learning how the human brain works. We have a rudimentary understanding of some issues – particularly those of significant clinical relevance that have been extensively researched. But to think that this limited knowledge translates into an existing opportunity to improve the tightly honed physical and mental subtleties of professional athletic performance is likely to be as disastrous as hiring a local amateur artist to restore a classic church fresco only to wind up with "Monkey Jesus" (Hurtado, 2012). We simply don't have a sufficiently complete understanding of the brain to avoid botching any such attempt.

1.6 Conclusion

I have argued above that while there are conceivable avenues for neurotechnology-assisted athletic performance enhancement, they tend to be quite restricted – either by their very nature or by our limited corresponding understanding of how the brain works in all its glorious detail. *Prima facie*, this lends some support to the notion that most of these avenues are closer to (legitimate) neurotraining than they are to (illegitimate) neurodoping. Basically, if a technology-assisted practice – such as frequency-range-detecting neurofeedback training using a consumer-grade EEG headband and a smartphone app – seems to be less effective for relevant forms of performance enhancement than simply engaging in a little mindfulness meditation, it seems rather difficult to find ethical fault with that practice, at least relative to WADA's anti-doping framework.

That said, other examples can just as well prime intuitions in the opposite direction: utilizing tACS to repeatedly engender neuronal entrainment of (let's assume) the ability to push a little further past training fatigue or sore muscles seems to be more ethically problematic. Arguing that such a practice is tantamount to neurodoping probably requires providing reasonably robust evidence that the ability in question actually *is* enhanced by the tACS (and not just believed to be so), although even here there is room for highly divergent conclusions.

Recall that WADA requires only two of its three criteria – that a substance (or technology) has a performance-enhancing effect, that it entails potential health risks to the athlete, and that it is against the "spirit of sport" – in order to include it on their *Prohibited list*. In other words, a performance-enhancing effect is not a necessary criterion, if repeated use of tACS might be considered to fulfill the health-risk and against-the-spirit-of-sport criteria. In addition, although WADA's precise decision-making process lacks transparency, there seems to at least potentially be room for quite a lax notion of what sort of evidentiary weight is required for something to be considered properly "performance-enhancing", such that even a widespread *perception* that it is may occasionally suffice to fulfill the performance-enhancing criterion (cf. Pugh & Pugh, 2021).

In other words, gaining a more grounded understanding of different neurotechnologies will not, in and of itself, remove the need for further ethical deliberation. It will, however, constrain what we might call the *argumentative space* somewhat, by disallowing arguments that clearly misconstrue the reality of those technologies. At this stage, this means that while we have not yet established a clear distinction between neurotraining and neurodoping, we're now better equipped to begin doing so.

Acknowledgments

Thank you to all the participants of the 2023 Barcelona UPF workshop on neurodoping – Alberto Carrio, Mirko Daniel Garasic, Gregory Krippa, Thomas Søbirk Petersen, Andrea Lavazza, and Jonathan Pugh – for helpful feedback and stimulating discussion on a (much earlier) version of this paper. And a particularly big thank you to Alberto, for organizing the event itself, in addition to an exquisite workshop dinner!

Notes

1 The information presented in this section is basic neuroscience knowledge, but any curious reader who wants more detail is directed toward essentially any of the many available introductory books on human neuroscience. If wanting for options, the magisterial (and exhaustively complex) choice would be Kandel et al. (2021).

2 In this and the following few paragraphs, I rely on Luck's (2014) introduction to a particular application of EEG: the *event-related potential* (ERP) technique. Rarely has a book on such a dry-sounding scientific topic been written in such a simultaneously definitive and engaging manner.

3 The information in this and the following few paragraphs is based on the comprehensive fMRI textbook by Huettel et al. (2014).

4 A more recent development has sought to use fNIRS not only for slow, blood-flow-related signals in the brain, but also for fast neural activity (Gratton et al., 1995). These sorts of *event-related optical signals* (EROS; sometimes also called *fast optical signals,* or FOS) have been reliably replicated in experiments done directly on neural tissue, but the technology's utility in non-invasive experiments on humans is more controversial, with several researchers voicing skepticism about its capacity to reliably track neural activity in such contexts (Radhakrishnan et al., 2009; Steinbrink et al., 2005). Perhaps tellingly, there has been very little research utilizing the technology over the past decade or so, which is why I chose not to include it in the previous section on passive direct technologies.

5 This is, it must be noted, not the way ECT is utilized in clinical contexts today (Espinoza & Kellner, 2022), but is certainly possible with sufficient current amplitude and length of stimulation. Note that standard current strengths for ECT are typically in the vicinity of 500–900 mA, so around two orders of magnitude larger than for TES.

6 Although there are also many important *structural* neurotechnologies, such as *computed tomography* (CT) and structural *magnetic resonance imaging* (MRI) in its many guises, including, e.g., diffusion tensor imaging (DTI), these are not directly relevant to enhancement of athletic performance, and so need not concern us further here.

References

Balardin, J. B., Zimeo Morais, G. A., Furucho, R. A., Trambaiolli, L., Vanzella, P., Biazoli Jr., C., & Sato, J. R. (2017). Imaging brain function with functional near-infrared spectroscopy in unconstrained environments. *Frontiers in Human Neuroscience, 11*, 258. https://doi.org/10.3389/fnhum.2017.00258

Bazanova, O. M., & Vernon, D. (2014). Interpreting EEG alpha activity. *Neuroscience & Biobehavioral Reviews, 44*, 94–110. https://doi.org/10.1016/j.neubiorev.2013.05.007

Berger, H. (1929). Über das elektroenkephalogramm des menschen. *Archiv für psychiatrie und nervenkrankheiten, 87*(1), 527–570.

Beyerstein, B. L. (1990). Brainscams: Neuromythologies of the new age. *International Journal of Mental Health, 19*(3), 27–36. https://doi.org/10.1080/00207411.1990.11449169

Chase, H. W., Boudewyn, M. A., Carter, C. S., & Phillips, M. L. (2020). Transcranial direct current stimulation: A roadmap for research, from mechanism of action to clinical implementation. *Molecular Psychiatry, 25*(2), 397–407. https://doi.org/10.1038/s41380-019-0499-9

Donoghue, T., Schaworonkow, N., & Voytek, B. (2022). Methodological considerations for studying neural oscillations. *European Journal of Neuroscience, 55*(11–12), 3502–3527. https://doi.org/10.1111/ejn.15361

Edwards, D. J., Cortes, M., Wortman-Jutt, S., Putrino, D., Bikson, M., Thickbroom, G., & Pascual-Leone, A. (2017). Transcranial direct current stimulation and sports performance. *Frontiers in Human Neuroscience, 11*, 243. https://doi.org/10.3389/fnhum.2017.00243

Espinoza, R. T., & Kellner, C. H. (2022). Electroconvulsive therapy. *New England Journal of Medicine, 386*(7), 667–672. https://doi.org/10.1056/nejmra2034954

Fertonani, A., & Miniussi, C. (2017). Transcranial electrical stimulation: What we know and do not know about mechanisms. *The Neuroscientist, 23*(2), 109–123. https://doi.org/10.1177/1073858416631966

Fonteneau, C., Mondino, M., Arns, M., Baeken, C., Bikson, M., Brunoni, A. R., Burke, M. J., Neuvonen, T., Padberg, F., Pascual-Leone, A., Poulet, E., Ruffini, G., Santarnecchi, E., Sauvaget, A., Schellhorn, K., Suaud Chagny, M.-F., Palm, U., & Brunelin, J. (2019). Sham tDCS: A hidden source of variability? Reflections for further blinded, controlled trials. *Brain Stimulation, 12*(3), 668–673. https://doi.org/10.1016/j.brs.2018.12.977

Fregni, F., El-Hagrassy, M. M., Pacheco-Barrios, K., Carvalho, S., Leite, J., Simis, M., Brunelin, J., Nakamura-Palacios, E. M., Marangolo, P., Venkatasubramanian, G., San-Juan, D., Caumo, W., Bikson, M. Brunoni, A. R., & Neuromodulation Center Working Group. (2021). Evidence-based guidelines and secondary meta-analysis for the use of transcranial direct current stimulation in neurological and psychiatric disorders. *International Journal of Neuropsychopharmacology, 24*(4), 256–313. https://doi.org/10.1093/ijnp/pyaa051

Gratton, G., Corballis, P. M., Cho, E., Fabiani, M., & Hood, D. C. (1995). Shades of gray matter: Noninvasive optical images of human brain responses during visual stimulation. *Psychophysiology, 32*(5), 505–509. https://doi.org/10.1111/j.1469-8986.1995.tb02102.x

Gross, J. (2019). Magnetoencephalography in cognitive neuroscience: A primer. *Neuron, 104*(2), 189–204. https://doi.org/10.1016/j.neuron.2019.07.001

Hallett, M. (2007). Transcranial magnetic stimulation: A primer. *Neuron, 55*(2), 187–199. https://doi.org/10.1016/j.neuron.2007.06.026

Hari, R., & Puce, A. (2023). *MEG-EEG primer*. Oxford University Press.

Hsu, T. Y., Juan, C. H., & Tseng, P. (2016). Individual differences and state-dependent responses in transcranial direct current stimulation. *Frontiers in Human Neuroscience, 10*, 643. https://doi.org/10.3389/fnhum.2016.00643

Huettel, S. A., Song, A. W., & McCarthy, G. (2014). *Functional magnetic resonance imaging* (3rd ed.). Sinauer.

Hurtado, M. (2012, August 24). Mal fresco! Botched Ecce Homo restoration woman has "anxiety attack". *The Guardian*. https://www.theguardian.com/world/2012/aug/24/spain-europe-news

Jeunet, C., Glize, B., McGonigal, A., Batail, J. M., & Micoulaud-Franchi, J. A. (2019). Using EEG-based brain computer interface and neurofeedback targeting sensorimotor rhythms to improve motor skills: Theoretical background, applications and prospects. *Neurophysiologie Clinique, 49*(2), 125–136. https://doi.org/10.1016/j.neucli.2018.10.068

Kandel, E. R., Koester, J. D., Mack, S. H., & Siegelbaum, S. A. (2021). *Principles of neural science* (6th ed.). McGraw Hill.

Krauss, J. K., Lipsman, N., Aziz, T., Boutet, A., Brown, P., Chang, J. W., Davidson, B., Grill, W. M., Hariz, M. I., Horn, A., Schulder, M., Mammis, A., Tass, P. A., Volkmann, J., & Lozano, A. M. (2021). Technology of deep brain stimulation: Current status and future directions. *Nature Reviews Neurology, 17*(2), 75–87. https://doi.org/10.1038/s41582-020-00426-z

Lakatos, P., Gross, J., & Thut, G. (2019). A new unifying account of the roles of neuronal entrainment. *Current Biology, 29*(18), R890–R905. https://doi.org/10.1016/j.cub.2019.07.075

Lilienfeld, S. O., Aslinger, E., Marshall, J., & Satel, S. (2017). Neurohype: A field guide to exaggerated brain-based claims. In L. S. M. Johnson & K. S. Rommelfanger (Eds.), *The Routledge handbook of neuroethics* (pp. 241–261). Routledge. https://doi.org/10.4324/9781315708652

Liu, A., Vöröslakos, M., Kronberg, G., Henin, S., Krause, M. R., Huang, Y., Opitz, A., Mehta, A., Pack, C. C., Krekelberg, B., Berényi, A., Parra, L. C., Melloni, L., Devinsky, O., & Buzsáki, G. (2018). Immediate neurophysiological effects of transcranial electrical stimulation. *Nature Communications, 9*(1), 5092. https://doi.org/10.1038/s41467-018-07233-7

Löwel, S., & Singer, W. (1992). Selection of intrinsic horizontal connections in the visual cortex by correlated neuronal activity. *Science, 255*(5041), 209–212. https://doi.org/10.1126/science.1372754

Luck, S. J. (2014). *An introduction to the event-related potential technique* (2nd ed.). MIT press.

Marzbani, H., Marateb, H. R., & Mansourian, M. (2016). Neurofeedback: A comprehensive review on system design, methodology and clinical applications. *Basic and Clinical Neuroscience, 7*(2), 143. https://doi.org/10.15412/j.bcn.03070208

Miller, K. J., Hermes, D., & Staff, N. P. (2020). The current state of electrocorticography-based brain–computer interfaces. *Neurosurgical Focus, 49*(1), E2. https://doi.org/10.3171/2020.4.focus20185

Muehllehner, G., & Karp, J. S. (2006). Positron emission tomography. *Physics in Medicine & Biology, 51*(13), R117. https://doi.org/10.1088/0031-9155/51/13/R08

Palm, U., Kumpf, U., Behler, N., Wulf, L., Kirsch, B., Wörsching, J., Keeser, D., Hasan, A., & Padberg, F. (2018). Home use, remotely supervised, and remotely controlled transcranial direct current stimulation: A systematic review of the available evidence. *Neuromodulation: Technology at the Neural Interface, 21*(4), 323–333. https://doi.org/10.1111/ner.12686

Pearson, J. (2024, May 28). Neuralink looks to the public to solve a seemingly impossible problem. *CBC.* https://www.cbc.ca/news/science/neuralink-compression-challenge-1.7216667

Pinti, P., Tachtsidis, I., Hamilton, A., Hirsch, J., Aichelburg, C., Gilbert, S., & Burgess, P. W. (2020). The present and future use of functional near-infrared spectroscopy (fNIRS) for cognitive neuroscience. *Annals of the New York Academy of Sciences, 1464*(1), 5–29. https://doi.org/10.1111/nyas.13948

Pugh, J., & Pugh, C. (2021). Neurostimulation, doping, and the spirit of sport. *Neuroethics, 14,* 141–158. https://doi.org/10.1007/s12152-020-09435-7

Radhakrishnan, H., Vanduffel, W., Deng, H. P., Ekstrom, L., Boas, D. A., & Franceschini, M. A. (2009). Fast optical signal not detected in awake behaving monkeys. *NeuroImage, 45*(2), 410–419. https://doi.org/10.1016/j.neuroimage.2008.12.014

Rashid, M., Sulaiman, N., Abdul Majeed, A. P. P., Musa, R. M., Nasir, A. F. A., Bari, B. S., & Khatun, S. (2020). Current status, challenges, and possible solutions of EEG-based brain-computer interface: A comprehensive review. *Frontiers in Neurorobotics, 14,* 25. https://doi.org/10.3389/fnbot.2020.00025

Regalado, A. (2020, August 30). Elon Musk's Neuralink is neuroscience theater. *MIT Technology Review.* https://www.technologyreview.com/2020/08/30/1007786/elon-musks-neuralink-demo-update-neuroscience-theater/

Rogers, A. (2020, September 4). Neuralink is impressive tech, wrapped in Musk hype. *WIRED.* https://www.wired.com/story/neuralink-is-impressive-tech-wrapped-in-musk-hype/

Shen, Y., Campbell, R. E., Côté, D. C., & Paquet, M. E. (2020). Challenges for therapeutic applications of opsin-based optogenetic tools in humans. *Frontiers in Neural Circuits, 14,* 41. https://doi.org/10.3389/fncir.2020.00041

Siebner, H. R., Funke, K., Aberra, A. S., Antal, A., Bestmann, S., Chen, R., Classen, J., Davare, M., Di Lazzaro, V., Fox, P. T., Hallett, M., Karabanov, A. N., Kesselheim, J., Beck, M. M., Koch, G., Liebetanz, D., Meunier, S., Miniussi, C., Paulus, W., Peterchev, A. V., & Ugawa, Y. (2022). Transcranial magnetic stimulation of the brain: What is stimulated? A consensus and critical position paper. *Clinical Neurophysiology, 140,* 59–97. https://doi.org/10.1016/j.clinph.2022.04.022

Sikander, G., & Anwar, S. (2018). Driver fatigue detection systems: A review. *IEEE Transactions on Intelligent Transportation Systems, 20*(6), 2339–2352. https://doi.org/10.1109/TITS.2018.2868499

Steinbrink, J., Kempf, F. C., Villringer, A., & Obrig, H. (2005). The fast optical signal: Robust or elusive when non-invasively measured in the human adult? *NeuroImage, 26*(4), 996–1008. https://doi.org/10.1016/j.neuroimage.2005.03.006

Tan, L. F., Dienes, Z., Jansari, A., & Goh, S. Y. (2014). Effect of mindfulness meditation on brain-computer interface performance. *Consciousness and Cognition*, *23*, 12–21. https://doi.org/10.1016/j.concog.2013.10.010

Tashiro, M., Itoh, M., Fujimoto, T., Masud, M. M., Watanuki, S., & Yanai, K. (2008). Application of positron emission tomography to neuroimaging in sports sciences. *Methods*, *45*(4), 300–306. https://doi.org/10.1016/j.ymeth.2008.05.001

Thompson, T., Steffert, T., Ros, T., Leach, J., & Gruzelier, J. (2008). EEG applications for sport and performance. *Methods*, *45*(4), 279–288. https://doi.org/10.1016/j.ymeth.2008.07.006

Vasiljevic, G. A. M., & De Miranda, L. C. (2020). *Brain-computer interface games based on consumer-grade EEG Devices: A systematic literature review. International Journal of Human-Computer Interaction*, *36*(2), 105–142. https://doi.org/10.1080/10447318.2019.1612213

Vöröslakos, M., Takeuchi, Y., Brinyiczki, K., Zombori, T., Oliva, A., Fernández-Ruiz, A., Kozák, G., Kincses, Z. T., Iványi, B., Buzsáki, G., & Berényi, A. (2018). Direct effects of transcranial electric stimulation on brain circuits in rats and humans. *Nature Communications*, *9*(1), 483. https://doi.org/10.1038/s41467-018-02928-3

WADA. (2004). *World anti-doping code international standard: Prohibited list 2024*. https://www.wada-ama.org/sites/default/files/2023-09/2024list_en_final_22_september_2023.pdf

Weisberg, D. S., Keil, F. C., Goodstein, J., Rawson, E., & Gray, J. R. (2008). The seductive allure of neuroscience explanations. *Journal of Cognitive Neuroscience*, *20*(3), 470–477. https://doi.org/10.1162/jocn.2008.20040

Chapter 2

Neuro-Doping, Effort, and Fairness

Jonathan Pugh and Christopher Pugh

2.1 Introduction

Whilst there is a voluminous literature on the ethics of doping in sport (Devine, 2011; Gleaves, 2011; Loland & McNamee, 2019; McNamee, 2012; Savulescu et al., 2004), the more specific ethical discussion concerning the use of neurostimulation for the enhancement of sporting performance is still in its relative infancy. Indeed, it is only just over a decade since Nick Davis' seminal paper identified the prospect of so-called neuro-doping (Davis, 2013). However, given the increasing interest amongst elite athletes in readily available transcranial direct current stimulation (tDCS) devices, the more specific discussion of "neuro-doping" warrants greater attention.[1] Furthermore, due to the wide range of tDCS' potential ergogenic effects, and the various possible mechanisms of action underlying those (potential) effects, we have previously suggested that neurostimulation "adds new dimensions to old questions about the ethics of doping in sport" (Pugh & Pugh, 2021). Of course, the prospect of harnessing the power of powerful (but potentially opaque) artificial intelligence systems to further refine the ergogenic effects of neuroenhancement naturally strengthens this point.

Although it is fair to say that the discussion of the ethics of neuro-doping is still in its relative infancy, that is not to say that significant progress has not been made. In particular, the past few years have seen nuanced discussions of the implications of tDCS for how we think about the role of effort in elite sport and the conception of fairness that we should employ in this domain. Our aim in this chapter is to provide something of an update about the recent ethical discussion on these points, in the light of some of the more recent scientific findings relevant to neuro-doping. We hope that this will serve as a useful background to some of the more focused chapters in this collection. With that in mind, we shall begin, in Section 2.2, with a very brief introduction to tDCS, before drawing out some themes of the recent ethical discussions about the relationship between tDCS, effort, and achievement in Section 2.3, before turning to consider arguments from fairness in the context of neuro-doping in Section 2.4. Over the course of the discussion

DOI: 10.4324/9781003520290-3

in this chapter, we will also provide something of an update on some of the scientific evidence regarding the ergogenic effects of tDCS that has emerged since the evidence overview that we provided as part of our 2021 paper on the topic of neuro-doping (Pugh & Pugh, 2021).

2.2 Introducing tDCS and an Evidence Update

Since other chapters in this collection will provide a more detailed examination of various neurotechnological interventions that might be deployed in sport, we shall limit ourselves here to only very brief introductory remarks about the nature of tDCS. The purpose of a tDCS device is to non-invasively deliver small amounts of electric current to areas of the brain. This current is delivered via electrodes incorporated into the device, which in turn is placed on the user's head. Notably, direct-to-consumer tDCS devices are now readily available on the consumer market (Wexler, 2017), and it is even possible to find online guidance about how to develop home-made, rudimentary devices that are capable of delivering non-invasive stimulation.

For a number of years, tDCS has been investigated as an experimental treatment for a range of neurological and psychological disorders (Bennabi & Haffen, 2018; Benninger et al., 2010; Ngernyam et al., 2013). Although studies have suggested that tDCS can be beneficial for several disorders, further research is still needed to understand the underlying mechanism of the beneficial effects observed in these studies and to optimise tDCS's therapeutic potential (Kang et al., 2024). Whilst the intervention is associated with some low risks of moderate adverse effects, it is widely accepted that tDCS has an acceptable safety profile when it is used within established safety parameters (Antal et al., 2017; Bikson et al., 2016). There has also been a growing number of studies investigating the effect of tDCS in enhancing elements of cognition in healthy adults (as well as clinical populations) (Looi et al., 2016; Mancuso et al., 2016). Indeed, the prospect of "cognitive enhancement" using tDCS appears to have played a significant role in prompting consumer interest in this intervention (Wexler, 2017).

The potential effect of any application of tDCS depends on several variables. Perhaps most importantly, tDCS can be used to target quite different areas of the brain, areas which may be implicated in quite different physiological and cognitive processes. Moreover, the device can be used to either excite neuronal activity in the targeted area (using anodal stimulation) or to inhibit activity in that area (via cathodal stimulation) (Stagg et al., 2018); the device can also be used to deliver stimulation of varying degrees of intensity. Indeed, studies investigating the ergogenic effects of tDCS have used a range of different targets and stimulation protocols in attempting to elicit different kinds of effects. As we shall detail further below, recent evidence suggests other important subject-specific variables that might influence the effect of stimulation in this context.

In our 2021 overview, we suggested that the evidence in favour of tDCS's ergogenic effects was highly mixed, and that there was substantial disagreement about tDCS's potential to enhance athletic performance (Pugh & Pugh, 2021). Although we shall provide details of some more recent systematic reviews that have been published since below, this general picture of the evidence base remains apt at the time of writing. Some studies fail to observe any significant ergogenic effects of tDCS, and critics have raised doubts about the ecological validity of those that do observe positive effects. For instance, concerns have been raised about, *inter alia*, the relevance of the primary outcome measures employed in some studies to elite sport performance, the reliance on non-elite athlete study participant pools, and difficulties in replicating key findings (Holgado et al., 2019; Lefaucheur, 2019; Machado et al., 2019). It is therefore important to exercise considerable caution in interpreting this evidence. Nonetheless, we should not dismiss the fact that there have been several positive findings across various studies, with some recent systematic reviews claiming that the available evidence suggests that certain tDCS protocols could potentially lead to sporting performance enhancement (Chinzara et al., 2022; Maudrich et al., 2022).

As we pointed out above, tDCS can be used to target different areas of the brain, with a view to eliciting different kinds of ergogenic effects. In a recent systematic review and meta-analysis, Chinzara et al. (2022) usefully divide the potential effects of tDCS in the sporting context into the following three domains: (i) strength, (ii) endurance, and (iii) visuo-motor skill. One notable finding in their analysis is that, although overall participants showed a small improvement in performance in these domains after application of tDCS across the studies analysed, the evidence suggesting a positive effect of tDCS over sham stimulation was strongest and most reliable in the strength domain. The evidence in favour of a positive effect on visuo-motor skill was weaker but still significant, whilst the evidence in favour of a positive effect on endurance only approached significance (Chinzara et al., 2022).

Even within each of these different domains, different studies have attempted to elicit these effects with different protocols and targets. As a result, even if one accepts that tDCS does have significant ergogenic effects, there is still "no consensus concerning the mode of action of tDCS as a function of specific stimulation sites" (Maudrich et al., 2022, p. 1525). We shall consider a few potential mechanisms that Maudrich *et al* identify in their systematic review below. At the outset though, it should be noted that a number of candidates for the mechanism of action underlying tDCS's enhancing effect in the domain of endurance are suggestive of the possibility that stimulation might serve to make the experience of exercise feel less aversive. For example, it has been hypothesised that stimulation of the motor cortex might prolong the onset of fatigue, and/or attenuate exercise-induced pain by increasing the subject's pain perception thresholds (Maudrich et al., 2022). The hypothesis that tDCS might make exercise feel less aversive is arguably somewhat supported by supplementary evidence in some studies, including observed decreases in the subject's rate of perceived exertion (RPE) accompanying enhanced performance (Angius et al., 2019), although such associations have not always been found. Nonetheless, much of the existing ethical literature on neuro-doping has proceeded on the assumption that tDCS could enhance sporting performance on the basis of these broad kinds of mechanisms and effects. For that reason, much of the recent discussion concerning the ethics of neuro-doping has concerned the role of effort in valuable sporting achievement, as we shall now explain.

2.3 The Argument from Effort

Any argument aiming to establish that a given performance-enhancing biotechnological intervention should be prohibited in elite sport faces an obvious consistency challenge; after all, a wide variety of performance-enhancing methods are permitted in elite sport. To illustrate, consider cycling; an elite cyclist today will follow a strict diet and training program. This training might have occurred at altitude, or involved the use of a hypoxic air tent to help stimulate the athlete's packed cell volume, which in turn will enable their muscles to receive more oxygen during exercise. Before a race, the cyclist might consume energy gels to help maintain stamina, and they will most likely be riding a bicycle with pneumatic tyres and a derailleur system, technological advances that will enable them to ride faster than their historical forebears. All of these performance-enhancing measures are currently permitted in elite cycling, and many of them are uncontroversial.

The challenge this raises is that any account of why a given biotechnology should be prohibited in sport must either (i) accept that this conclusion could have highly revisionist connotations for what else should be permitted in elite sport if we are to maintain consistency, or (ii) explain why the biotechnology in question differs from other widely accepted forms of performance enhancement. Much of the literature on the ethics of conventional forms of doping (such as EPO) generally amounts to an attempt to provide such explanations (Loland, 2018; Loland & McNamee, 2019).

In the current context, it might be thought that if tDCS serves to reduce the aversiveness of sporting performance (as explored above), this might be understood to demarcate it from other permissible forms of performance enhancement in sport. Although "hard work" is not included in the World Anti-Doping Agency's understanding of the spirit of sport (which informs that organisation's judgements about which ergogenic interventions should be prohibited in elite sport), some theorists have suggested that hard work should be understood as a necessary component of the Spirit of Sport (Imperatori et al., 2018) or more broadly of praiseworthy achievements.

Indeed, this sort of view is supported by philosophical work on the nature of achievement that gives a central role to effort in defining the nature and/

or value of achievements. For instance, Gwen Bradford argues that "achievements are comprised by a process and product, where the process is difficult, and competently causes the product" (Bradford, 2015, p. 25). Difficulty is, therefore, a necessary component of any achievement for Bradford, and she construes difficulty as pertaining to the intensity and duration of effort that the process involves. In turn, as Erler notes in his insightful discussion of the nature of effort, perceived effort can be understood as the "familiar experience of strenuous striving towards a certain goal", and professional competitive sporting performance will typically "require the athlete to experience substantial effort" (Erler, 2021) and the aversive phenomenology that this entails.

With this in mind, one might develop the following initial argument in favour of the claim that the use of tDCS would undermine sporting achievement:

P1 – Hard work is a necessary component of praiseworthy sporting achievement.
P2 – The use of tDCS would undermine the need for hard work in sporting performance.
C – The use of tDCS would undermine the possibility of praiseworthy sporting achievements.

What should we make of this argument? Interestingly, both premises have been challenged in the recent ethical literature. With respect to P1, the general claim that difficulty is necessary for valuable achievement has been subject to various criticisms in the philosophical sphere (Douglas, 2019; Forsberg & Skelton, 2020; Hirji, 2019). More specifically in the neuro-doping literature, competing accounts of praiseworthiness do not include effort or difficulty as a *necessary* condition for praiseworthiness. For example, Bowman-Smart and Savulescu (2021) have suggested that whilst praiseworthy achievements must be costly in some sense, the relevant cost need not be the aversive experience of effort. Instead, praiseworthy sporting achievement must involve (i) a voluntary costly commitment to a particular valuable end, that is (ii) reached via actions that surpass a minimum threshold of agential contribution, as defined by the (mutable) parameters of the sport, such that (iii) the costs incurred are directly related to that agential contribution (Bowman-Smart et al., 2021). On this account, neuro-doping would serve to undermine praiseworthy sporting achievements if it diminished the athlete's agential contribution below this minimum threshold, or if it rendered the performance to be lacking in costs that were directly related to the agent's contribution. As Bowman-Smart and Savulescu suggest, motivational doping, or the use of tDCS to reduce the aversive experience of sporting performance *could* have these sorts of effects in extreme cases; however, they claim that it is more plausible that current methods would only serve to slightly diminish the agent's contribution to a sporting performance, and not in such a way that the contribution would fall below the minimum threshold that is necessary for the user's sporting achievement to qualify as being praiseworthy.

However, one of the complicating factors for Bowman-Smart and Savulescu's analysis is that it appears that the cost of effort can be more or less closely related to the kind of minimal agential contribution that we take to define different sports. For example, in an endurance sport like marathon running, we might take even quite small biotechnological diminishments in effort to threaten the crucial minimal agential contribution that the athlete makes to performance in a marathon. The reason for this is that the ability to overcome the aversive experience of effort plays such a key role in what constitutes successful performance in that sport. However, in other sports, it may be more plausible to suppose that the need for the athlete to exert effort plays a less significant role in what we value and want to celebrate in that sport. Indeed, it might even be the case that the need to exert effort could represent an obstacle to the athlete's ability to contribute to other excellences that successful performance in the sport plausibly requires. Consider, for example, tennis; it is true that mental and physical endurance are crucial elements of successful performance in elite tennis (Erler, 2021). However, there are a huge number of other skills and excellences that the sport celebrates; we also assess and praise players on a range of other abilities, including their technique, tactics, shot selection, and mental fortitude. In this case, it might be that a more significant reduction in the need to exert effort could still be compatible with the agent's contribution to successful performance in the sport, given the importance of these other skills to what we take to determine successful performance. In view of this sort of complication, some theorists have defended a sport-specific approach to thinking about the role or effort in the value of sport and the ethics of neuro-doping (Devine, 2011; Pugh & Pugh, 2021; Shaw, 2021).

Turning now to P2, we might also question whether the use of tDCS would in fact undermine the need for hard work in sporting performance. One obvious rejoinder to this is that tDCS just might not have significant effects on the athlete's experience of effort. As explored above, the evidence in favour of tDCS's having an ergogenic effect is mixed, and there is a lack of understanding of the underlying mechanisms of action when it is observed to have ergogenic effects. In their recent detailed discussion of the potential mechanisms of action that might underlie the ergogenic effects of tDCS, Maudrich et al. (2022) suggest that stimulation of the motor cortex might cause these effects by prolonging the onset of fatigue; however, they also point out that pain tolerance is also potentially mediated by this area of the brain, and that stimulation of this area might instead enhance performance by attenuating exercise-induced pain. Whilst prolonging the onset of fatigue might straightforwardly reduce the need for "hard work", it is less clear that this would be true of increasing an athlete's pain tolerance. There are also significant epistemological obstacles to ascertaining these mechanisms and to establishing a good test for determining when a performance enhancement does in fact undermine the need for hard work (Pugh & Pugh, 2021).

That said, there is some evidence that the use of tDCS to stimulate some targets (particularly the motor cortex) can have ergogenic effects, and that at least some of these effects might plausibly be associated with a reduction in perceived effort. However, this is only of limited use for those advocating P2 in a manner that would allow for a generalised conclusion about the permissibility of tDCS in elite sport. The reason for this is that tDCS can be used to target quite different areas of the brain in pursuit of ergogenic effects that do not appear to have a plausible association with a reduction in the aversive experience of performance. For example, Maudrich et al. (2022) report that some studies have investigated the ergogenic effects of stimulating the cerebellum and the prefrontal cortex (PFC); these areas have less straightforward neurological implications for the athlete's experience of effort during sporting performance. For example, cerebellar tDCS has been associated with reducing errors during motor tasks, and it has been suggested that these effects may be attributable to improvements in postural adjustment that stimulation evinces, and reductions in tremor (Maudrich et al., 2022, p. 1527). Now, it might be that there could be something problematic about this sort of use of tDCS in a precision sport such as shooting; however, it is somewhat debatable whether the stimulation here is problematic *because* it is reducing the athlete's need to expend effort *per se*.

Finally, even if we assume that tDCS achieves an ergogenic effect by modulating the experience of effort during performance, this obviously does not entail that it would completely circumvent the need for the athlete to exert at least *some* effort during performance. Accordingly, a charitable interpretation of P2 should understand it to raise the concern that tDCS would undermine hard work by *significantly reducing* (rather than circumventing) the need for effort. Yet, even on this charitable understanding, one still might question P2 on the basis that tDCS might simply serve to increase the performance pay-off that an athlete receives for exerting the same level of effort they would have exerted in the absence of stimulation. In such a scenario, tDCS would not reduce the athlete's aversive experience of effort during performance; rather, to use Erler's memorable phrase, it would enable them to get "more bang for their effortful buck" (Erler, 2021, p. 196). Notably, since the publication of Erler's analysis, this interpretation has received some empirical support in one study investigating stimulation of the PFC (Pollastri et al., 2020), the findings of which Maudrich et al suggest could indicate that "tDCS may have reduced the cognitive effort needed to exert inhibitory control, allowing for higher levels of performance with the same perceived effort" (Maudrich et al., 2022, p. 1525). To be clear, this is just one study, suggestive of just one proposed mechanism of one particular montage of tDCS. However, it does, we suggest, illustrate the importance of nuance in analysing the way tDCS might evince a performance-enhancing effect that appears to involve a reduction in perceived effort, before moving to moral conclusions about the permissibility of tDCS in elite sport.

As the preceding discussion illustrates, it is far from clear that the argument from effort can straightforwardly provide a firm basis for a generalised prohibition of tDCS in elite sport. However, considerations of fairness might also plausibly be invoked in support of this claim, as we shall now explore.

2.4 The Argument from Fairness

Considerations of fairness are frequently invoked to ground moral arguments about the use of performance-enhancing interventions in sport (Schermer, 2008). In the context of neuro-doping specifically, Petersen and Lippert-Rasmussen have explained that there are several ways of cashing out an argument against neuro-doping from considerations of fairness (Petersen & Lippert-Rasmussen, 2020). Indeed, one of the permutations of the argument from fairness they consider (namely, "Lenk's Equality of Opportunity Fairness Argument") bears a considerable degree of overlap with the argument from effort considered in the previous section. The reason for this is that Lenk's Equality of Opportunity Fairness argument relies on the premise that fairness "requires that athletes do not enjoy decisive advantages over others to perform best in sports that are not the result of their own training and performance but the result of enhancement technology" (Petersen & Lippert-Rasmussen, 2020, p. 185). Whilst Petersen and Lippert-Rasmussen reject this premise, those who are sympathetic to the argument from effort considered in the previous section might plausibly claim that the unfairness alluded to in this premise is best explained by the lack of effort involved in advantages that are not secured via training and performance (Imperatori et al., 2018).

Here though, we shall consider a somewhat simpler argument from fairness as requiring something like a "level playing field". Suppose it were true that tDCS merely enables an athlete to obtain "more bang for their effortful buck" in the manner that Erler suggests. One might yet complain that it would still be unfair for one athlete using tDCS to get this greater pay-off for their effort, in a way that provides them with an advantage over a competitor who is *not* using tDCS. This thought captures the essence of what Petersen and Lippert-Rasmussen call the "Unfair Inequality of Opportunity Argument", which they formalise as follows (Petersen & Lippert-Rasmussen, 2020, p. 181):

P1: Fairness requires that athletes have equal opportunities to win.
P2: The use of neuro-doping by some athletes creates greater inequality in the opportunities to win.
P3: If P1 and P2, then the use of neuro-doping by athletes should be banned.
C1: Thus, the use of neuro-doping by athletes should be banned.

Whilst Petersen and Lippert-Rasmussen suggest that all three of the above premises are problematic, for our purposes here we can just focus on P1 and P2.

As these authors explain, the interpretation of these premises depends a great deal on the sense of equality that they are understood to invoke. First, one might interpret the premises to be invoking what the authors call "formal equality of opportunity" (Petersen & Lippert-Rasmussen, 2020, p. 182). In the sporting context, this sense of equality can be understood to require that no one is excluded from competing, and that the victor should be determined by identifying the competitor who best meets the victory conditions of the sport in question. However, the premises could also be understood to be invoking what the authors call "substantive equality of opportunity" (Petersen & Lippert-Rasmussen, 2020, p. 182). In the sporting context, this sense of equality can be understood to require that people have fair opportunities to develop the abilities that are necessary to best meet the victory conditions of the sport in question. Importantly, the authors suggest that substantive equality of opportunity can be understood in either a moderate or radical sense. The moderate view claims that substantive equality requires "counteracting the differential effects of social class"; in contrast, the substantive view claims that substantive equality also requires "counteracting luck in the differential" lottery (Petersen & Lippert-Rasmussen, 2020, p. 182).

With these distinctions in mind, we can now understand why Petersen and Lippert-Rasmussen believe that P1 and P2 are problematic. Suppose that we interpret the premises to be invoking a radical view of substantive equality; on this interpretation, P1 is very plausibly false, as success in elite sport can clearly depend on various factors that are the outcome of the genetic lottery. Michael Phelps and Eero Mantyranta are frequently invoked examples of highly successful athletes who happened to be born with unusual physiological features that made them particularly well-placed to succeed in their chosen sports (Jennings & Braun, 2023; Savulescu et al., 2004). They thus enjoyed a considerable competitive advantage over their competitors who did not share these traits. The point is that if we believe that it was not unfair for such athletes to dominate their respective sports, then it is hard to see how P1 could be true. More broadly, the authors suggest that these cases (and others) give us reasons to doubt that we should invoke a radical view of substantive equality in discussions of what fairness requires in elite sport.

In contrast, if we interpret the premises to be invoking either moderate substantive equality or formal equality alone, then Petersen and

Lippert-Rasmussen argue it is much less clear that P2 will be true. Consider first moderate substantive equality. If the concern about fairness pertains to the differential effects of social class, then the authors argue that it may be possible to regulate the use of neuro-doping in a manner that facilitates fairness:

> (If neuro-doping) were permitted in poor countries, but banned in rich countries – it could mitigate these athletes' lack of luck in the social lottery and thus decrease moderate, substantive inequality of opportunity. (Petersen & Lippert-Rasmussen, 2020, p. 183)

Consider now, formal equality of opportunity. The authors first raise some doubts about whether P1 would be true if it were to invoke this sense of equality, since many ascriptive properties (such as sex and disability) form the basis for competitive categorisation in sport (Petersen & Lippert-Rasmussen, 2020, p. 182). However, since such categorisation is not universally endorsed, the authors' main critique of invoking formal equality of opportunity in the argument we are considering in this section is that one could suitably ensure formal equality of opportunity by ensuring that *all* athletes have an equal opportunity to access the intervention. The note that:

> As long as all athletes are permitted to use neuro-doping, then fairness, as presently understood, has no quarrel with neuro-doping. (Petersen & Lippert-Rasmussen, 2020)

The thought here is that if athletes are not prohibited from neuro-doping, then all athletes will have an equal opportunity to avail themselves of its benefits, thus satisfying the demands of formal equality of opportunity.

Of course, one might plausibly raise the concern that ensuring only formal equality of opportunity is to ensure a somewhat impoverished version of equality; to put the point another way, giving all athletes equal permission to use neuro-doping techniques does not entail giving all athletes equal opportunity to receive the *ergogenic benefits* of these interventions. One permutation of this general line of response might appeal to financial impediments that some athletes may face; not all athletes will be able to afford to purchase expensive forms of neuro-doping, and so it is unclear that merely making it permissible to use neuro-doping interventions amount to giving all athletes fair equality of opportunity to access these benefits. However, as we saw with the discussion of substantive equality of opportunity above, it is important to somewhat contextualise this concern; indeed, it is an objection that could be raised against a whole host of non-biomedical forms of enhancement. Although authorities have taken measures to prevent the use of certain kinds of equipment that are considered prohibitively expensive, it is undeniable that financial investment still plays a powerful role in elite sport. Accordingly, given the relatively low cost of tDCS devices in comparison to other forms of advanced performance-enhancing technologies that are permitted in sport, it is unclear that concern about financial fair equality of opportunity can mount a compelling objection to neuro-doping without having highly revisionary implications for other seemingly permissible forms of performance enhancement. Moreover, as the authors themselves point out, neuro-doping could be regulated in a manner that would mitigate the financial impediments that some athletes might face.

A different permutation of this general argument might instead appeal to biological rather than financial impediments that some athletes might face in benefiting from neuro-doping techniques. It is well-documented that there can be significant differences in the effectiveness of tDCS for different users. In their recent analysis of tDCS in sporting performance, Chinzara and colleagues highlight work showing that the initial state of the performer (i.e., their initial arousal or level of fatigue) modulates the effectiveness of tDCS (Chinzara et al., 2022, p. 470). They also highlight the need for further work to flesh out how participant charactersistics (such as gender and genetics) might contribute to the heterogeneous effects of tDCS (Chinzara et al., 2022, pp. 481–482). Again, evidence of these heterogeneous effects might be thought to raise doubts about the claim that merely making neuro-doping permissible for all athletes is sufficient to secure true equality of opportunity. Indeed, Andreas Lavazza has argued that those who cannot sufficiently benefit from tDCS in sport due to the differential effectiveness of the intervention should be compensated for this fact (Lavazza, 2019).

However, this permutation of the general line of response also appears to be susceptible to the same concerns raised against radical substantive equality above. As Petersen and Lippert-Rasmussen point out in their own response to Lavazza's paper, athletes differ in their degree of responsiveness to conventional forms of performance enhancement, including nutrition and training, and yet, it seems implausible to claim that this precludes fair competition (Petersen & Lippert-Rasmussen, 2021). Indeed, in view of the highly revisionist implications of a consistent applications of Lavazza's view, Petersen and Lippert-Rasmussen suggest that it is largely "conventions that determine which inequalities in responsiveness are unfair and which are not" (Petersen & Lippert-Rasmussen, 2021, p. 717) rather than some general principle of fairness (such as the luck egalitarianism that Lavazza appears to espouse, and that plausibly undergirds other quite radical views of substantive equality of opportunity in the literature). Moreover, they claim that "as long as these conventions are public and generally respected, there is nothing inherently unfair" about refraining from redressing such inequalities in sport (Petersen & Lippert-Rasmussen, 2021).

We are sympathetic to Petersen and Lippert-Rasmussen's rebuttal of the Unfair Inequality of Opportunity Argument to this point, and to their claims about the role of conventions in determining our understanding of fairness in sport. One might further suggest that perhaps part of the explanation of the conventional nature of understanding of fairness in sport may lie in the idea that in the ethics of sport certain values (such as the value of "natural performance") are often promoted that not only compete with philosophical principles of fairness, but may in fact be mutually incompatible with them. In his discussion of tension between the value of fairness and the natural, Alexandre Erler nicely captures this thought in the following passage:

> Many people, it seems, want to hold both that the athletes they admire should only rely on a combination of talent and grit to achieve success, and that these athletes should be able to take full credit for the determinants of that success. A truly consistent approach, however, must acknowledge that these two ideals cannot be fully realized together. Either we must drop one in favour of the other, or, if we wish to retain some commitment to both, trade-offs between them will be required.
>
> (Erler, 2018)

Our conventional understanding of sport is arguably then a reflection of the fact that our understanding of fairness in this context involves a trade-off with other values. A unilateral commitment to a principled philosophical conception of fairness in sport would, in contrast, likely require us to sacrifice a commitment to other values that some may wish to uphold in sport.

The upshot of this for the ethics of neuro-doping is that evidence pertaining to the differential ergogenic effects of tDCS might support a fairness-based objection that appeals to a broadly luck egalitarian conception of fairness in sport. However, there are strong reasons to doubt that such a principled understanding of fairness could plausibly be operative in sport as we know it today. If we instead adopt the conventionalist approach to fairness in sport that Petersen and Lippert-Rasmussen adopt, and accept the kind of balance that our current conventions appear to forge between fairness and other values, then this kind of fairness-objection to neuro-doping loses much of its force.

Yet, it would be a mistake to claim that the objection will have lost *all* force if we take this approach. The reason for this is that conventions in sport, including conventions of fairness, are malleable, and the nature of the trade-offs that we want to make in sport can evolve along with our societal values. Indeed, recent controversies pertaining to the classification of female athletes with differences of sexual development (DSD) have forced regulators and ethicists to grapple with questions about what fairness in sport requires. We shall conclude our discussion here by suggesting that we are plausibly in a period in which our conventions about fairness in sport are being subjected to deep societal debates of the sort that give us reason to be cautious about relying on our extant conventions when considering whether contemporaneous technological developments in performance enhancement are compatible with fairness.

As Jennings and Braun discuss in a recent feature article on the classification of female athletes with DSD, the latest World Athletics regulations require:

> female athletes with DSD and sufficient androgen sensitivity to lower their testosterone levels to below 2.5 nmol/L over a period of at least 24 months in order to compete in the women's category of any international athletics event.
>
> (Jennings & Braun, 2023, p. 1)

Crucially, as these authors point out in the paper, World Athletics has sought to justify these regulations (and their attendant impositions on some female athletes' natural physiology) by appealing to principles of fairness that afford salience to the roles of dedication, talent and hard work in seeking to ensure a level playing field.

Notably, in a similar vein, Sigmund Loland has previously invoked a luck egalitarian fair equality of opportunity norm to frame his discussion of World Athletics' approach to the well-publicised case of Caster Semenya (Loland, 2020). In this discussion, Loland argues that such a norm "justifies restricting the women's class to runners below a certain testosterone level" as "the lesser evil" (Loland, 2020, p. 588), and that such a norm admits of historical, socio-cultural, and moral justification. More specifically, with respect to the latter, Loland suggests that the norm can be justified by appeal to "(neo-) Kantian conceptions of persons as autonomous moral agents entitled to respect and to be treated in fair and just ways" (Loland, 2020, p. 587). Crucially, he also observes that existing classification regimes may not adequately reflect the fair equality of opportunity norm, and that "several sports could reconsider their practice" if they were to follow the norm (Loland, 2020).

The point of this discussion is not to suggest that Loland is correct to invoke a luck egalitarian fair equality of opportunity norm in this context. Nor is it to claim that this norm does in fact justify World Athletics' approach to classification in the Semenya case. Indeed, in their analysis, Jennings and Braun themselves assume World Athletics' understanding of fairness for the sake of argument, and conclude that this conception does *not* lend support to requiring female athletes with DSD to suppress their testosterone levels (Jennings & Braun, 2023). Instead, they argue that this conception of fairness supports a revisionary categorical system in elite sport that a number of theorists have proposed, in which all athletes (regardless of gender) are categorised into classes based on properties that lead to significant performance advantages (Jennings & Braun, 2023). Rather the point of this discussion is that the recent debates over female athletes with DSD is one in which theorists and regulators have had to revisit the manner in which we conventionally trade-off values associated with fairness and "the natural" in sport. Moreover, it is a context in which some theorists have advocated that we should perhaps challenge some of our existing conventions to better safeguard the fairness that sport ought to instantiate. It is these points about challenges to existing conceptions of fairness in sport that we suggest are relevant to thinking about fairness in the context of neuro-doping.

Of course, these arguments can themselves be challenged, and there may also be good reasons for why the sort of revisionism we are seeing advocated in the context of debates about athlete classification need not translate to our conventional understanding of fairness in the context of performance enhancement and neuro-doping. However, they are perhaps indicative of the possibility that our conventional understandings of fairness in sport are less stable than they have previously been. Accordingly, a fairness-based argument against neuro-doping might yet be somewhat resistant to consistency-based objections that might be levelled against it. Whenthese objections appeal largely to our existing practices and conventional understanding of fairness in sport to ground an appeal to consistency, they are perhaps weakened when those very conventions are being challenged for other reasons.

2.5 Conclusion

Our aims in this chapter have been quite limited, and there are several important dimensions to the debate on the ethics of neuro-doping that we have not been able to address here. Most notably, we have focused only on one particular neuro-technology (namely tDCS), and we have not addressed practical concerns about the feasibility of prohibiting or even regulating that technology in elite sport.

We have, however, sought to address two salient ethical concerns that should, we believe, be addressed before we consider the non-idealised question of what the correct regulatory approach to neuro-doping might be in practice. Drawing on recent work in both the ethical and scientific literature, we have suggested that neither the argument from effort nor the argument from fairness straightforwardly provides a firm basis for a generalised prohibition of tDCS in elite sport. This is perhaps a somewhat significant conclusion for how we should currently approach regulatory questions about neuro-doping, but it is a conclusion that is contingent on the technology that is currently widely available for neuro-doping purposes, what we currently know about how that technology appears to potentially evince its apparent ergogenic effects, and our current conventions about the nature of fairness in sport. Naturally, all of these factors are likely to evolve, especially as we countenance the possibility of merging neurotechnology with artificial intelligence.

Therefore, it would of course be a mistake to assume that the conclusions we have drawn about tDCS in this chapter will translate straightforwardly to technologies from which it might quite radically differ. Nonetheless, it seems plausible to predict that concerns about both fairness and the implications that such future technologies may have for the athlete's effort and its role in their sporting performance will likely be of relevance. Accordingly, we hope that our discussion in this chapter can serve as a useful backdrop to discussions of more advanced forms of AI-informed neuro-doping.

Note

1 As Møller and Christiansen (2021) point out, this is technically a misnomer, since doping is technically defined as that which the World Anti-Doping Agency deems to be an anti-doping violation. Since neurostimulation has not yet been deemed to constitute such a violation, it does not meet this definition of doping. Whilst acknowledging that the authors are correct on this definitional point, the terminology of "neuro-doping" to describe the use of neurostimulation in sport is now widespread, so we shall also adopt it for the purposes of ourdiscussion here.

References

Angius, L., Santarnecchi, E., Pascual-Leone, A., & Marcora, S. M. (2019). Transcranial direct current stimulation over the left dorsolateral prefrontal cortex improves inhibitory control and endurance performance in healthy individuals. *Neuroscience, 419*, 34–45. https://doi.org/10.1016/j.neuroscience.2019.08.052

Antal, A., Alekseichuk, I., Bikson, M., Brockmöller, J., Brunoni, A. R., Chen, R., Cohen, L. G., Dowthwaite, G., Ellrich, J., Flöel, A., Fregni, F., George, M. S., Hamilton, R., Haueisen, J., Herrmann, C. S., Hummel, F. C., Lefaucheur, J. P., Liebetanz, D., Loo, C. K., … Paulus, W. (2017). *Low intensity transcranial electric stimulation: Safety, ethical, legal regulatory and application guidelines*. 1774–1809.

Bennabi, D., & Haffen, E. (2018). *Transcranial Direct Current Stimulation (tDCS): A promising treatment for major depressive disorder?* https://www.ncbi.nlm.nih.gov/pmc/articles/PMC5977072/

Benninger, D. H., Lomarev, M., Lopez, G., Wassermann, E. M., Li, X., Considine, E., & Hallett, M. (2010). *Transcranial direct current stimulation for the treatment of Parkinson's disease*. 1105–1111.

Bikson, M., Grossman, P., Thomas, C., Zannou, A. L., Jiang, J., Adnan, T., Mourdoukoutas, A. P., Kronberg, G., Truong, D., Boggio, P., Brunoni, A. R., Charvet, L., Fregni, F., Fritsch, B., Gillick, B., Hamilton, R. H., Hampstead, B. M., Jankord, R., Kirton, A., … Woods, A. J. (2016). *Safety of transcranial Direct Current Stimulation: Evidence based update 2016*. 641–661.

Bowman-Smart, Hilary, Savulescu, & Julian. (2021). The ethics of motivational neuro-doping in sport: Praiseworthiness and prizeworthiness. *Neuroethics, 14*(2), 205–215. https://doi.org/10.1007/s12152-020-09445-5

Bradford, G. (2015). *Achievement*. Oxford University Press.

Chinzara, T. T., Buckingham, G., & Harris, D. J. (2022). Transcranial direct current stimulation and sporting performance: A systematic review and meta-analysis of transcranial direct current stimulation effects on physical endurance, muscular strength and visuomotor skills. *The European Journal of Neuroscience, 55*(2), 468–486. https://doi.org/10.1111/ejn.15540

Davis, N. J. (2013). *Neurodoping: Brain stimulation as a performance-enhancing measure*. 649–653.

Devine, J. W. (2011). Doping is a threat to sporting excellence. *British Journal of Sports Medicine, 45*(8), 637–639. https://doi.org/10.1136/bjsm.2009.070862

Douglas, T. (2019). Enhancement & desert. *Politics, Philosophy and Economics, 18*(1), 3–22.

Erler, A. (2018). *'Natural' athletic performance or a level playing field? You can't have both*. 30–31.

Erler, A. (2021). Neuro-doping and the value of effort in endurance sports. *Neuroethics, 14*(2), 191–203. https://doi.org/10.1007/s12152-020-09450-8

Forsberg, L., & Skelton, A. (2020). Achievement and enhancement. *Canadian Journal of Philosophy, 50*(3), 322–338. https://doi.org/10.1017/can.2019.43

Gleaves, J. (2011). *The ethics of doping and anti-doping: Redeeming the soul of sport?* 75–78.

Hirji, S. (2019). Not always worth the effort: Difficulty and the value of achievement. *Pacific Philosophical Quarterly, 100*(2), 525–548. https://doi.org/10.1111/papq.12257

Holgado, D., Vadillo, M. A., & Sanabria, D. (2019). *The effects of transcranial direct current stimulation on objective and subjective indexes of exercise performance: A systematic review and meta-analysis*. 242–250.

Imperatori, L. S., Milbourn, L., & Garasic, M. D. (2018). *Would the use of safe, cost-effective tDCS tackle rather than cause unfairness in sports?* 377–387.

Jennings, K., & Braun, E. (2023). Beyond suppressing testosterone: A categorical system to achieve a "level playing field" in sport. *The American Journal of Bioethics, 1*. https://doi.org/10.1080/15265161.2023.2232750

Kang, J., Lee, H., Yu, S., Lee, M., Kim, H. J., Kwon, R., Kim, S., Fond, G., Boyer, L., Rahmati, M., Koyanagi, A., Smith, L., Nehs, C. J., Kim, M. S., Sánchez, G. F. L., Dragioti, E., Kim, T., & Yon, D. K. (2024). Effects and safety of transcranial direct current stimulation on multiple health outcomes: An umbrella review of randomized clinical trials. *Molecular Psychiatry*, 1–13. https://doi.org/10.1038/s41380-024-02624-3

Lavazza, A. (2019). *Transcranial electrical stimulation for human enhancement and the risk of inequality: Prohibition or compensation?* 122–131.

Lefaucheur, J.-P. (2019). *Boosting physical exercise with cortical stimulation or brain doping using tDCS: Fact or myth?* Elsevier Masson SAS.

Loland, S. (2018). *Performance-enhancing drugs, sport, and the ideal of natural athletic performance*. 8–15.

Loland, S. (2020). Caster semenya, athlete classification, and fair equality of opportunity in sport. *Journal of Medical Ethics, 46*(9), 584–590. https://doi.org/10.1136/medethics-2019-105937

Loland, S., & McNamee, M. J. (2019). *The 'spirit of sport', WADAs code review, and the search for an overlapping consensus*. 325–339.

Looi, C. Y., Duta, M., Brem, A.-K., Huber, S., Nuerk, H.-C., & Kadosh, R. C. (2016). *Combining brain stimulation and video game to promote long-term transfer of learning and cognitive enhancement*. 22003.

Machado, D. G. da S., Unal, G., Andrade, S. M., Moreira, A., Altimari, L. R., Brunoni, A. R., Perrey, S., Mauger, A. R., Bikson, M., & Okano, A. H. (2019). *Effect of transcranial direct current stimulation on exercise performance: A systematic review and meta-analysis*. 593–605.

Mancuso, L. E., Ilieva, I. P., Hamilton, R. H., & Farah, M. J. (2016). Does transcranial direct current stimulation improve healthy working memory?: A meta-analytic review. *Journal of Cognitive Neuroscience, 28*(8), 1063–1089. https://doi.org/10.1162/jocn_a_00956

Maudrich, T., Ragert, P., Perrey, S., & Kenville, R. (2022). Single-session anodal transcranial direct current stimulation to enhance sport-specific performance in athletes: A systematic review and meta-analysis. *Brain Stimulation, 15*(6), 1517–1529. https://doi.org/10.1016/j.brs.2022.11.007

McNamee, M. J. (2012). *The spirit of sport and the medicalisation of anti-doping: Empirical and normative ethics*. 374–392.

Møller, V., & Christiansen, A. V. (2021). Neuro-doping – A serious threat to the integrity of sport? *Neuroethics, 14*(2), 159–168. https://doi.org/10.1007/s12152-020-09446-4

Ngernyam, N., Jensen, M. P., Auvichayapat, N., Punjaruk, W., & Auvichayapat, P. (2013). *Transcranial direct current stimulation in neuropathic pain*. https://www.ncbi.nlm.nih.gov/pmc/articles/PMC4193292/

Petersen, T. S., & Lippert-Rasmussen, K. (2020). Neuro-doping and fairness. *Neuroethics, 14*(2), 179–190. https://doi.org/10.1007/s12152-020-09447-3

Petersen, T. S., & Lippert-Rasmussen, K. (2021). Doping, fairness, and unequal responsiveness: A response to Lavazza. *Bioethics, 35*(7), 714–717. https://doi.org/10.1111/bioe.12908

Pollastri, L., Gallo, G., Zucca, M., Filipas, L., Torre, A. L., Riba, U., Molino, L., & Geda, E. (2020). *Bilateral dorsolateral prefrontal cortex high-definition transcranial direct-current stimulation improves time-trial performance in elite cyclists*. https://doi.org/10.1123/ijspp.2019-0910

Pugh, J., & Pugh, C. (2021). Neurostimulation, doping, and the spirit of sport. *Neuroethics, 14*(Suppl 2), 141—158. https://doi.org/10.1007/s12152-020-09435-7

Savulescu, J., Foddy, B., & Clayton, M. (2004). *Why we should allow performance enhancing drugs in sport*. 666–670.

Schermer, M. (2008). *On the argument that enhancement is "cheating"*. 85–88.

Shaw, E. (2021). Neurodoping in chess to enhance mental stamina. *Neuroethics, 14*(2), 217–230. https://doi.org/10.1007/s12152-020-09456-2

Stagg, C. J., Antal, A., & Nitsche, M. A. (2018). Physiology of transcranial direct current stimulation. *The Journal of ECT, 34*(3), 144–152. https://doi.org/10.1097/YCT.0000000000000510

Wexler, A. (2017). *Who uses direct-to-consumer brain stimulation products, and why? A study of home users of tDCS devices*. 1–21.

Chapter 3

AI-Driven Neurostimulation in Sport

A Critical Approach

Alberto Carrio

3.1 Introduction

Improving athletic performance has always been a key issue in sport. A great deal of research, involving various fields of science and technology, has been carried out to this end. Although the initial focus was on improving physical performance, there is a growing interest in the importance of the psychological side of athletic performance. To achieve psychological improvements in athletes, traditional methods have been explored, followed by the incorporation of the latest technologies. In this way, neurostimulation, and in particular the use of smart neurostimulation devices, has become the penultimate method for improving athletic skills and performance. The use of this technology opens up new opportunities for athletes, coaches and sports sponsors. But it also raises many ethical concerns about its safe use, the ability of athletes to refuse them and their impact on the fairness of sport.

This chapter, like others in this book collection, aims to contribute to and stimulate the ongoing debate about the increasing importance of high technology in sport. In particular, the role of artificial intelligence-driven technology in enhancing athletic performance and the ethical concerns it raises. However, unlike other contributions, this chapter analyses this issue adopting an internal point of view of sport. That is, it examines the use of intelligent neurostimulation technologies through the lens of the internal values of sport and their consistency with the rationale of the World Anti-Doping Agency (WADA) Code.

The chapter is divided into four main sections. In the first part (Section 3.2), I give a broad overview of neurostimulation in sport, from natural and chemical substances to modern AI-driven devices. The second part (Section 3.3) examines the increasing incorporation of high technology in sport in the light of WADA's current anti-doping policy and takes a critical approach to the rationale behind the WADA Code and Prohibited List. The third part (Section 3.4) presents and discusses the arguments for and against considering AI-powered neurostimulation as a prohibited method under the rationale of the WADA Code. The chapter concludes (Section 3.5) by suggesting an

DOI: 10.4324/9781003520290-4

exploratory way for WADA to monitor the enhancing effect and safe use of these devices in elite sport.

3.2 An Overview of Neurostimulation in Sport

Most efforts to improve athletic performance have traditionally focused on the physical body, on the mechanics of movement. As such, improving muscular endurance through hard training and proper nutrition has always been the basic norm for athletic success. Throughout the history of sport, training has often been supplemented by the use of certain substances, such as alcohol, herbs and some animal parts, which were thought to improve athletic performance (Conti, 2010). Similarly, the use of psychotropic substances to intervene in the psyche, which has a long tradition in human culture, is not alien to sport.

In modern sport, however, the ideal of athletic performance is linked to the demonstration of excellence. In this sense, an excellent athlete must respect the internal values of sport, such as effort, concentration, self-improvement, fair play and teamwork, which also requires a strong self-control of mental abilities. It's no coincidence that top athletes work hand in hand with coaches and psychologists to gain control of their mental abilities, thereby strengthening their performance and improving their mental health and resilience.

According to Tännsjö, who agrees with previous pro-enhancement proposals such as those of Miah (2004) and Savulescu (Savulescu, Foddy & Clyton, 2004; Savulescu, 2014), the use of modern neurostimulation technologies, provided they are safe, is not only convenient but should be mandatory in order to level sports competition, allowing athletes with less natural endowments to improve themselves, which would make sports competition much fairer.

But the assumption of Tännsjö is going too far. That's why it's important to understand what the role of neurostimulation has been in sport and how smart neurostimulation currently works in sport before making a decision on whether to allow or ban it in and out of sports contests. In what follows, I will review the literature on neurostimulation from less to more invasive techniques, focusing on how they work in sport.

3.2.1 Intervening in the Sport Psyche: From Drugs to Brain Control

As mentioned above, the use of psychotropic substances, including their alleged performance-enhancing effects in sport, has a long history in humanity. More recently, improvements in pharmaceutical design have led to the development of new synthetic drugs that can stimulate the central nervous system (CNS) in a variety of ways. A common feature of these drugs is their therapeutic purpose, such as treating age-related neurodegenerative disorders or improving attention and concentration deficits. However, CNS stimulants have also been shown to improve cognitive performance in healthy people by increasing alertness and attention in stressful situations.

Let's first look at how these stimulant drugs work, before looking at other ways of stimulating the brain.

3.2.1.1 *The Chemistry of Athletic Success?*

The most popular chemical stimulants are probably methylphenidate and modafinil. Methylphenidate is a central nervous system (CNS) stimulant with several therapeutic uses, including attention deficit disorder and narcolepsy. Because methylphenidate is an effective blocker of dopamine reuptake by neurons, it has been prescribed to treat bipolar disorder and other major depressive disorders (Dell'Osso et al., 2014). Methylphenidate has also proved its effectiveness as a cognitive and athletic performance enhancer (Spencer et al., 2015; Berezanskaya et al., 2022).

However, the use of methylphenidate for athletic performance requires high doses and alternative routes of administration outside medical control and prescription, which can lead to unintended and serious adverse effects.

Modafinil has been used primarily for the treatment of narcolepsy and to stimulate wakefulness in sleep apnoea.[1] Like methylphenidate, modafinil is a CNS stimulant that has been used for military purposes and as a smart drug by students and workers to increase alertness (Van Rooyen et al., 2021). Although the ability of both methylphenidate and modafinil to act as effective cognitive enhancers is debated due to the stimulant nature of both, they have many contraindications and adverse side effects. Both are banned in competition by the World Anti-Doping Agency (WADA).[2] However, perhaps WADA should also consider banning their use in and out of competition, given the various adverse effects they can have on athletes' health, and in accordance with the rationale of the WADA Code, which I will discuss later in this chapter.

3.2.1.2 *Neurofeedback Training in Sport*

Neurofeedback training is a relatively new method of improving athletic performance. Neurofeedback has been investigated outside of sport for many years and can be defined as a method of teaching people to consciously control their brain waves (Marzbani et al., 2016). That's because it has been described as a biological way of feedback (Xiang et al., 2018). Currently, neurofeedback is becoming increasingly popular with athletes and coaches, and has even been considered the best way to improve cognitive and motor performance, and to achieve peak athletic performance (Wilson et al., 2006; Gruzelier, 2014). Neurofeedback training was initially recommended as an effective therapy for psychological and cognitive disorders, such as attention deficit, hyperactivity and so on. However, given the results of neurofeedback in improving motor and cognitive skills, several works recommend its use in sport as a way of optimising the overall psychological status of athletes (Gruzelier, 2014; Cheng et al., 2015; Wang et al., 2020).

One of the best-known effects of neurofeedback training is the stimulation of the vagus nerve, the longest and most complex of the cranial nerves. The main function of the vagus nerve is to control the parasympathetic system, i.e. the regulation of rest and digestion. It is responsible for linking sensory activity and motor information, helping to regulate the function of other organs such as heart rate, breathing and digestive process. The vagus nerve plays an important role in brain-body communication and also in athletic performance, as it affects the reduction of the sympathetic nervous system and can therefore also lower blood pressure, improve cognition and concentration, reduce inflammation and so on (Clancy et al., 2014). In recent years, however, improvements in science and technology have paved the way for new forms of neurostimulation that are already having a major impact in the world of sport.

3.2.2 *Brain Interventions to Boost Athletic Performance*

Apart from the use of synthetic drugs and other chemical forms of neurostimulation in sport, there are many other different types of intervention that have been explored for this purpose. Following Merkel (Merkel et al., 2007), these interventions can be divided into three broad categories, namely, genetic, electromagnetic and surgical interventions. The application of gene transfer and neurosurgery with restorative and enhancing purposes is manifold but also raises several ethical issues in and outside of sport.

Gene therapy has aroused great interest due to its promising application in the treatment of neurological impairments and diseases such as Alzheimer's (Rafii et al., 2014) and Parkinson's (Saraiva et al., 2016), or with restorative purposes such as neuroprotective effects in spinal muscular atrophy (Olivan et al., 2016) or enhancement of tissue regeneration after brain injury (Kwon et al., 2016). However, the natural blood barrier protection of the CNS and the unpredictability of the vectors acting as gene delivery vehicles raise several ethical and safety concerns that need to be clearly understood before approving such interventions in healthy populations (Puhl et al., 2019). That's why, all things considered, gene therapy is not currently a suitable option for improving athletic performance in sport.

With regard to brain surgery, advances in science and technology have paved the way for a new generation of high-tech implantable devices that are showing promising results for patients with brain damage. New brain-implantable devices undoubtedly represent a great opportunity for brain-injured people, including Paralympic athletes. They will open up an attractive future for Paralympic sports once their effectiveness and safety have been proven. Today, however, brain implants for regular athletes in sports competition are nothing more than a futuristic elucidation without any real possibility. Moreover, the use of these devices in today's professional sports would be immediately recognised as a form of brain doping and a means of cheating. In any case, many of the articles in this collection deal with this issue and the possibilities it opens up for the future of sport.

However, there are many other less invasive brain stimulation techniques that are already being used in elite and professional sports.

3.2.2.1 Brain Stimulation Techniques in Sport

Brain stimulation techniques have long been popular in professional and even amateur sports. In spite of the initial scepticism with which these techniques were met, they have gained quite widespread acceptance in the field of sport (Goodall, 2012). Brain stimulation in sport aims to improve key physical and psychological performance skills such as motor learning, muscle strength, fatigue reduction and concentration. In other words, brain stimulation has similar effects to those of drugs in the past and, according to some authors, poses fewer risks when used properly (Davis, 2013).

As with the brain interventions mentioned above, brain stimulation techniques have been developed for therapeutic purposes. Again, only a few of them can realistically be applied to current sport, apart from foreseeable future applications in Paralympic sport. In any case, below I will look at some of the most popular current brain stimulation techniques and their viability in sport.

3.2.2.1.1 DEEP BRAIN STIMULATION

The first candidate to be considered is deep brain stimulation (DBS). This is a type of neurostimulation that involves the surgical implantation of a neurostimulator device and electrodes connected to different regions of the brain. In its current state, the nature of DBS makes it useless for sporting competition, but even if it could be successfully applied to sport, DBS deserves the same treatment as brain implants, as its use would be considered a form of brain doping and also a clear unfair use in sport. Quite apart from the risk they pose to the health of athletes.

3.2.2.1.2 TRANSCRANIAL MAGNETIC STIMULATION

Transcranial magnetic stimulation (TMS) is another brain stimulation technique that is less invasive than DBS. TMS is used to study the functioning of the prefrontal cortex (Hallett, 2007). Although there are many different types of TMS, they mainly consist of inducing electrical currents in the underlying cortex (Rossini et al., 2015). That is, TMS uses short electrical pulses to stimulate specific parts of the brain that regulate mood, and can also influence long-term reorganisation of brain activity if stimulated regularly (Davis, 2013). TMS is therefore capable of altering the activity and connections between various areas of the brain (Bergmann et al., 2021). Combining TMS and DBS is a promising way to learn about both the cortex and other brain regions and how the connections between them influence neurological conditions (Johnson et al., 2020). However, as in the previous cases, TMS alone or in combination with DBS is far from being used in current sport.

3.2.2.1.3 TRANSCRANIAL ELECTRICAL STIMULATION

Transcranial electrical stimulation (tES) is a non-invasive neurostimulation technique that aims to alter some areas of the brain by passing electrical currents through the cortex (Reed et al., 2018). Under the common denominator of tES, different techniques of neurostimulation coexist, including transcranial direct current stimulation (tDCS), alternating current stimulation (tACS) and random noise stimulation (tRNS).

The use of tES in sports has increased in recent years in both professional and amateur sports. In fact, there are many companies that are openly marketing various devices with the aim of using them as a kind of "do-it-yourself" neurostimulation in sports. Commercial devices are usually an off-the-shelf product that adapts tDCS, which originally involved applying low-intensity current directly to different parts of the skull through electrodes (anodes). The low intensity of tDCS is used to modulate the excitability of the selected brain region, providing the neurons with the necessary stimulation to keep them at their firing threshold. It has also been shown that tDCS reduces the concentration of γ-aminobutyric acid (GABA), which is the main inhibitory neurotransmitter in the mammalian CNS (Bachtiar et al., 2015; Hunter et al., 2015).

Indeed, tDCS has been tested in different groups of individuals, both healthy and clinical (Berryhill & Martin, 2018), demonstrating that low current stimulation is able to modulate the resting membrane potential, producing both increasing and decreasing neuronal activity (Nitsche & Paulus, 2000).

On the other hand, tDCS neurostimulation seems to have an accumulative effect on neural networks, with different effects on the whole cardiovascular system. Even if more research is needed in this field, some studies suggest that the use of tDCS in young healthy adults increases the modulation of cerebral blood (Catchlove et al., 2018; Figeys et al., 2021), which may have important implications for sports performance. In this sense, some researchers claim that brain stimulation is becoming a key technology for improving sports performance. According to Davis (2013), tDCS neurostimulation has at least two important and distinct effects in sport. The first is the immediate improvement in performance for a short period of time after using the technology. This short period of time would be sufficient to improve concentration and accuracy in many sports competitions, such as goal and basket shooting, jumping and so on. In fact, this is what some well-known commercial brands are promoting, reporting satisfactory results in elite athletes. On the other hand, the ability of tDCS to improve the acquisition of athletic skills during training and to use these skills more efficiently in athletic competition raises new hopes for athletic performance, but also raises serious ethical concerns. In other words, tDCS is being used as a training aid to increase the ability to learn athletic skills faster and reproduce them later in competition, which should be welcomed, but also handled with care because it affects other important values in sport (Carrio & Pérez Triviño, 2017).

3.2.3 *The Rise of AI-Driven Smart Neurostimulation in Sport ...*

As a result of the impressive improvement in knowledge of the structure and function of the brain, partly as a result of the "decade of the brain" (1990–1999), a great deal of research has been carried out into neurostimulation as a possible alternative to drug treatment for brain disorders. Indeed, Delgado (1952) was a pioneer in the implantation of electrodes in the brain for the recording of its activity and stimulation of the brain as a possible therapy for brain disorders.

At present, the rapid pace at which AI is being developed everywhere is opening up new opportunities for a new and more complete understanding of the complexity of how the brain works, as well as new possibilities for neurostimulation. In fact, some important advances have been made in the decoding of brain activity through the use of brain computer interface (BCI) systems. BCIs are a combination of hardware and software designed to transfer information from the brain to a computer, enabling the localisation and decoding of activity in brain regions (Mirabella, 2017).

On the other hand, the emergence of AI and machine learning (ML) systems is of great interest for a relatively new field such as computational neuroscience and psychiatry. In this sense, ML is a very useful tool for analysing and classifying electroencephalography (EEG) and finding proportional correlations between the activity of brain regions and responses to stimulation. There is no doubt that advances in ML and AI have great potential in healthcare to improve diagnosis and prognosis in brain health. Indeed, ML and AI systems are expected to play an important role in identifying the connections between different brain regions and providing accurate results for individualised therapy according to individual responses in patients with brain disorders (Khosla et al., 2019).

In this sense, the emergence of relatively new techniques in AI, such as Explainable Artificial Intelligence (XAI), is already having a very positive impact on neurostimulation. The potential of XAI, combining the most sophisticated ML algorithms with a satisfactory explanation of how to apply these technologies to healthcare in general and to brain healthcare in particular, opens up a promising future (Holzinger et al., 2018; Langlotz et al., 2019). In fact, the importance of individual responses to stimulation and environmental situations makes ML and AI an optimal tool for understanding how brain therapy works in each individual. That's why XAI is now a promising technique to provide an adequate explanation of the brain network and open up possibilities to manipulate stimulus and reward through reinforcement in motor learning, cognition and memory enhancement (Jiang et al., 2019).

However, this is only one side of the coin. The other side refers to the many clinical and ethical concerns that the use of AI and ML raises in healthcare in general (Romero-Brufau et al., 2020), and in neurostimulation in particular, such as its long-term efficacy and safety, its impact on the self, the autonomy of the patient to decide on treatment and the well-being after removal of the stimulator devices (Gilbert et al., 2023).

3.2.4 ... and the Ethical and Regulatory Concerns It Raises

Although most of these new technologies in neurostimulation are not suitable for current mainstream sports competition, apart from the potential in Paralympic sports, less invasive AI-driven devices, such as smart tDCS, are currently in use. There is no doubt that these devices open up new possibilities for improving performance, accuracy, reducing fatigue and accelerating the acquisition of athletic skills, as we have seen. In fact, these and many other advantages are what brands promote when advertising their products, even reporting the satisfactory results of elite athletes.

That's why the impact of tDCS on athletic performance is becoming a big issue among researchers. While some of them report improvements in reducing fatigue and can help to alleviate the perception of sport stress, they still maintain a strong scepticism about its ability to push athletes beyond the average of human psychological limits (Berthelot et al., 2015). Others argue that the use of tDCS for training enhances motor learning and the acquisition of athletic skills, which has an important impact on sports performance and can provide a competitive advantage in elite athletes (Reardon, 2016; Reis et al., 2009; Borducchi et al., 2016).

Whatever its implications for sports performance, tDCS has been increasingly used by elite athletes, coaches and sports psychologists over recent years. Indeed, alongside tDCS, many other intelligent neurostimulation technologies have recently emerged, such as commercial vagus nerve stimulators and even closed-loop BCIs. This explosion of do-it-yourself neurostimulation could easily get out of hand in sport, if it is not already out of control. On the one side, these devices can open up new opportunities for athletes. However, their widespread use also exposes athletes to new risks that must be minimised and poses new ethical challenges for sport governance that should be addressed before it is too late. As was the case years ago with the widespread use of performance-enhancing drugs and the serious problems they caused for athletes' health and integrity in sport.

The question that remains, therefore, is whether the use of this technology in sport should be allowed and even encouraged, or whether, on the contrary, it should be regulated and even banned on the grounds of unfairness. In other words, are we witnessing the emergence of a new type of brain enhancement that should be banned by sports governing bodies (SGBs) and, in particular, labelled by WADA as a prohibited method and, consequently, as brain doping?

3.3 Bringing High-tech to Sport: A Critical Approach to Smart Stimulation in the Light of WADA Foundations

Sport has always sought cutting-edge technology for many reasons. Improving performance is at the top of the list, but technology has also played an important role in assisting referees, providing sports medicine, engaging fans and making sport safer. In fact, the evolution and progress of sport can't be understood without reference to technological improvements. Think, for example, of the improvements in sports clothing and footwear, balls, track and field surfaces, finishing control technologies and so on. There is no doubt that the fulfilment of the Olympic motto – faster, higher and stronger (*Citius, Altius, Fortius*) – wouldn't have been possible without the help of technological improvements. That's because it makes sense adding "together" (*Communiter*) to this motto, as it is read from July 2020. After all, sport is a human activity and, as in many other areas of human endeavour, technology has played a key role in it.

In this sense, it is worth mentioning the well-known anthropological contrast drawn by Huizinga (1949) between *"homo ludens"* and *"homo faber"*. According to Huizinga, human beings are better defined as players than as workers. In other words, according to Huizinga, human nature is primarily a cultural activity that begins and develops through play. But even if Huizinga's contraposition makes sense identifying play as a cultural activity that "contributes to the well-being of the group" (Huizinga, 1949, p. 9), the truth is that, as Huizinga himself characterises it, play is a human artificial activity because "it creates order, it is order" (Huizinga, 1949, p. 10). In other words, play is the imposition of order where chaos reigns. And it is this characteristic of play as order, and in particular of games and sport as an activity governed by rules, as defined by Suits (1978), that brings sport closer to a technical activity. That's because sport could be better defined as the meeting point between *homo ludens* and *homo faber*. A highly technical human activity that imitates natural actions, as Plato (2016) defined technè, or even better, an activity in which "technè sometimes completes what nature cannot lead to an end, and others imitate nature", according to Aristotle's (2014) definition of technological artefacts.

In any case, both technology and sport are broad concepts that can be understood in many different ways that need to be clarified beforehand in order to have a clear understanding of what kind of sport and what uses of technology we are referring to when we put the two together. While a complete theory of technology in sport is needed, an interesting approach to enhancing technology in sport has been taken by Loland (2009). In his work, Loland distinguishes three views of enhancing technologies in sport, which he calls (i) the relativist theory, (ii) the narrow theory and iii) the broad theory. This distinction has been widely accepted by sport ethicists and scientists.

According to Loland, each of these theories encompasses different approaches to sport. The first, the relativist theory, takes an external view of sport, where sport is seen as a social practice that serves various purposes, such as the economic or political side of sport. In other words, the internal values of sport and the moral basis of individual effort, natural performance, etc. are worthy of consideration as long as they don't interfere with other external goals.

The narrow theory of performance-enhancing technologies in sport is based on the assumption that the main objective of sport, and of professional sport in particular, is the enhancement of athletic performance. Consequently, performance-enhancing technologies and substances are perfectly in line with this objective and should be permitted as long as they are available to athletes, in accordance with the principle of equal opportunities. The narrow theory, often referred to as the liberal theory, argues in favour of the freedom of athletes to make informed choices and to select the methods or substances that will allow them to better achieve their goals. We can consider Savulescu (2004 & 2006) and Tännsjö (2021) referred above as representatives of this theory since they take an optimistic view of technology. This approach has been criticised by Loland and McNamee (2016) and labelled as a naive approach to sport.

Finally, the wide or broad theory of performance-enhancement technologies in sport emphasises the intrinsic values of sport. In this sense, sport has been defined as a virtuous practice that has the aim of promoting individual effort, the learning of skills and abilities, and moral excellence (Loland, 2009). Indeed, Devine (2011 & 2022) has defined sport as a social practice aimed at achieving and demonstrating excellence. Consequently, Devine refers to doping and the use of artificial performance-enhancing substances and methods as "eroders of excellence" (Devine, 2022). While the narrow and broad theories require further elaboration beyond the scope of this chapter, the truth is that the broad theory is now the only one that is compatible with the internal view of sport that I also endorse in this chapter, and with the concept of doping that the WADA Code currently addresses. For this reason, the next section aims to provide a critical examination of the WADA Code and the concept of doping that it supports.

3.3.1 *The Rationale Behind the WADA Code*

The use of performance-enhancing substances has a long history in and out of sport, as we have seen above. However, while the use of performance-enhancing substances and methods may be ethically questionable, they have not been banned by the SGBs for a long time and therefore can't technically be considered a case of doping. It was not until 1967 that the IOC Medical Commission adopted a definition of doping, after the Council of Europe had raised serious concerns about the increasing use of performance-enhancing substances in sport. And, in particular, by the occurrence of tragic situations, such as the death of the British cyclist Tommy Simpson during the Tour de France, when the use of amphetamines and alcohol was detected in the athlete's blood.

The first definition of doping, adopted by both the Council of Europe and the IOC Medical Commission, embraced a normal functioning account of the human body and also a naturalistic approach to sport, prohibiting the use of any substance or method "unnatural or alien to the body" or administered in "an abnormal amount or by abnormal methods" with the aim of achieving an unnatural or unfair performance in competition (Kremenik et al., 2006; Dikic et al., 2015; Vlad et al., 2018). That was also the time of the first publication of the prohibited list of substances by the IOC.

However, new performance-enhancing substances and methods have emerged as a result of scientific and pharmaceutical progress, and this list had to be updated by the IOC Medical Commission until the creation of WADA in 1999. WADA's anti-doping policies, expressed in the well-known WADA Code, have always aimed to protect two fundamental issues in sport, namely the fairness and integrity of sporting competition and the potential harm to athletes' health. While the inclusion of new substances and methods in the prohibited list has always been a matter of controversy, the protection of athletes' health and the inherent paternalism associated with it have raised several criticisms. This clearly highlights the important ethical dimension of anti-doping policies.

Nowadays, WADA includes in the Prohibited List (PL) several stimulant substances, such as the aforementioned modafinil, which have similar aims and effects to tDCS (Brühl et al., 2019) and vagus nerve stimulation in and out of sport (Hatik et al., 2023). However, the PL doesn't include any kind of technological neurostimulation. So, the question remains: should WADA include it?

While the exclusion of current neurostimulation technologies from the PL should be welcomed due to the lack of conclusive scientific evidence of their efficacy as a performance-enhancing method, a different approach could be taken given the proliferation of smart AI-driven devices available for use in competition, in many cases without medical or expert supervision.

In this sense, the rationale of the WADA's Code and the principle of prudence that should guide WADA policy when considering whether to include a substance or method in the PL could apply to both the inclusion and exclusion of these devices from the PL. Let's see below how the arguments for and against inclusion would work. But first, it is worth looking at the current definition of doping in the WADA Code.

3.3.2 The Constitutive Role of Anti-doping Rules

According to Art. 1 of the WADA Code, doping consists in the "occurrence of one or more of the anti-doping rule violations set forth in Article 2.1 through Article 2.11 of the Code".[3] As it is easy to see, this definition of doping, rather than endorsing a single concept of doping, describes a number of situations that may end up being qualified as doping. That's because Art. 1 plays the role of a constitutive rule, according to which doping is any circumstance labelled as such by WADA.

The canonical form of constitutive rules, according to Searle (1969), is: "X counts as Y in context C". Constitutive rules, as Searle affirms, constitute (and also regulate) an activity that is logically dependent on the rules (Searle, 1969, pp. 33–34). Examples of constitutive rules are the rules of games, since it is not possible to explain the game without reference to the rules that constitute it. Another important feature of constitutive rules is that they allow us to distinguish between brute facts and institutional facts. The former, i.e. picking up a ball with your hands or using performance-enhancing substances or methods, are brute facts that can be described without the existence of human institutions. The existence of institutional facts, on the other hand, depends entirely on the constitutive rules that transform these brute facts into institutional facts, such as a penalty in football or a case of doping in sport. That's why the definition of doping given by WADA in Art. 1 is constitutive of all the cases of doping that it regulates. In other words, in professional sport, doping is whatever WADA, at its sole discretion, decides it is.

Although I won't go into detail here about constitutive rules in sport,[4] it is important to retain that the role of constitutive rules requires a clear definition of the institutional actions they constitute, otherwise it would be difficult to correctly identify the institutional facts. This is important in the context of the WADA definition of doping, as the actions and situations listed in Art. 2.1-11 of the Code are described very broadly, and it is difficult to assess what constitutes a case of doping. Consider, for example, the following situations:

1. Attempted use of a prohibited substance or method (Article 2.2). But, what exactly does "attempted use" mean under this rule? Would it be considered an attempted use to evaluate the possibilities of the enhancement

effect of a substance or method and, in the end, discard it after evaluating the risk of using it? If so, WADA would be penalising a state of mind for which no action has been taken. However, it is almost impossible to know in advance what can be considered an "attempted use", since "the success or failure of the Prohibited Substance or Prohibited Method is immaterial" (Article 2.2.2) and the violation can be established by other reliable means.

2. Possession of such substances or methods by Athletes or Athlete Support Personnel (Article 2.6). Even though WADA argues that an acceptable justification for such possession could be asserted, i.e., possession to deal with emergency situations, this Article imposes an important obligation on Athletes for actions that they could easily ignore, such as possessing the prohibited substance or method for the doctors or other support personnel around them.

Additionally, the violation of the rules imposes a strict liability on the athlete, from which it is almost impossible to escape.

Finally, it is also worth mentioning that WADA has wide discretion to place a substance or method on the PL. As I have just mentioned, WADA can decide at its sole discretion whether a substance or method should be included in the Prohibited List if it meets any of the following three criteria:

"4.3.1.1 Medical or other scientific evidence, pharmacological effect or experience that the substance or method, alone or in combination with other substances or methods, has the potential to enhance or enhances sport performance;

4.3.1.2 Medical or other scientific evidence, pharmacological effect or experience that the Use of the substance or method represents an actual or potential health risk to the Athlete;

4.3.1.3 WADA's determination that the Use of the substance or method violates the spirit of sport described in the introduction to the Code".[5]

In other words, WADA is free to include any substance or method on the PL even if that substance or method does not have an enhancing effect but may have that effect in combination with other substances or methods or may mask the use of other prohibited substances or methods.

In addition, WADA may also place a substance or method on the PL if it determines, in its sole discretion, that the substance or method is contrary to the "spirit of sport" as described in the Code. But the spirit of sport, like any other spirit, is difficult to capture in human language, despite the Code's best efforts to define it as "the celebration of human spirit, body and mind. It is the essence of Olympism and is reflected in the values we find in and through sport".[6]

These values include health, excellence, ethics and fair play, fun and joy. But again, all of these concepts are not easily captured in words. In fact they are all "thick concepts", i.e. concepts that are both evaluative and descriptive (Williams, 1985), the meaning of which is neither precise nor easy to grasp in words. It is perhaps for this reason that the rationale of the Code regarding the "spirit of sport" is finally expressed "in the way we play true" and ends up stating that "doping is fundamentally contrary to the spirit of sport", which clearly implies a circular argument, a *petitio principii* fallacy.

Unsurprisingly, several authors, both from internal and external perspectives of sport, have criticised the definition of doping in the WADA Code.

3.4 Arguments for and against the Inclusion of Neurostimulation as a Prohibited Method under the WADA Code

Even if the definition of doping that the WADA Code addresses can be criticised in several ways, as we have seen, it doesn't invalidate the rationale of anti-doping policies, namely the protection of the intrinsic values of sport, the health of athletes and the ethics of playing fair. The aim of criticism should be to improve these policies and the correct application of the anti-doping rules, rather than to question their validity.

In what follows, I will briefly consider whether WADA should include smart neurostimulation as a prohibited method in sport. In order to do this, I will first examine the arguments against inclusion and then the arguments for inclusion. Later, I will attempt to weigh both arguments in order to draw a conclusion that explores a third approach.

3.4.1 The Argument against the Inclusion

In line with the critics of WADA's concept of doping, the argument against the inclusion (AAI) of smart neurostimulation devices as a prohibited method would be based on three key premises, namely (i) the lack of conclusive scientific evidence of enhancement effect; (ii) the non-invasive nature of these devices; and (iii) the excessive burden of proof that the prohibition would place on the athlete.

Thus, the argument against inclusion would support and challenge all of the criteria set forth in Article 4.3 of the WADA Code for the inclusion of a substance or method in the PL and could be formulated as follows:

> AAI: Smart neurostimulation and current non-invasive stimulation technologies do not meet any of the three criteria listed in Article 4.3, as there is no significant scientific evidence that they actually enhance athletic performance, nor do these devices pose an actual or potential risk to athletes' health. Consequently, the inclusion of these devices in the Prohibited List

> at WADA's sole discretion could only be based on the alleged assumption that they violate the thick concepts that the "spirit of sport" embraces, such as "the way we play true" or, alternatively, on a *petitio principii* fallacy as exposed above. Moreover, the inclusion would impose a burden of proof on athletes that is almost impossible to meet and could therefore be considered a diabolic proof (*probatio diabolica*).

The AAI certainly makes a strong case against the inclusion of intelligent neurostimulation devices without deviating from the rationale of the WADA Code. Indeed, the argument would be in line with the increasing use of technology in sport to explore new ways of achieving new levels of athletic performance and even enhancing the resilience of athletes.

3.4.2 *The Argument for Inclusion*

The inclusion of smart neurostimulation devices and other current technologies for neurostimulation in sport in the PL, could be argued, is already covered by Art. 4.3 of the WADA Code. To demonstrate this, it is only necessary to slightly modify the three key premises on which the AAI is based, according to the rationale of the WADA Code. The argument for Inclusion (AFI) in the PL could easily challenge the AAI by arguing that there is broad scientific disagreement about intelligent neurostimulation devices, which implies that (i) there is at least reasonable doubt that these devices could have a direct or indirect impact on sport performance; (ii) they also pose a potential health risk to athletes; and consequently (iii) according to the current state of the art, the use of these devices is against the "spirit of sport".

Following this line, the AFI, as a reasonable response to the AAI, could be worded as follows:

> AFI: Even if the current scientific knowledge is divided about the enhancement effect of smart neurostimulation devices and other modern technologies on athletic performance, there is at least a reasonable doubt about the potential of these technologies to act as athletic performance enhancers. Furthermore, given the current state of neuroscience, it can be argued that these devices improve blood oxygenation and have a positive effect on the functioning of the human cardiovascular system by stimulating the entire CNS. In this context, and taking into account the broad disagreement in the scientific community on the effects and safe use of this technology, it can be concluded that its use in sport represents a potential risk to the health of athletes. It can therefore be argued that, according to the WADA Code, the use of modern smart neurostimulation devices is contrary to the "spirit of sport", as it raises many ethical and medical issues and can also be considered as an artificial enhancement of athletic performance, which

is contrary to the goal of pursuing human excellence in sport and the "way we play true sport".

As we can see, AFI's challenge to AAI is based on two key issues, namely the strong defence of the rationale of the WADA Code and the reasonable doubt raised by the lack of scientific consensus. In addition, AFI also raises concerns about the combined effects of intelligent neurostimulation throughout the CNS, which reinforces the importance of monitoring scientific and technological progress in order to preserve the intrinsic values of sport, such as human excellence and fairness. Contrary to AAI, which takes an external and more liberal approach to sport, AFI clearly supports the internalist view of sport and the so-called naturalist approach to sport.

3.4.3 Balancing the Pros and Cons

Both AAI and AFI address the key requirements of Art. 4.3, namely, (i) the enhancement effect, (ii) the actual or potential risk to the health of athletes and (iii) "the spirit of sport". However, they also strongly disagree on other key issues, such as the scope and meaning of (i) scientific consensus and (ii) the potential of these devices to both enhance athletic performance and put athletes' health at risk.

Therefore, while the AAI sees the lack of scientific consensus on the enhancement effect of intelligent neurostimulation devices as an opportunity to incorporate them into sport, the AFI focuses on the disagreement as evidence of their actual or potential use as enhancers of athletic performance, as well as the actual or potential risk they pose to athletes' health. Furthermore, AFI emphasises the combined effect of smart neurostimulation on blood oxygenation and the impact it has on the whole CNS as a proof of the actual or potential risk these devices imply both for fairness in sport and for the health of athletes.

In the same vein, the AAI takes an optimistic view of the use of technology in sport. It also adopts a liberal approach to the freedom of athletes to give informed consent to the use of these devices. This brings AAI very close to what Loland calls the narrow theory of technology in sport that I mentioned above. AFI, for its part, embraces the internal view of sport, which focuses on the human value of sport by adopting a naturalistic approach to athletic performance. In other words, AFI endorses a conservative approach to technology in sport in line with what Loland calls the broad theory of technology in sport, also outlined above.

In summary, both the AAI and the AFI raise important issues that deserve consideration and make it difficult to decide whether or not to include smart neurostimulation devices in the PL. However, both arguments also have some weaknesses that need to be pointed out. In this sense, the AAI disregards the side effects of intelligent neurostimulation, which, as mentioned above, have a positive effect on blood oxygenation and the entire NSC and can contribute to the improvement of motor learning and the acquisition of athletic skills, as do other prohibited substances and methods, giving athletes an unfair advantage. Apart from the potential impact they can have currently or in the long term on the health of athletes.

AFI, for its part, ignores the potential and effectiveness of neuroscience in sports performance and takes a very conservative approach to the use of modern technology in sport. In addition, AFI also takes a strongly paternalistic view of the autonomy and freedom of athletes to give informed consent to the substances and methods they wish to use to improve their athletic performance, even if this may negatively affect their health.

That's because in what follows, I'm going to try to briefly explore a third approach that brings together the strong points that AAI and AFI address and leaves out the weak ones.

3.5 Exploring a Third Approach

It seems that both the AAI and the AFI are interested in preserving the logic of the WADA Code. Even if the AAI adopts a more liberal and critical approach to the logic of the WADA Code, it is far from supporting a free doping approach to sport, as Tännsjo (2021) and Petersen (2021) seem to do, fuelling the aspirations of the so-called "Enhanced Games" movement, which emerged in 2023, raising the flag of athletes' freedom and right to monetise their performance.[7] That is, a purely market-oriented view of sport.

However, there are important disagreements between the two arguments that each of them doesn't want to ignore. Therefore, in order to bridge the gap between them, it is important to keep in mind the key issues that each of these arguments addresses.

On the AAI side, (i) the importance of technology in sport and the need to incorporate the latest scientific and technological improvements that can safely enhance athletic performance, (ii) the freedom of athletes to choose whether or not to use it for this purpose and, consequently, (iii) the avoidance of the essentialism that "human excellence" performance-based destiles.

On the side of AFI, it is imperative to keep in mind the toxic environment surrounding sport, especially elite sport. That's because AFI focuses its attention on (i) protecting the health and well-being of athletes and, consequently, (ii) their autonomy to freely refuse the use of substances and methods that could put them at risk. That's because it is necessary to maintain a certain paternalistic policy based on the idea of human excellence in sport. In other words, the AFI doesn't deny the positive impact of technology in sport and the need to respect the freedom and autonomy of athletes. But it also points out the difficult situation that the lack of regulation of smart stimulation would put athletes in, as they would not be able to reject the use of these devices for the sake of protecting their health, putting them at a competitive disadvantage that would jeopardise their careers.

Therefore, taking all these issues seriously, an appropriate and at least temporary solution would be to include smart neurostimulation devices and other current neurostimulation technologies in the monitoring programme that WADA publishes annually. According to Art. 4.5 of the WADA Code, WADA establishes a monitoring programme for some substances that are not included in the Prohibited List but are monitored by WADA "in order to identify potential patterns or misuse in sport". In fact, this programme already includes some stimulant substances with similar effects to smart neurostimulation and could easily include current neurostimulation devices.

This proposal would respect the freedom of athletes to use them within the monitoring programme, as required by the AAI, while allowing the programme to gather information about the actual or potential enhancing effect of these devices, as well as the potential risk to athletes' health that they pose. This would also increase the autonomy of athletes to give informed consent to the use of intelligent neurostimulation technology and, in any case, the ability to adopt more appropriate policies in this regard.

3.6 Conclusion

Modern advances in neuroscience have added a new dimension to the importance that psychological skills have always had in sport. There is no doubt that new horizons for the future of sport are being opened up by the constant improvements in this field and the rapid pace at which AI is growing. Indeed, modern neurostimulation techniques are already in widespread use at the professional level. However, the scientific community is divided on their efficacy, although some elite athletes report interesting benefits in improving athletic performance and accuracy. In any case, the increasing use of this technology in sport raises important ethical and regulatory concerns about the safety of its use, the freedom of choice of athletes, and the fairness and integrity of sports competition.

This chapter has first examined the evolution of neurostimulation in sport and provided an overview of the technologies currently used in sport, mainly to enhance athletic performance and skill. As I have shown, while there remains strong disagreement about the ability of this technology to effectively improve athletic performance in healthy adults, there is also consensus about how it affects brain activity and stimulates the entire CNS, raising serious questions about its compatibility with WADA's anti-doping policy.

I have then examined the integration of intelligent neurostimulation into sport as part of the wider debate on the role of high technology in sport and the different perspectives from which it is examined. In this sense, two arguments have been presented that address the main concerns of two opposing views on the use of technology in sport. The first, the argument against the inclusion of intelligent neurostimulation as a prohibited method in the WADA Code (AAI), is closer to what Loland calls the liberal or narrow theory of technology in sport. Conversely, the second, the argument for inclusion (AFI), takes a more conservative approach, embracing the postulates of what Loland calls the broad theory of technology in sport. Each of these arguments presents key issues and also some weaknesses that I have tried to balance in order to seriously consider the claims that each of them addresses.

Finally, in an attempt to combine the strengths of both arguments, I have explored a third way by proposing the inclusion of intelligent neurostimulation in the WADA monitoring programme. As I have argued, the inclusion of neurostimulation in the monitoring programme would satisfy the main claims of each argument while providing valuable information about its impact on both athletic performance and the health of athletes.

Clearly, the protocol for monitoring smart neurostimulation, the appropriate composition of the commissions to carry out this task, the selection of athletes and the requirements for their informed consent to participate in the programme need further elaboration, which I cannot address in this chapter. This is an interesting topic for further research.

Notes

1 "Modafinil Monograph for Professionals". *Drugs.com*. American Society of Health-System Pharmacists. September 23, 2023. Archived from the original on March 30, 2019. Retrieved August 1, 2024).
2 WADA's prohibited list can be checked a at the side https://www.wada-ama.org/sites/default/files/2023-09/2024list_en_final_22_september_2023.pdf S6. Stimulants)
3 https://www.wada-ama.org/sites/default/files/resources/files/2021_wada_code.pdf
4 For a detailed account of the role of constitutive rules in sport see Carrio, 2023.
5 See Art. 4.3 WADA Code, p. 34.
6 See Introduction of WADA Code, p. 13.
7 The information about that organisation is available at its webpage https://enhanced.org/

References

Aristotle. (2014). Physics (The Revised Oxford Translation). In J. Barnes (Ed.), The complete works of Aristotle, Vol. 1. Princeton University Press.

Bachtiar, V., Near, J., Johansen-Berg, H., & Stagg, C. J. (2015). Modulation of GABA and resting state functional connectivity by transcranial direct current stimulation. eLife, 4, e08789. https://doi.org/10.7554/eLife.08789

Berezanskaya, J., Cade, W., Best, T. M., Paultre, K., & Kienstra, C. (2022). ADHD prescription medications and their effect on athletic performance: A systematic review and meta-analysis. Sports Medicine - Open, 8(1), 5. https://doi.org/10.1186/s40798-021-00374-y. PMC 8755863. PMID 35022919.

Bergmann, T. O., Varatheeswaran, R., Hanlon, C. A., Madsen, K. H., Thielscher, A., & Siebner, H. R. (2021). Concurrent TMS-fMRI for causal network perturbation and proof of target engagement. NeuroImage, 237, 118093. https://doi.org/10.1016/j.neuroimage.2021.118093

Berryhill, M. E., & Martin, D. (2018). Cognitive effects of transcranial direct current stimulation in healthy and clinical populations: An overview. Journal of ECT, 34(e1), e25–e35. https://doi.org/10.1097/YCT.0000000000000534

Berthelot, G., Sedeaud, A., Marck, A., Antero-Jacquemin, J., Schipman, J., Saulière, G., et al. (2015). Has athletic performance reached its peak? Sports Medicine, 45(9), 1263–1271. https://doi.org/10.1007/s40279-015-0347-2

Borducchi, D., Gomes, J. S., Akiba, H., Cordeiro, Q., Borducchi, J. M., Valentin, L., et al. (2016). Transcranial direct current stimulation effects on athletes' cognitive performance: An exploratory proof of concept trial. Frontiers in Psychiatry, 7, 183. https://doi.org/10.3389/fpsyt.2016.00183

Brühl, A. B., d'Angelo, C., & Sahakian, B. J. (2019). Neuroethical issues in cognitive enhancement: Modafinil as the example of a workplace drug? Brain and Neuroscience Advances, 3, 1–13. https://doi.org/10.1177/2398212818816018

Catchlove, S. J., Macpherson, H., Hughes, M. E., Chen, Y., Parrish, T. B., & Pipingas, A. (2018). An investigation of cerebral oxygen utilization, blood flow and cognition in healthy aging. PLoS ONE, 13(1), e0197055. https://doi.org/10.1371/journal.pone.0197055

Carrio Sampedro, A. (2023). Reglas constitutivas, prácticas irregulares y errores arbitrales: Un análisis comparativo entre la filosofía del derecho y del deporte. In Á. Ródenas & V. García Yzaguirre (Eds.), Jurisdicción y teoría del sistema jurídico. Homenaje a Juan Ruiz Manero (pp. 471–467). Palestra/Marcial Pons.

Carrio Sampedro, A., & Pérez Triviño, J. L. (2017). On the compatibility of brain enhancement and the internal values of sport. *Sport, Ethics and Philosophy, 11*(3), 307–322. https://doi.org/10.1080/17511321.2017.1320687

Cheng, M. Y., Huang, C. J., Chang, Y. K., Koester, D., Schack, T., & Hung, T. M. (2015). Sensorimotor rhythm neurofeedback enhances golf putting performance. Journal of Sport & Exercise Psychology, 37(6), 626–636.

Clancy, J. A., Mary, D. A., Witte, K. K., Greenwood, J. P., Deuchars, S. A., & Deuchars, J. (2014). Non-invasive vagus nerve stimulation in healthy humans reduces sympathetic nerve activity. Brain Stimulation, 7(6), 871–877. https://doi.org/10.1016/j.brs.2014.07.031. Epub 2014 Jul 16. PMID: 25164906.

Conti, A. A. (2010). Doping in sports in ancient and recent times. Med Secoli, 22(1–3), 181–190. https://pubmed.ncbi.nlm.nih.gov/21560989/. PMID: 21560989.

Davis, N. J. (2013). Neurodoping: Brain stimulation as a performance-enhancing measure. *Sports Medicine, 43*(8), 649–653. https://doi.org/10.1007/s40279-013-0027-z

Delgado, J. M., Hamlin, H., & Chapman, W. P. (1952). Technique of intracranial electrode implacement for recording and stimulation and its possible therapeutic value in psychotic patients. *Confinia neurologica, 12*(5–6), 315–319.

Dell'Osso, B., Dobrea, C., Cremaschi, L., Arici, C., & Altamura, A. C. (2014). Wake-promoting pharmacotherapy for psychiatric disorders. *Current Psychiatry Reports, 16*(12), 524. https://doi.org/10.1007/s11920-014-0524-2. PMID 25312027. S2CID 26314915.

Devine, J. W. (2011). Doping is a threat to sporting excellence. *British Journal of Sports Medicine, 45*(8), 637–639.

Devine, J. W. (2022). Elements of excellence. *Journal of the Philosophy of Sport, 49*(2), 195–211.

Dikic, N., Djurdjevic, N., & McNamee, M. J. (2015). Doping. In H. ten Have (Ed.), Encyclopedia of Global Bioethics. Springer. https://doi.org/10.1007/978-3-319-05544-2_156-1

Figeys, M., Zeeman, M., & Kim, E. S. (2021). Effects of transcranial direct current stimulation (tDCS) on cognitive performance and cerebral oxygen hemodynamics: A systematic review. Frontiers in Human Neuroscience, 15, 623315. https://doi.org/10.3389/fnhum.2021.623315 PMID: 33897392; PMCID: PMC8058208)

Gilbert, F., Ienca, M., & Cook, M. (2023). How I became myself after merging with a computer: Does human-machine symbiosis raise human rights issues? Brain Stimulation, 16, 783–789.

Goodall, S., Howatson, G., Romer, L., & Ross, E. (2014). Transcranial magnetic stimulation in sport science: A commentary. European Journal of Sport Science, 14(Suppl 1), S332–S340.

Gruzelier, J. H. (2014). EEG-neurofeedback for optimising performance. I: A review of cognitive and affective outcome in healthy participants. Neuroscience & Biobehavioral Reviews, 44, 124–141.

Hallett, M. (2007). Transcranial magnetic stimulation: A primer. Neuron, 55(2), 187–199. https://doi.org/10.1016/j.neuron.2007.06.026

Hatik, S. H., Arslan, M. T., Demirbilek, Ö., & Özden, A. V. (2023). The effect of transcutaneous auricular vagus nerve stimulation on cycling ergometry and recovery in healthy young individuals. Brain and Behavior. Advance online publication. https://doi.org/10.1002/brb3.3332

Holzinger, A., Kieseberg, P., Weippl, E., & Tjoa, A. M. (2018). Current advances, trends and challenges of machine learning and knowledge extraction: From machine learning to explainable AI. In A. Holzinger, P. Kieseberg, A. M. Tjoa, & E. Weippl (Eds.), Machine Learning and Knowledge Extraction. Springer, p. 1–8.

Huizinga, J. (1949). Homo ludens: A study of the play-element in culture. Routledge & Kegan Paul.

Hunter, M. A., Coffman, B. A., Gasparovic, C., Calhoun, V. D., Trumbo, M. C., & Clark, V. P. (2015). Baseline effects of transcranial direct current stimulation on glutamatergic neurotransmission and large-scale network connectivity. Brain Research, 1594, 92–107.

Jiang, L., Stocco, A., Losey, D. M., Abernethy, J. A., Prat, C. S., & Rao, R. P. N. (2019). BrainNet: A multi-person brain-to-brain interface for direct collaboration between brains. Scientific Reports, 9, 6115. https://doi.org/10.1038/s41598-019-41895-7

Johnson, L. A., Wang, J., Nebeck, S. D., Zhang, J., Johnson, M. D., & Vitek, J. (2020). Direct activation of primary motor cortex during subthalamic but not pallidal deep brain stimulation. Journal of Neuroscience, 40(11), 2166–2177. https://doi.org/10.1523/JNEUROSCI.2480-19.2020

Khosla, M., Jamison, K., Ngo, G. H., Kuceyeski, A., & Sabuncu, M. R. (2019). Machine learning in resting-state fMRI analysis. Magnetic Resonance Imaging, 64, 101–121. https://doi.org/10.1016/j.mri.2019.05.031

Kremenik, M., Onodera, S., Nagao, M., Yuzuki, O., & Yonetani, S. (2006). A historical timeline of doping in the olympics (Part 1 1896–1968). *Kawasaki Journal of Medical Welfare, 12*(1), 19–28.
Kwon, E. J., Skalak, M., Lo Bu, R., & Bhatia, S. N. (2016). Neuron-targeted nanoparticle for siRNA delivery to traumatic brain injuries. ACS Nano, 10(8), 7926–7933. https://doi.org/10.1021/acsnano.6b03858
Langlotz, C. P., Allen, B., Erickson, B. J., Kalpathy-Cramer, J., Bigelow, K., Cook, T. S., et al. (2019). A roadmap for foundational research on artificial intelligence in medical imaging: From the 2018 NIH/RSNA/ACR/The academy workshop. *Radiology, 291*, 781–791. https://doi.org/10.1148/radiol.2019190613
Loland, S. (2009). The ethics of performance-enhancing technology in sport. *Journal of the Philosophy of Sport, 36*(2), 152–161. https://doi.org/10.1080/00948705.2009.9714754
Loland, S., & McNamee, M. J. (2016). Anti-doping, performance enhancement and 'the spirit of sport': A philosophical and ethical critique. In V. Møller, I. Waddington, & J. Hoberman (Eds.), Doping and public health (pp. 111–123). Routledge.
Mansfield, A. (2016). *Do the warriors owe some of their success to these "brain-zapping" headphones?* Complex.
Marzbani, H., Marateb, H. R., & Mansourian, M. (2016). Neurofeedback: A comprehensive review on system design, methodology and clinical applications. Basic and Clinical Neuroscience, 7(2), 143–158. https://doi.org/10.15412/J.BCN.03070208. PMID: 27303609; PMCID: PMC4892319.
Merkel, R., Boer, G., Fegert, J., Galert, T., Hartmann, D., Nuftin, D., & Rosahl, S. (2007). Intervening the brain: Changing psyche and society. Springer.
Miah, A. (2004). *Genetically modified athletes. Biomedical ethics, gene doping and sport*. Routledge.
Mirabella, G., & Lebedev, M. A. (2017). Interfacing to the brain's motor decisions. *Journal of Neurophysiology, 117*, 1305–1319. https://doi.org/10.1152/jn.00051.2016
Nitsche, M. A., & Paulus, W. (2000). Excitability changes induced in the human motor cortex by weak transcranial direct current stimulation. *The Journal of Physiology, 527*, 633–639. https://doi.org/10.1111/j.1469-7793.2000.t01-1-00633.x
Oliván, S., Calvo, A. C., Rando, A., Herrando-Grabulosa, M., Manzano, R., Zaragoza, P., Tizzano, E. F., Aguilera, J., & Osta, R. (2016). Neuroprotective effect of non-viral gene therapy treatment based on tetanus toxin C-fragment in a severe mouse model of spinal muscular atrophy. Frontiers in Molecular Neuroscience, 9, Article 76. https://doi.org/10.3389/fnmol.2016.00076
Petersen, T. S. (2021). *Doping in sport. A defence*. Routledge.
Plato. (2016). Laws (M. Schofield, Ed., T. Griffith, Trans.). Cambridge University Press.
Puhl, D. L., D'Amato, A. R., & Gilbert, R. J. (2019). Challenges of gene delivery to the central nervous system and the growing use of biomaterial vectors. Brain Research Bulletin, 150, 216–230. https://doi.org/10.1016/j.brainresbull.2019.05.024. Epub 2019 Jun 5. PMID: 31173859; PMCID: PMC8284997.
Rafii, M. S., Baumann, T. L., Bakay, R. A. E., Ostrove, J. M., Siffert, J., Fleisher, A. S., Herzog, C. D., Barba, D., Pay, M., Salmon, D. P., Chu, Y., Kordower, J. H., Bishop, K., Keator, D., Potkin, S., & Bartus, R. T. (2014). A phase 1 study of stereotactic gene delivery of AAV2-NGF for Alzheimer's disease. Alzheimer's & Dementia, 10(5), 571–581. https://doi.org/10.1016/j.jalz.2013.09.004

Reardon, S. (2016). 'Brain doping' may improve athletes' performance. *Nature, 531*, 283–284. https://doi.org/10.1038/nature.2016.19534

Reed, T., & Cohen Kadosh, R. (2018). Transcranial electrical stimulation (tES) mechanisms and its effects on cortical excitability and connectivity. Journal of Inherited Metabolic Disease, 41(6), 1123–1130. https://doi.org/10.1007/s10545-018-0181-4. Epub ahead of print. PMID: 30006770; PMCID: PMC6326965.

Reis, J., Schambra, H., Cohen, L., Buch, E., Fritsch, B., Zarahn, E., et al. (2009). Noninvasive cortical stimulation enhances motor skill acquisition over multiple days through an effect on consolidation. *Proceedings of the National Academy of Sciences of the United States of America, 106*, 1590–1595. https://doi.org/10.1073/pnas.0805413106

Romero-Brufau, S., Wyatt, K. D., Boyum, P., Mickelson, M., Moore, M., & Cognetta-Rieke, C. (2020). A lesson in implementation: A pre-post study of providers' experience with artificial intelligence-based clinical decision support. International Journal of Medical Informatics, 137, 104072. https://doi.org/10.1016/j.ijmedinf.2019.104072

Rossini, P. M., Burke, D., Chen, R., Cohen, L. G., Daskalakis, Z., Di Iorio, R., Di Lazzaro, V., Ferreri, F., Fitzgerald, P. B., George, M. S., et al. (2015). Non-invasive electrical and magnetic stimulation of the brain, spinal cord, roots and peripheral nerves: Basic principles and procedures for routine clinical and research application. An updated report from an I.F.C.N. committee. Clinical Neurophysiology, 126(6), 1071–1107. https://doi.org/10.1016/j.clinph.2015.02.001

Saraiva, C., Paiva, J., Santos, T., Ferreira, L., & Bernardino, L. (2016). MicroRNA-124 loaded nanoparticles enhance brain repair in Parkinson's disease. Journal of Controlled Release, 235, 291–305. https://doi.org/10.1016/j.jconrel.2016.06.005

Savulescu, J. (2006). Justice, fairness and enhancement. Annals of the New York Academy of Sciences, 1093(1), 321–338.

Savulescu, J. (2014). Performance optimization and physiological doping. *Substance Use & Misuse, 49*(9), 1186–1189. https://doi.org/10.3109/10826084.2014.904124

Savulescu, J., Foddy, B., & Clayton, M. (2004). Why we should allow performance enhancing drugs in sport. *British Journal of Sports Medicine, 38*(6), 666–670. https://doi.org/10.1136/bjsm.2003.005249

Searle, J. R. (1969). *Speech acts. An essay in the philosophy of language*. Cambridge University Press.

Spencer, R. C., Devilbiss, D. M., & Berridge, C. W. (2015). The cognition-enhancing effects of psychostimulants involve direct action in the prefrontal cortex. Biological Psychiatry, 77(11), 940–950. https://doi.org/10.1016/j.biopsych.2014.09.013. PMC 4377121. PMID 25499957

Suits, B. H. (1978). The grasshopper: Games, life, and utopia. University of Toronto Press.

Tännsjö, T. (2021). Neuro-doping as a means to avert fascistoid ideology in elite sport. Neuroethics, 14(Suppl 2), S169–S178. https://doi.org/10.1007/s12152-020-09443-7

Van Rooyen, L. R., Gihwala, R., & Laher, A. E. (2021). Stimulant use among prehospital emergency care personnel in Gauteng Province, South Africa. South African Medical Journal, 111(6), 587–590. https://doi.org/10.7196/SAMJ.2021.v111i6.15465. PMID 34382572. S2CID 236402826.

Vlad, R. A., Hancu, G., Popescu, G. C., & Lungu, I. A. (2018). Doping in sports, a never-ending story? Advanced Pharmaceutical Bulletin, 8(4), 529–534. https://doi.org/10.15171/apb.2018.062. Epub 2018 Nov 29. PMID: 30607326; PMCID: PMC6311632.

Wang, K. P., Cheng, M. Y., Chen, T. T., Huang, C. J., Schack, T., & Hung, T. M. (2020). Elite golfers are characterized by psychomotor refinement in cognitive-motor processes. Psychology of Sport and Exercise, 50, 101739. https://doi.org/10.1016/j.psychsport.2020.101739

Wilson, V. E., Peper, E., & Moss, D. (2006). "The Mind Room" in Italian soccer training: The use of biofeedback and neurofeedback for optimum performance. Biofeedback, 34(3), 79–81.

Williams, B. (1985). *Ethics and the limits of philosophy*. Harvard University Press.

Xiang, M. Q., Hou, X. H., Liao, B. G., Liao, J. W., & Hu, M. (2018). The effect of neurofeedback training for sport performance in athletes: A meta-analysis. Psychology of Sport and Exercise, 36, 114–122. https://doi.org/10.1016/j.psychsport.2018.02.004

Chapter 4

AI, Performance Enhancement and Agential Limits

A Functionalist Evaluation Framework

Niko Vuorinen and Sigmund Loland

4.1 Introduction

The technologies that fall under the concept of artificial intelligence (AI) have recently taken great leaps forward. AI technologies also have many applications in the realm of competitive sports (Chmait & Westerbeek, 2021). Ethical questions arise from the use of AI in sport, but have yet remained unanswered, including those relating to performance enhancement (Carrio Sampedro, 2023).

In this chapter, we will explore and attempt to define what limitations should be put on the use of AI to enhance sport performance in the context of agency. Using an AI system in sport can be seen as transferring agency from the user to the system. Sport performance, on the other hand, is typically perceived as being about the athlete's natural talent and performance capabilities. A tension emerges: is it acceptable for an AI to govern the decision-making processes that enhance performance, or should it be about the athlete's own mental capacities? Who should have the ownership of the actions? How does a training setting differ from a competition? A need for a general framework is apparent.

Examples involving electroencephalography (EEG) based brain-computer interface (BCI) technologies in epee fencing[1] will be used in an attempt to provide answers. As the development of AI is fast paced, the framework should be able to provide answers to the use of existing, but also potential technologies. The first example involves a hypothetical EEG-tDCS closed-loop BCI system with a similar idea to Leite et al. (2017) that optimally and constantly modulates fatigue during an instance of sport. tDCS is a prominent technology to enhance performance in sports by modulating brain activity with small electric currents (Edwards et al., 2017; Kadosh, 2013). A portable, lightweight EEG system provides the system with the user's EEG signal for optimization purposes. EEG is considered as "one of the most accurate and objective indicators" of fatigue (Wang et al., 2023).

The second example involves a neurofeedback system, an existing technology used in sport (Hung & Cheng, 2019). Neurofeedback training uses

DOI: 10.4324/9781003520290-5

visual and auditory cues to help the user learn to control their brainwave states. Neurofeedback improves concentration in sport (Rydzik et al., 2023). Both examples can be said to have a performance-enhancing effect in epee fencing but, agentially speaking, they are different.

The work towards an evaluation framework consists of three steps. First, a causal model of agency based on Davidson's (1978) model and a classification for agency displacement types are defined. Then, the concept of a performance fundamental is presented with a functionalist machinery to establish a connection between agency displacement and performance enhancement. Last, a contractualist theory of sport is presented for normative application.

4.2 Conceptual Groundwork

AI, understood broadly, is "a cross-disciplinary approach to understanding, modelling, and replicating intelligence and cognitive processes by invoking various computational, mathematical, logical, mechanical, and even biological principles and device" (Frankish & Ramsey, 2014). According to Bryson (2020), intelligence is "the capacity to do the right thing at the right time". Cognitive processes involve things such as information processing, reasoning and decision-making any of the mental functions assumed to be involved in the acquisition, storage, interpretation, manipulation, transformation and use of knowledge. These processes encompass such activities as attention, perception, learning and problem solving (American Psychological Association, 2024). The concepts are somewhat overlapping.

Replicating intelligence and cognitive processes with machines opens possibilities to enhance performance in sport in ways that surpass human speed and precision capacities. While being more efficient is typically unproblematic, and in fact usually desirable, in fields such as medicine or engineering, competitive sport builds on a series of rules defining internal limitations, such as rules on the standardization of equipment to create equality among competitors, or rules concerning doping use. Allowable ways to enhance performance follow what Suits (1978) has described as a particular non-instrumental games logic in which players engage in the voluntary attempt to overcome "unnecessary obstacles" to reach a goal for the sake of the realization of the goal itself.

Following the earlier definition, using an AI system to enhance performance in competitive sport would effectively mean letting the system take care of a cognitive process or processes that would normally be handled by the athlete or the coach – a human agent. AI is a technology, and the use of technology in sport is not in itself right or wrong; in fact, it is a necessary condition for most sports, making them possible in the first place (Loland, 2018). However, if some part of the agent's cognitive processing is handed over to an AI in sport, a question arises whether this contradicts the internal logic of and common practice in (a specific) sport, or more broadly, the *ethos* of (a specific) sport: the common, socially accepted interpretation of on how the goals of a sport are to be agentially achieved (D'Agostino, 1981: Loland & McNamee, 2000).

Agency should be understood here as a broad, hybrid concept that has a descriptive and a normative component. Following Davidson (1971), agency is a capacity tied to the mental state of intentionality, where reasons cause the intention, and intention causes the action. For an agent to act in a certain rational, purposeful way – in contrast to something happening randomly – requires intentionality, which stems from the agent's reasons. A reason is constituted by a desire – or more generally, a pro attitude – and a belief such that the intentional action will lead to the desire of the agent (Davidson, 1978). Performance-enhancing effect is a clear example of a desire in a competitive sport context; a desire can be understood as a goal of the action. Agency is thus understood as a causal chain. Such a formulation of agency constitutes the descriptive component. The benefit of Davidson's formulation is its simplicity: it merely posits that agential actions have roots in the agent's reasons, which may or may not be conscious, and not necessarily even good ones (Davidson, 1978).

Additionally, the responsibility, or the ownership, of the agential act cannot be attributed to someone or something else. According to Zeiser (2024), attributability is essential for decision ownership: attributability "assumes that actions express the character of an agent, and decisions reflect certain qualities that belong to that agent" and "[m]ore specifically, decisions reflect a decision-maker's value-judgements". Attributability is typically understood as the chain of mental events and attitudes leading or being directed towards the action, or constituting it, in such a way that they are identifiable with the agent (Zheng, 2016). The descriptive and normative components may seem overlapping or redundant, but it intends to signify that agency comes with moral responsibility understood causally. Intentionality and reasoning begin from and belong to the agent.[2]

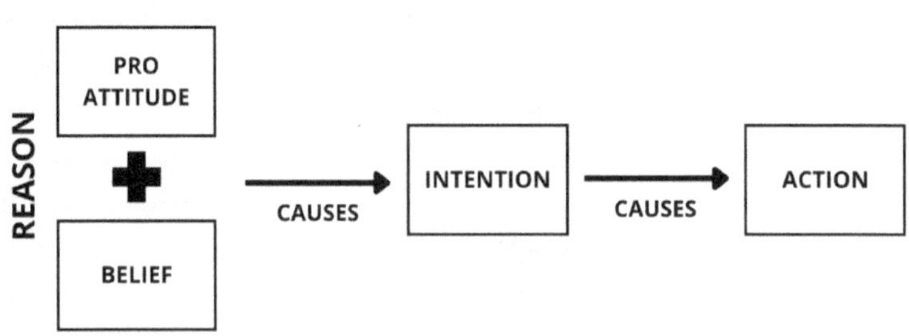

Figure 4.1 Davidson's causal chain of agency

To approach the issue of handing over cognitive processing to an AI in competitive sport, let us first define *agency displacement* of an athlete within their sport. Simply put, agency displacement refers to the change in an athlete's agential presence as a result of using an AI system. To illustrate agential presence, consider the men's epee fencing Leipzig 2017 World Championships final between Nikolai Novosjolov of Estonia and Paolo Pizzo of Italy. Both were already world champions, Novosjolov having won two individual gold medals, while Pizzo secured his second by beating Novosjolov 15-13. In fencing, the rules forbid the use of electronic communication devices during the bout[3] and giving advice while the time is running.[4] If one considers just those instances of the Leipzig final bout when time was running, there was then nothing external that could have affected their agency – they were agentively fully present, making all their decisions themselves.

One could, however, think of an extreme situation where the control of the fencers' actions was transferred to highly advanced brain implants governed by a sophisticated AI. The implants make all the decisions, and the fencers have essentially been reduced to puppets, while the system acts as a puppet master to their respective fencers. The systems' cognitive capabilities are identical to the two fencers' capabilities, meaning that the level of fencing skill stays the same compared to the fully agential situation. In this extreme case, the fencers have no agentive presence. Such a system should then be understood as a perfectly agentially displacing system – the agent part of the athlete is figuratively removed from the driver's seat and placed in a passenger one during an instance of sport.

4.3 Displacement Type Classification for Agency Attribution

It is not always straightforward to differentiate whether the decision to act originated from the agent or from somewhere else. Human beings are complex beings that are influenced by the societal norms and values and those around us, in sport, especially by coaches, teammates and other competitors. For the purpose of analysing agency within the context of AI and performance enhancement, however, it is useful to establish an analytic distinction between agency that originates from the human agent, which implicitly contains the non-AI attributable complexity, and what is displaced by an AI.

Therefore, in the case of a perfectly displacing system presented earlier, the answer is clear, as the intention and the reason to act originate externally of the agent in full, but such a system currently belongs to the realm of science fiction and is highly unlikely to be met in the real sport world anytime soon. On the other hand, if a hypothetical tool for tactical analysis provides a vital piece of information for the athlete that will cause a change in their actions during the upcoming bout, could it then be said that the decision to act originated from the agent?

Zeiser (2024) writes that, in fact, "most AI systems today actually operate as decision-support systems", where "humans are technically the final decision-makers". Decision-support systems then can be divided into descriptive and prescriptive systems (Zeiser 2024.). The first one merely provides information of the situation at hand, whereas the latter one gives suggestions on how to proceed. In this sense, most current AI systems then concern the reason-producing part of agency. It is, however, easy to imagine an advanced system that, for example, replaces parts of a football coach's work by actually deciding on team composition and tactics, in which case it is not merely a decision-support system. Another example could be an automatic dispenser of a performance-enhancing medical substance similar to the Omnipod DASH insulin management system[5] that is used for type 1 diabetes treatment.

Information production is a major function of contemporary AIs, as established in the previous paragraph. In general, information plays an important role in the dynamics of agency that is not well presented in Davidson's model and needs to be addressed, in the sense that it creates an ongoing flow between the different aspects of agency. This calls for a modified version of the model. But first a definitional clarification: instead of talking about desires or pro attitudes, it is better to describe them as *value attitudes* to incorporate the attributabilist idea of agency as reflecting the value-judgements of the agent. A value attitude here should not be read as a value itself, but as the willingness to realize a value through action in certain ways and to a certain extent. Even if the agent holds a value, it is not obvious that the agent is prepared to act according to it. Value attitudes should also be understood as restrictors for the belief set for intentional actions. The total belief set is the set of all possible value-realizing beliefs about actions that the agent can do, best described as a set of "should you want to realize X, then do this". It is built on the information available to the agent – it reveals what, at least in theory, is possible action-wise for the agent. A value attitude then limits the set to those beliefs that potentially realize the value behind the attitude, the beliefs described as "*since* you want to realize X, then do this", forming a restricted belief set. The restricted set can be understood as a dispositional layer that gives the likely direction for taking an action in relation to the attitude. The descriptive information available to the agent then supports the beliefs within the restricted set to a varying degree, and the belief that is best supported results in an action.

The descriptive information available to the agent has several other functions. It also directs the value attitudes: new information might change the attitudes of the agent, which again transforms the restricted belief set. Also, as seeking new information is an intentional act, it is directed by the value attitudes – attitudes affect the information acquisition, and information affects the attitudes. On the other hand, a realized action necessarily provides information for the agent, contributing to the overall process, even if the aim of the action wasn't information acquisition.

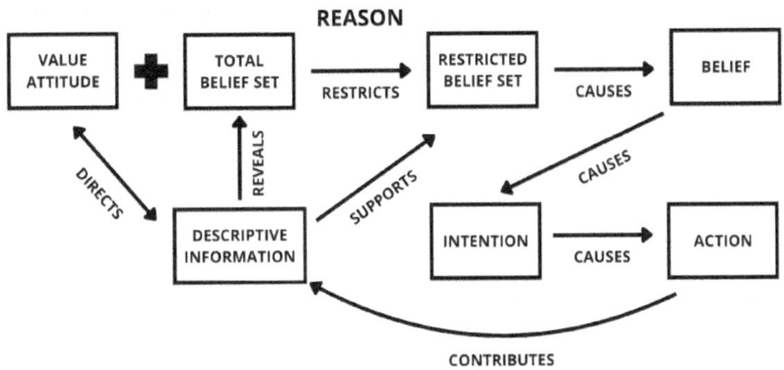

Figure 4.2 Modified Davidson's model for causal agency

When considering the displacing effect of an AI system, building on Zeiser and the modified model (Figure 4.2), the following displacement type classification for agency attribution can be presented:

i. Information-producing: The system automates descriptive information production that can be used to support the belief decision or direct the value attitudes of the reason for an intentional act. The agent forms the belief or the attitude on their own. A smart watch keeping track of the user's heart rate levels would be an information-producing system that supports a belief. A hypothetical analysis tool for fencing team competitions that provides injury and physical condition information about the opposing team's fencers could direct the willingness of the coach to push for a strategy that emphasizes attempting to gain a lead against a certain fencer.[6]
ii. Attitude producing: The system automates normative information production concerning attitudes. It suggests an attitude for the user, such as aiming for an optimal body composure or presents particular areas to concentrate on while developing their sport performance – speed, explosivity, for example – without providing a plan to achieve it is an attitude-producing system. The user may or may not accept the suggestion at face value. As an attitude represents a willingness to realize a value, the value is also implicitly embedded within the system.
iii. Belief-producing: The system automates normative information production concerning beliefs about actions. It suggests how the user should act, which implicitly contains an attitude, and an explicit belief that supports the plan. In other words, it generates ready-to-use beliefs for the user that are not dependent on the available information of the agent. The user may or may not follow the plan at face value. An AI gym coach

that creates training plans or a tactical advisor are examples of a belief-producing systems.

iv. Intention-producing: The system automates intention production. It causes an action based on a belief and an attitude, which are also implicitly present, similar to a belief-producing system. An intention-producing system acts on its own, regardless of the user's will. An automatic transmission of a race car or the earlier presented, hypothetical brain implant for fencing are examples of intention-producing systems.

In essence, the previous classification tells us how the agential action should be normatively attributed between the user and the AI system. It is important to note that all AI systems automate *something* – in the sense that the automated process is external to the user; it happens independently from the user and without their effort or capabilities. This is a logical necessity, as it algorithmically replicates an aspect of intelligence or a cognitive process, removing the need for a human agent to rely on their own capacities to govern that particular aspect. An AI system that does not replicate intelligence or cognitive processes is not an AI system. From the agential perspective, it also means that every AI system used in sport is also an agentially displacing system, as it by definition takes over some aspect of agency as it falls under some of the presented displacement type classes.

Should agency then be allowed to be displaced by an AI system in sport, or should we advocate for a wholly puristic stance? Considering performance enhancement, intention-producing displacement seems the most problematic one as it removes the agent from the process, but the distinction is not that clear-cut. Bryson (2020) states that intelligence is a special case of computation, and natural and artificial intelligence are not different in this sense. Considering the previous, a coach can be seen as a naturally intelligent system that automates an aspect of sport-relevant attitude and belief production, as the coach guides the athlete's skill acquisition and tactical

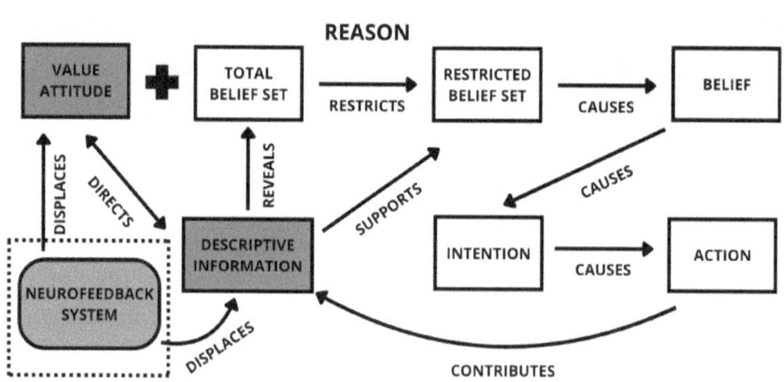

Figure 4.3 Aspects of agency displaced by a neurofeedback system (coloured red)

decision-making, which reduces the athlete's agency in the attitude- and belief-producing sense.[7] Few would, however, claim that coaching should not be allowed in sport.

Then again, returning to fencing, using a system that gives sound cues of passed time during a bout – an example of an information-producing system – is forbidden. The fencer is supposed to rely only on their own sense of time and the timer on the scoring machine in the middle of the piste, which is often difficult to see during active fencing. This could be achieved with a Bluetooth earpiece connected to a computer with access to the scoring machine or just by having someone yell the current time left. Functionally, the outcome is the same, and the potential difference lies only in how effectively the system fulfils the function. Then, if agential displacement is not universally prohibited in sport, it is necessary to establish a framework for the limits of acceptable displacement.

4.4 Functionalism and Performance Fundamentals

AI develops at a great pace and already has a wide variety of different approaches for improving sport performance (see e.g. Araújo et al., 2021 and Munoz-Macho et al., 2024). Purely from the agency displacement perspective, it should not matter *how* agency is being displaced – e.g. by a machine learning algorithm or another human being – if a capacity is supposed to be governed by the athlete in the first place. Functionalism is a general doctrine in philosophy of mind, positing that mental states are not defined by their internal constitution, but by their causal roles (Block, 2007). Mathematically speaking, a function is a transformation rule from an input set to an output set (Gowers, 2008). A performance-enhancing AI system, then, can be understood as a rule that, given an input, produces an output that enhances performance by displacing agency in one of the four ways presented in the displacement type classification.

Looking at agency displacement from a functionalist perspective makes it possible to evaluate agency displacement of different AI technologies in a neutral way, meaning that it does not matter what kind of algorithm or physical setup the system is realized on. It is important to note that the question of *the form* of an agentially displacing system is a separate one from the question of agency displacement itself: even if displacing agency is not prohibited in some particular situation, the way it is created or built, the setup, might be. A system might, for example, cause physical harm to the user or violate the user's right to privacy by sharing sensitive data with outsiders.

Agency displacement is also different from *de-skilling*, which refers to the situation where technological innovations make it easier to perform the required skills for a sport (Miah, 2006), as being able to use a de-skilling technology during an instance of a sport means that the capacity governed by that technology is already acceptable from the agency displacement point of view. It is also clear that the form of the system must be introduced in sporting practice before it becomes meaningful to discuss the question of de-skilling effects. Hierarchically then, questions of agency displacement come first, form second, and de-skilling third.

A system might have several functional definitions. For example, an EEG headset combined with a piece of software is used for neurofeedback training in sport (Hung & Cheng, 2019). Such a system could be functionally defined as "taking electrical activity generated by neurons in the brain as input and producing real-time information about the user's brainwave states and giving visual or auditory cues to help the user to reach the optimal brain state as output" – an expected definition. But the definition could as well just be "takes electrical power from a power outlet as input and produces heat as output", since all electronic systems produce heat when used, making it functionally identical to, for example, a PlayStation console, or an electric kitchen stove under this definition. Therefore, it is necessary to examine the nature of the sport under examination and introduce the concept of a performance fundamental (PF) to evaluate the relevancy of the definitions.

4.4.1 Performance Fundamentals

Simply put, a PF is a sport-specific property of an athlete that can be deemed important for performing well and reaching the goal of the sport. For example, in fencing, the goal would be making a touché, whereas in football, it would be scoring a goal. If athlete A is identical to athlete B in every other way except that A has a higher capacity in some property P compared to B, and during an instance of a sport A has a higher chance of reaching the goal of the sport than B, and the difference in chance is significant and systematic, then P can be considered a PF within the sport that A and B are participating.

To exemplify: in fencing, broadly speaking, such properties as concentration, accuracy and complex reaction time are performance fundamentals. All the mentioned can be understood in a general and a sport-specific sense. Since the above comparison condition is based on the chance of reaching the goal of a specific sport and thus should be understood in the latter sense, reflecting the sporting actions the performance is built on, such as the accuracy of tip control in fencing. Specificity and practical applicability of a PF rely on the knowledge about the sport: being able to distinguish fundamentals in a sport is a core ambition in applied exercise science and requires a deep understanding of the sport.

If the output of the functional definition of an AI system *can be shown to map into a PF* in such a way that the capacity of the athlete concerning the said PF increases significantly when they use the system, the definition is relevant for evaluating agency displacement. This mapping can be understood as another function that provides a causal link from the output to the increased performance within a PF. Formally speaking:

Let $\mathcal{F}_1$ be the set of possible functions of an AI system and $\mathcal{F}_2$ be the set of possible performance fundamental mapping functions. Then,

$$f_1 \in \mathcal{F}_1 : \mathrm{I} \mapsto \mathrm{O}$$
$$f_2 \in \mathcal{F}_2 : \mathrm{O} \mapsto \mathrm{PF},$$

where f_1 is the function of the AI system, f_2 is the PF mapping function, I is the input, O is the output and PF is a performance fundamental. I is restricted by f_1 in the sense that not everything can be used as an input. For example, an EEG headset cannot have the heart rate of the user as input, as it measures brainwaves.

Using the expected f_1 definition for a neurofeedback system presented earlier, with brainwave states and visual or auditory cues as outputs, an f_2 then exists, as neurofeedback improves concentration in sport (Rydzik et al., 2023), and concentration is a performance fundamental in fencing. Such an f_1 would then be relevant for agency displacement evaluation. It is important to note that as f_1 and f_2 are separate functions, the PF that f_2 maps into is not the same thing as the O of f_1 – this output should be understood as something physical, a product of *the system*, whereas a PF represents a measurable abstraction, such as endurance, which is a capacity of *the user*. It would be quite a stretch to claim that, for example, a visual cue would be a performance fundamental of any sport. Instead, as inputs of f_2s, they operate as the bases of explanation for the operation of f_2s. An f_2 then bridges the AI system, the athlete and performance in a sport.

Not every system is an intelligent system and therefore doesn't fit within the f_1 / f_2 framework. Using a doping example, erythropoietin (EPO) increases the user's red cell count, which in turn increases endurance (Jelkmann, 2020). But EPO has neither inputs or outputs, nor a rule that governs its operation; in a way, it's an input in itself, should the human body be considered a function. It is passive and does not have the capacity of doing the right thing at the right time, but instead it always causes an increase in the red cell count if the conditions are right; e.g. there are no medical conditions that cause EPO resistance, such as iron deficiency or inflammation (Macdougall & Cooper, 2002). An AI-operated EPO dispenser would, of course, count as an intelligent system. In this case a user-optimized amount of EPO would be the output O in f_1 of the system.

4.4.2 *Analysing Agency Displacement*

Evaluating agency displacement concerns the output of f_1 if f_1 is relevant. This output is reflected against the four-part displacement type classification presented earlier to determine how agency is displaced and attributed to the AI system. Recalling that the output of the neurofeedback system is (1) real-time information about the user's brainwave states and (2) visual and auditory cues, it is clear that (1) falls under information-producing agency displacement as it produces descriptive information about the brain states of the user but does not produce suggestions for action, whereas (2) is not as clear-cut. This is because (2) exhibits information-producing features in the sense that the visual or auditory cues are pieces of information that describe the proximity of the user's current brain state to some other state, yet these cues seem to imply a normative perspective as the they implicitly imply a hierarchy of desirability among different brain states, which seems to lean closer to attitude-producing displacement. In other words, there is an implicit suggestion for an attitude that restricts the total belief set into beliefs that result in actions that promote certain brainwave states over others. Figure 4.3 presents the displaced aspects of agency.

Having an implied hierarchy of desirability, however, does not mean that the system is producing plans of action, as is with a belief-producing system. The cues of the neurofeedback system, to continue with the example, direct the user towards the value(s) embedded to the system: it essentially states that a brain state of a certain type is more valuable than some other brain state, and that the user should be willing to act in a way that realizes that value. Should the user proceed to use the system as intended – one could of course use it in an unintended way, for example by mirroring the cue information, but this is again an unlikely curiosity – they then accept the system's value encoding, and attitude production is thus agentially displaced. Using cues is implicit attitude-wise, as mentioned earlier, but the system could as well be explicit about expressing a value proposition – stating that the user should have a certain attitude. An AI coach for physical conditioning, for example, might state explicitly that the user should aim for a certain weight and body composition to optimize their endurance to suit the specific requirements of a fencing competition. Producing normative information about attitudes differs from belief production, as attitudes can exist without an idea of an action to achieve it, a belief, but a belief is tied to an action.

4.4.3 An Evaluative Framework

The classification of the output of an f_1 does not alone reveal whether it should be allowed in a sport, as mentioned earlier. It needs to be reflected against the ethos of the particular sport, or, as defined above, of the socially accepted interpretation of how the goals of a sport are to be agentially achieved. It has to be noted that we do not build on an essentialist ethos account here. The ethos of a sport is the outcome of a constant negotiation in words and action between practitioners on how to play the sport well and where to draw the limits between what are acceptable and non-acceptable methods and means (Loland & McNameee, 2000). Morgan (1994) emphasizes the role of a deliberating practitioner community in this respect: practitioners interactively shaping, protecting and also developing the ethos of their sport.

As a sporting ideal shared by a sporting community, an ethos has normative and prescriptive force. Actually, from a contractualist point of view, the ethos of a sport can be considered the definition of a more or less tacit contract among competitors (Loland, 2002). There is a pragmatic reason for competitors to keep to the contract. If some competitors systematically violate and break the ethos, meaningful competition is difficult to realize at all. This leads to an ethical justification of ethos compliance. Based on neo-Kantian premises, Rawls (1971) formulates a basic fairness obligation. When voluntarily engaged in a rule-governed practice, a moral obligation arises to keep the rules. The premise is this: It is unfair to benefit from the collaboration of others without doing one's own share. Meaningful competition depends upon that most competitors keep the shared ethos most of the time. Intentional ethos violators depend upon other competitors' ethos compliance for a sport to be realized at all. They then enjoy the value and potential payoffs of sport participation without doing their fair share. The act unfairly.

This does not mean that a sport ethos is unconditionally morally binding. Competitors may gradually develop an increased acceptance for violence, or for discriminatory practices, or, as the AI case, for breaches of ethical norms of privacy and autonomy. An ethically acceptable ethos, then, must meet basic requirements in the form of general, ethical principles.

Our task here is to develop an evaluative framework for the use of AI to enhance sport performance. Obviously, if such use violates general ethical principles, it should be rejected. The critical question concerns the narrow, sport-specific part of an ethos, that is, the socially accepted interpretation of how the goals of a sport are to be agentially achieved, and how the sport is to be played well.

This sport-specific ethos can be further conceptualized with the help of Ngyuen (2019). In games, an agential skeleton, practical agency, is engineered into to the game, this being the abilities, goals and values the player has, created in relation to the rules, goals and practical environment. In Ngyuen's view, agency is layered, and during a game, the player temporarily takes the engineered agency as a layer operating on top of their overall agency. Within the ethos of a sport, then, there is an engineered, restricted agency that the competitors must immerse themselves in during an instance of a sport if they agree to the contract – a specific way of instantiating the sporting performance. It tells the competitors where and how agency must be instantiated in a sport – and where it can be displaced and attributed to an AI, for example. The limits of the acceptable ways of enhancing performance, including agential attributability, are then also governed by the restricted agency. As mentioned earlier, PFs are measurable abstractions that bring about the performance, hence their acceptable agential attributability is governed by the engineered agency of the sport.

In the following analysis, this will be our tentative, normative rule of thumb. To establish whether an AI system is agentially acceptable in a sport from performance enhancement perspective, it is necessary to go through the following steps:

i. Formulate the function f_1 of the AI system
ii. Establish the connection between O and PF in a performance-enhancing way via f_2
iii. Classify the output O of the system using the agency displacement type classification
iv. Extract the allowable agency displacement types concerning the PF from the ethos of the sport in question
v. Compare the displacement type(s) of O with the acceptable displacement types to decide on the acceptability

Again, being agentially acceptable does not mean being acceptable from other ethical aspects. For example, if a system causes harm to others, then it might not be acceptable even if it doesn't break the agency requirement. The last chapter applies the presented framework to a hypothetical EEG-based AI technology in the context of epee fencing in competition and training settings.

4.5 Applying Example: EEG-Based Technologies in Epee Fencing

4.5.1 *EEG-tDCS*

As mentioned in the introduction, the first example is a hypothetical EEG-tDCS closed-loop BCI system that keeps the user's fatigue levels constantly at a minimum. Modulable factors with tDCS include "sensory perception and processing, fatigue, perceived exertion, multiple aspects of executive function including dual tasking and response inhibition, and neural recovery" (Zhu et al., 2019). Functionally speaking, the system's f_1 input is the EEG signal, and the output is an optimized direct current to the brain.

Fatigue declines skilled performance in sport, including speed and accuracy of decision-making (Sun et al., 2021). Mental fatigue also reduces willingness to take risks (Jia et al., 2022). In fencing, a situation must be analysed and reacted to in a fraction of a second, and simple and choice reaction times play a key role (Johne, 2021). Therefore, as tDCS reduces fatigue, it is plausible to suggest that the function of the imagined EEG-tDCS system maps into certain PFs of epee fencing, namely decision-making speed and accuracy, meaning that there is an f_2.

The system is clearly an intention-producing one: it operates on its own, bypassing the user's will. It neither produces descriptive information nor makes suggestions. It is different, for example, from taking a caffeine supplement – an accepted substance – which also reduces fatigue (Calvo et al., 2021), as the decision on timing and dosing is done by the athlete, even if advised by a nutritional specialist. This kind of specialist advice would fall under attitude- and belief-producing displacement, which is a separate discussion.

The next step is to extract the information on whether the contract has agency requirements for these fundamentals. In the case of fencing, this should be done by looking at the interpretations of the stakeholders participating in the world cup series – the highest level of competitive fencing – and the International Fencing Federation (FIE) governing the world cup series. As in any competitive sport, but especially in an Olympic sport, the competition is fierce on the highest level, and the limits of the sport are constantly being tried. Always looking for ways to gain an advantage means that the contract must be defined in a very precise manner for it to hold, and it must be quick to adapt to new situations. The top-level fencers and their coaches are the stakeholders that are most deeply involved in the sport in its current form – their interpretations should be taken as a close description of the ethos. The FIE, on the other hand, is responsible for maintaining the rules by providing referees for competitions and creating rule committees. Maintaining the rules is also, of course, an interpretational act related to the ethos and should be considered when extracting the agency requirements. The rules tend to develop in response to new situations and needs. The rule changes, then, also influence the interpretations of the other stakeholders, creating a mutual dynamic for the evolution of the ethos.

Looking at interviews of elite-level fencers makes it possible to deduce that mental capability and tactical decision-making are a core part of fencing, e.g. describing it as chess at 200 kilometres per hour (see e.g. Chirashnya, 2020; Majendie, 2021; Taguchi, 2018). Additionally, the passivity rule[8] encourages active fencing and risk-taking by sanctioning inactivity. An individual fencing world cup is two days long, typically lasting anywhere from eight to twelve hours per day. The competition begins with a pool of five to six bouts, typically followed by eight to nine rounds of direct elimination within two days, which also emphasizes the importance of being able to maintain a high level of decision-making performance over a long period of time.

It is thus reasonable to suggest that there is an agential requirement on decision-making speed and accuracy – it is something that a fencer should be able to produce and control on their own, meaning that such a system should not be used during competitions. How about training, then? From the practical perspective, it is next to impossible to prevent the use outside the competition setting as tDCS use is virtually undetectable (Davis, 2013). The previous does not entail acceptability, however.

Competitive sport is not just a set of singular competitive events: in fencing, the athletes typically have competitive careers lasting years or even decades, and attend the competitions one after another, as a continuum. Training plays an integral part in this continuum, with an aim to enhance one's chances to succeed in the competitions. It doesn't exist in isolation. At least on the world cup level, the contract should be seen as covering participation as a continuum, not just applying to particular events. The rules of a sport are not in itself agential: it is not necessary that there is always a competition going on. But a competitor subscribed to a contract cannot separate themselves from the agential requirements the contract even if they are not currently in a competition. The logical outcome would then be that the system violates the agential requirements in training as well.

Nothing, of course, prevents the contract from taking such a form that training has different agential requirements for enhancing these PFs. In the case of fencing, it is impossible to tell whether there are different agential requirements for training, as no such information exists yet – it is also likely that this part of the contract is not well defined, since tDCS technology is not mainstream knowledge among athletes and other stakeholders. Lack of definition underlines the importance of stakeholder involvement in finding the agential requirements that correspond with the ethos.

4.5.2 Neurofeedback

In the case of neurofeedback, the f_1 input was earlier defined as "electrical activity generated by neurons" and output as "real-time information about the user's brainwave states and giving visual or auditory cues". The PF concerning f_2 is concentration, as established earlier in the text. It was also established that the system belongs to the information-producing and attitude-producing displacement classes.

Concentration is rather close to decision-making speed. One could say that good concentration is a necessity for good decision-making speed and accuracy. The earlier presented analysis about the (part of the) ethos of epee fencing can be utilized here as well – concentration is at the core of epee fencing and should be at the responsibility of the athlete. But since the system is not an intention-producing one, the same reasoning as with the EEG-tDCS system cannot be used for neurofeedback. Then again, a neurofeedback system is not very far from having a mental performance coach training the athlete's concentration, except that a coach is likely to also provide concrete techniques or strategies to maintain the concentration, which falls into the belief-producing displacement class. The use of mental coaches in fencing is commonplace and accepted in training and in competition.

A neurofeedback system allows the athlete to develop their capacity of concentration through their own effort, facilitated and guided by the system. Therefore, it can be said that using a neurofeedback system does not violate the agential requirement of epee fencing, as this is similar to coaching, regardless of it being used in training or in competition. In fact, such a system could even be seen as valuable by allowing the athlete to enhance the manifestation of their sporting capabilities in an agentially ethos-abiding way.

4.6 Concluding Remarks

We have now established a framework for analysing whether the use of an AI system for performance enhancement is acceptable agentially, which touches the very core of sport. Looking at the system from a functionalist perspective allows for the creation of a causal link between the system and a performance fundamental, which opens it up for displacement evaluation. The evaluation involves ethos reflection and involves the different stakeholder groups and the rules.

It is intuitive to say that the biggest issues concern intention-producing systems, as these systems completely displace the user's agency. Those systems that displace smaller portions of agency are more likely to be agentially acceptable. It is more likely that if they face issues, the issues will be form or de-skilling related. In any case, a thorough understanding of the system and the sport at hand must be accompanied by the use of the framework, as a universal limit, covering all sports, cannot be set. Instead, AI use should be considered in relation to a specific sport.

Notes

1 Fencing-related knowledge is provided by one of the authors, Niko Vuorinen, who is a former professional epee fencer and a multiple time world cup medalist.
2 From a metaphysical perspective, causality is a challenged concept (e.g. Russell [1919]). Discussing the issues is not within the scope of this text. However, to attribute normative, intentional actions to an agent, it is necessary to establish an ownership link between the agent and the action, which is best described as the agent – or their mental states – being the cause, the origin, of the action, regardless of the metaphysical status of causality.
3 T.64.6. Technical Rules. International Fencing Federation.
4 T.109. Technical Rules. International Fencing Federation.
5 Insulet Corporation, https://www.omnipod.com.
6 A team match in fencing consists of 9 relay bouts, meaning that even a single bout won with a big score difference can provide a significant, hard-to-overcome. advantage. See for example from the 2024 Olympics Games the 8th bout (Foconi vs. Nagano in Italy against Japan) in the men's foil and the 7th bout (Rabb vs. Do in Hungary against Korea) in the men's sabre final. In both cases a 5-0 bout win turned the equally scored match into a clear victory for Japan and Korea.
7 A coach, of course, is a person, and much more than just an algorithmically driven tool, but serves as an exemplification in this case to establish an analogy.
8 T.124. Technical Rules. International Fencing Federation.

References

American Psychological Association. (2024). Cognitive process. https://dictionary.apa.org/cognitive-process.

Araújo, D., Couceiro, M., Seifert, L., Sarmento, H., & Davids, K. (2021). *Artificial intelligence in sport performance analysis*. Routledge.

Block, N. (2007). *What is functionalism? Functionalism, consciousness, and representation: Collected papers, Volume I.* The MIT Press.
Bryson, J. J. (2020). The artificial intelligence of the ethics of artificial intelligence: An introductory overview of law and regulation.In Dubber, M., Pasquale, F. &amp Das, S. (eds.), *The Oxford handbook of ethics and AI.* Oxford University Press. https://doi.org/10.1093/oxfordhb/9780190067397.013.1
Calvo, J. L., Fei, X., Domínguez, R., & Pareja-Galeano, H. (2021). Caffeine and cognitive functions in sports: A aystematic review and meta-analysis. *Nutrients, 13*(3), 868. https://doi.org/10.3390/nu13030868
Carrio Sampedro, A. (2023). The ethics of AI in sport: Taking athlete's rights and wellbeing seriously. *Final Report for The IOC Olympic Studies Centre.* https://library.olympics.com/Default/doc/SYRACUSE/3025522/the-ethics-of-ai-in-sport-taking-athletes-rights-and-wellbeing-seriously-alberto-carrio-sampedro
Chirashnya, I. (2020). Estonian Epee champion Erika Kirpu teaches us about flexibility and coming back from disappointment. *Academy of Fencing Masters.* https://academyoffencingmasters.com/blog/erika-kirpu/
Chmait, N., & Westerbeek, H. (2021). Artificial intelligence and machine learning in sport research: An introduction for non-data scientists. *Frontiers in Sports and Active Living, 3.* https://doi.org/10.3389/fspor.2021.682287
D'Agostino, F. (1981). The ethos of games. *Journal of the Philosophy of Sport, 8*(1), 7–18. https://doi.org/10.1080/00948705.1981.9714372
Davidson, D. (1971). I. Agency. *Agent, action, and reason.* University of Toronto Press.
Davidson, D. (1978). Intending. *Philosophy of history and action.* D. Reidel Publishing Company.
Davis, N. (2013). Neurodoping: Brain stimulation as a performance-enhancing measure. *Sports Medicine, 43*(8), 649–653. https://doi.org/10.1007/s40279-013-0027-z
Edwards, D. J., Cortes, M., Wortman-Jutt, S., Putrino, D., Bikson, M., Thickbroom, G., & Pascual-Leone, A. (2017). Transcranial direct current stimulation and sports performance. *Frontiers in Human Neuroscience, 11.* https://doi.org/10.3389/fnhum.2017.00243
Frankish, K., & Ramsey, W. M. (2014). Introduction. *The Cambridge handbook of artificial intelligence.* Cambridge University Press.
Gowers, T. (2008). The language and grammar of mathematics. *The Princeton companion to mathematics.* Princeton University Press.
Hung, T-M., & Cheng, M-Y. (2019). Neurofeedback in sport: Theory, methods, research, and efficacy. *Handbook of sport neuroscience and psychophysiology.* Routledge.
Jelkmann, W. (2020). Erythropoietin doping: Cardiovascular effects in athletes. *Annals of Sports Medicine and Research, 7*(1), 1142.
Jia, H., Lin, C. J., & Wang, E. M. (2022). Effects of mental fatigue on risk preference and feedback processing in risk decision-making. *Scientific Reports, 12*(1). https://doi.org/10.1038/s41598-022-14682-0
Johne, M. (2021). The impact of fencing training symmetrisation on simple reaction time. *Biomedical Human Kinetics, 13*(1), 231–236. https://doi.org/10.2478/bhk-2021-0028

Kadosh, R. (2013). Using transcranial electrical stimulation to enhance cognitive functions in the typical and atypical brain. *Translational Neuroscience, 4*(1). https://doi.org/10.2478/s13380-013-0104-7

Leite, J., Morales-Quezada, L., Carvalho, S., Thibaut, A., Doruk, D., Chen, C., Schachter, S. C., Rotenberg, A., & Fregni, F. (2017). Surface EEG-Transcranial Direct Current Stimulation (TDCS) closed-loop system. *International Journal of Neural Systems, 27*(06), 1750026. https://doi.org/10.1142/s0129065717500265

Loland, S. (2002). *Fair play in sport: A moral norm system.* Routledge.

Loland, S. (2018). Ethics of technology in sport. *Ethics in sport.* Human Kinetics.

Loland, S., & McNamee, M. (2000). Fair play and the ethos of sports: An eclectic philosophical framework. *Journal of the Philosophy of Sport, 27*(1), 63–80. https://doi.org/10.1080/00948705.2000.9714590

Macdougall, I. C., & Cooper, A. C. (2002). Erythropoietin resistance: The role of inflammation and pro-inflammatory cytokines. *Nephrology Dialysis Transplantation, 17*(suppl_11), 39–43. https://doi.org/10.1093/ndt/17.suppl_11.39

Majendie, M. (2021). Discuss: Fencing's like chess at 200kph while dressed as an astronaut. *Red Bull.* https://www.redbull.com/gb-en/fencing-champion-olga-kharlan-interview

Miah, A. (2006). Rethinking enhancement in sport. *Annals of the New York Academy of Sciences, 1093*(1), 301–320. https://doi.org/10.1196/annals.1382.020

Morgan, W. J. (1994). *Leftist theories of sport.* University of Illinois Press.

Munoz-Macho, A. A., Domínguez-Morales, M. J., & Sevillano-Ramos, J. L. (2024). Performance and healthcare analysis in elite sports teams using artificial intelligence: A scoping review. *Frontiers in Sports and Active Living, 6.* https://doi.org/10.3389/fspor.2024.1383723

Nguyen, C. T. (2019). Games and the art of agency. *The Philosophical Review, 128*(4), 423–462. https://doi.org/10.1215/00318108-7697863

Rawls, J. A (1971). *Theory of justice.* Harvard University Press.

Russell, B. (1919). On the notion of cause. *Mysticism and logic and other essays.* Longmans, Green and Co.

Rydzik, Ł., Wąsacz, W., Ambroży, T., Javdaneh, N., Brydak, K., & Kopańska, M. (2023). The use of neurofeedback in sports training: Systematic review. *Brain Sciences, 13*(4), 660. https://doi.org/10.3390/brainsci13040660

Suits, B. (1978). *The grasshopper: Games, life and utopia.* University of Toronto Press.

Sun, H., Soh, K. G., Roslan, S., Wazir, M. R. W. N., & Soh, K. L. (2021). Does mental fatigue affect skilled performance in athletes? A systematic review. *PLoS ONE, 16*(10), e0258307. https://doi.org/10.1371/journal.pone.0258307

Taguchi, S. (2018). Naoki YASU x Yuki OTA. *GO Journal,* (2). https://www.parasapo.tokyo/gojournal/en/issue02/interview03/

Wang, F., Wan, Y., Li, M., Huang, H., Li, L., Hou, X., Pan, J., Wen, Z., & Li, J. (2023). Recent advances in fatigue detection algorithm based on EEG. *Intelligent Automation & Soft Computing, 35*(3), 3573–3586. https://doi.org/10.32604/iasc.2023.029698

Zeiser, J. (2024). Owning decisions: AI decision-support and the attributability-GAP. *Science and Engineering Ethics, 30*(4). https://doi.org/10.1007/s11948-024-00485-1

Zheng, R. (2016). Attributability, accountability, and implicit bias. *Implicit bias and philosophy: Volume 2: Moral responsibility, structural injustice, and ethics*. Oxford University Press.

Zhu, Z., Zhou, J., Manor, B., Wang, X., Fu, W., & Liu, Y. (2019). Commentary: "Brain-doping," is it a real threat? *Frontiers in Physiology, 10*. https://doi.org/10.3389/fphys.2019.01489

Chapter 5

The Ethical Challenges of Brainchips and Extended Minds in Sport

Where Does Doping Begin?

Mirko Daniel Garasic

5.1 Introduction

This chapter will use Clark and Chalmers' thesis of the Extended Mind to question the boundaries of our technological identities and selves and – in doing so – assess if and how we should redefine doping in the years to come. The advent of brain-computer interfaces (BCIs) like Neuralink presents unprecedented opportunities and ethical dilemmas in various fields, including sport. Here, I want to explore the ethical challenges associated with the use of brainchips in sport, focusing on how such technology could be considered a form of doping, especially under the prism of the Extended Mind Thesis (EMT) – and the specific way in which this reshapes our understanding of the self. Thus, the discussion will include an overview of EMT and neural implants in relation to identity, the potential benefits and risks, the definition and implications of doping, and the ethical considerations that arise from integrating such advanced technologies in our conceptualization of the self and, consequently, their implementation in competitive sport.

5.2 Brain-Computer Interfaces (BCIs) and Neural Implants: An Overview

Brainchips can be more accurately divided into brain-computer interfaces (BCIs) and neural implants – both representing cutting-edge advancements in neuroscience and biomedical engineering. These technologies hold the potential to revolutionize medical treatments, augment human capabilities, and enhance our understanding of the brain. Though limited, in this section of the chapter, I will aim to provide a comprehensive overview of BCIs and neural implants, detailing their mechanisms, current technological state, and applications as well as the differences between the two.

DOI: 10.4324/9781003520290-6

5.2.1 *What Are They?*

A brain-computer interface (BCI) is a direct communication pathway between the brain and an external device. BCIs are designed to bypass conventional neural pathways, such as muscles and nerves, to enable direct interaction with computers or other devices. This technology is particularly valuable for individuals with motor disabilities, allowing them to control prosthetic limbs, computer cursors, or other assistive devices through thought alone. BCIs function by detecting and interpreting neural signals from the brain, typically by following five steps. First of all, there must be a signal acquisition. This involves capturing brain signals using non-invasive (e.g., EEG – electroencephalography) or invasive (e.g., intracortical electrodes) tools. Next, said signals need to be processed. Hence, raw brain signals are filtered and amplified to remove noise and enhance relevant neural activity. Third, specific patterns or features within the brain signals are identified and extracted. This step is crucial for differentiating between various intended actions or thoughts. The following move will thus be that of "translating" such information. The extracted features are translated into commands that can be understood by an external device. Not surprisingly, machine learning algorithms are often employed to improve the accuracy of these translations. Lastly, there is a device output. The translated commands are used to control an external device, such as a robotic arm, computer cursor, or communication software.

Neural implants, on the other hand, are devices implanted into the brain or nervous system to modulate, record, or stimulate neural activity. These implants can be used for a variety of purposes, including restoring lost sensory functions, controlling prosthetic devices, or treating neurological disorders such as Parkinson's disease, epilepsy, and chronic pain. Neural implants can operate through the following four levels. First, electrodes are surgically implanted in specific brain regions or along the spinal cord to target precise neural circuits. Second, the implanted device can deliver electrical impulses to stimulate or inhibit neural activity. This modulation can help restore normal function in damaged or dysfunctional neural circuits. Third, some neural implants are designed to record neural activity, providing valuable data for understanding brain function and disease progression. Fourth, advanced neural implants can incorporate feedback systems to adjust stimulation parameters in real-time, enhancing therapeutic outcomes.

5.2.2 *Where Are We with the Technology?*

As widely shown in the media (Neuralink is a leader in this), BCIs and neural implants provide high hopes for medical rehabilitation and are already used to restore motor function in patients with spinal cord injuries, stroke, and neurodegenerative diseases. Moreover, for individuals with severe communication impairments, such as those with amyotrophic lateral sclerosis (ALS),

BCIs can enable communication through thought-controlled typing or speech synthesis. On the nontherapeutic side, BCIs are being explored for cognitive training, mental health treatment, and enhancing focus and attention in healthy individuals. In addition, neural implants can be used (with all the ethical concerns connected to it) as research tools, providing valuable data for neuroscience research, helping scientists understand brain function, neural plasticity, and the mechanisms underlying neurological disorders.

Brainchips represent transformative technologies with the potential to significantly impact medicine, neuroscience, and human augmentation. While considerable challenges remain, ongoing research and technological advancements continue to push the boundaries of what is possible, bringing us closer to a future where these technologies become integral parts of our lives. Recent advancements in BCIs have been driven by improvements in materials, signal processing algorithms, and machine learning techniques – yet, much must be done still, and, in order to better understand where this technology is going, we need to grasp some differences within the BCIs universe. First of all, we should divide them into invasive and non-invasive BCIs. Neuralink falls under the former category. Intracortical BCIs, involving microelectrode arrays implanted directly into the brain, have shown promising results in clinical trials. Companies like Neuralink are working on high-density electrode arrays that offer precise control over prosthetic devices. As for the latter, Electroencephalography (EEG)-based BCIs have become more sophisticated, offering improved signal resolution and user comfort. Commercial products such as Emotiv and NeuroSky have made non-invasive BCIs more accessible for research and consumer applications. Deep brain stimulation (DBS) – only possible through neural implants – is widely used to treat Parkinson's disease and epilepsy. Advances in closed-loop systems connected to the devices, which adjust stimulation based on real-time neural feedback, are improving therapeutic outcomes. Last, we have neuroprosthetics: bionic limbs controlled by BCIs have demonstrated significant progress, allowing amputees to perform complex tasks with prosthetic hands or legs. Sensory feedback integration is an ongoing area of research, aiming to provide users with a more natural sense of touch.

Despite such inspiring achievements, it should not go unnoticed that several limitations are still in place. To begin with, both invasive and non-invasive BCIs are susceptible to signal noise and interference, which can reduce accuracy and reliability. Secondly, invasive procedures for implanting neural devices carry risks, including infection, inflammation, and potential damage to brain tissue. As often is the case with technology, making these devices widely available and affordable remains a significant hurdle – creating various ethical concerns for their legitimacy. Ethical concerns extend further when the ability to read and modulate brain activity raises ethical issues related to privacy, consent, and the potential for misuse. These are the technical challenges that brainchips bring with them. Before moving to analysing some of the conceptual ones (especially in relation to sport), we shall first introduce a recent theory that has challenged our understanding of identity, the mind and the self.

5.3 Extended Mind Thesis

The Extended Mind Thesis (EMT), formulated by Andy Clark and David Chalmers in their 1998 paper "The Extended Mind", proposes that the mind is not confined within the boundaries of the brain or even the body. Instead, it extends into the external environment, encompassing tools, devices, and other aspects of the physical and social world that contribute to cognitive processes.

The thesis is built on the idea that objects in the environment can function as integral components of our cognitive system. For example, when a person uses a notebook to store information, the notebook becomes a part of their memory system. Similarly, in contemporary society – it is quite astonishing to see the level of vision that Clark and Chalmers had! – when someone uses a smartphone to navigate, solve problems or, more simply, remember a phone number, the device acts as an extension of their cognitive abilities. Clark and Chalmers (1998) argue that these external aids are not merely supplementary but can be considered genuine parts of the mind because they perform functions that, if done internally, would be undoubtedly regarded as cognitive.

To support their argument, Clark and Chalmers introduce the concept of "active externalism", which suggests that the environment actively shapes and supports cognitive processes. To provide support for their innovative thesis (then more than now) they present a thought experiment involving two characters named Inga and Otto. The former remembers the location of a museum by recalling it from her biological memory, the latter, who has Alzheimer's disease, relies on a notebook to remember the same information. According to EMT, Otto's notebook serves the same functional role as biological memory, and thus it should be considered part of his mind. With its revolutionary approach to the conceptualization of cognitive processes – as well as identity and boundaries – the EMT challenges traditional views of cognition that strictly separate the mind from the external world. It emphasizes the fluid boundaries between internal mental processes and external aids, suggesting that cognition is a dynamic interplay between the brain, body, and environment.

Summing up, we could at least list three key implications of the EMT. First of all, EMT redefines cognition, expanding it to include interactions with external tools and artefacts, blurring the line between what is considered internal and external to the mind. Secondly, EMT highlights the significant role of technology and other external resources in enhancing and extending human cognitive capabilities. Finally, EMT raises questions about personal identity, the nature of mind, and the ethical treatment of individuals who rely heavily on external aids for cognitive tasks – leading us more directly to begin to see the connection between fairness, enhancement, and identity in sport contexts.

Clark and Chalmers' EMT proposes that the mind extends beyond the brain and body, incorporating external objects and tools that participate in cognitive processes. This perspective fundamentally rethinks the nature and boundaries of the mind, emphasizing the importance of the environment in shaping human cognition as well as identity. Both dimensions are crucial for athletes as they are for laymen, but here we want to focus on the impact that such an approach would have in sport. Hence, we will now move to elaborate on the implications that the EMT would bring in sport competition and doping. In order to do that, we will first delve into the effects that the EMT has on our ways of defining the boundaries between the natural and the artificial.

5.4 Between Natural and Artificial

Central to the philosophical discourse on sport is the concept of nature, which encompasses the inherent capabilities and limitations of the human body and mind. Sporting competition is often celebrated for its embodiment of natural human talents, such as strength, agility, and skill, cultivated through years of training and dedication. From a philosophical perspective, sport is regarded as a reflection of human excellence and endeavour, rooted in the values of fairness, integrity, and respect for the natural capacities of athletes.

The integration of brainchips into cognitive processes challenges conventional notions of what is "natural", as well as what should be defined as identity, prompting a reevaluation of what it means to be a distinct individual. In an EMT paradigm where cognitive functions are distributed across biological and artificial substrates, traditional markers of identity such as memory, agency, and autonomy take on new meanings. The potential for brainchips to facilitate shared or networked cognition complicates the boundaries between individual and collective identity. As individuals become interconnected through neural interfaces, forming networks of shared cognition, the traditional conception of the isolated, autonomous self becomes increasingly untenable. Instead, identity may be understood as emergent from the complex interactions between interconnected minds and technological systems, challenging traditional notions of personal autonomy and agency.

Relevantly, in 2004 Clark (independently from Chalmers) further expanded on his interpretation of the implications of the EMT (Clark & Erickson, 2004, p. 471), exploring the idea that humans are essentially "cyborgs" from birth, meaning that our cognitive processes are inherently intertwined with technology and external tools. The term "cyborg" typically refers to a cybernetic organism, a being that combines both biological and artificial components. Clark argues that humans have a natural predisposition to integrate with and exploit external resources, such as tools, language, and cultural practices, to enhance their cognitive abilities. He contends that our cognitive architecture is not limited to the biological brain but extends into the external world through our interactions with technology and other external supports. Among other points, in his book Clark extends the ideas presented in his earlier work with Chalmers to argue that the mind's extension into the external environment is not just a contingent or learned behaviour but is deeply ingrained in human nature. More relevantly for the present work, he also emphasizes the importance of the body in shaping cognition. Clark argues that our cognitive processes are not confined to the brain but are distributed across the brain, body, and the environment. The body and its interactions with the world play a crucial role in shaping our mental processes. He then discusses how humans have been augmenting their cognitive abilities through the use of tools and technologies throughout history. He explores examples of how writing, mathematics, and various external artefacts have become integral parts of human cognitive processes to argue that our interactions with technology are not just a recent development or a result of cultural evolution but are deeply embedded in our evolutionary history. Clark encourages a perspective that sees humans as beings naturally inclined to integrate with and rely on external resources for cognitive enhancement.

Notably, although from a different angle, two decades earlier Donna Haraway had already approached the issue of cyborgs (Haraway, 2013), outlining some of their innovative and yet natural features in her important work "A Cyborg Manifesto" in 1985. Both Haraway and Clark reject binary oppositions and dualisms that separate the natural from the artificial, the organic from the technological. While Haraway's work is more focused on challenging conventional distinctions between human and machine, nature and culture, Clark's concept of the Extended Mind challenges the separation between internal cognition and external tools.

In Haraway's work as well as in Clark's there is an emphasis on the importance of embodiment in understanding the relationship between humans and technology. Haraway's cyborg is not a disembodied entity but a being that is intimately connected with its material and technological context. Clark also underscores the role of the body in shaping cognition, arguing for an embodied and enactive approach to understanding the mind's extension into the world. Moreover, both perspectives highlight the idea of augmentation and hybridity. Haraway's cyborg is a hybrid creature, a melding of machine and organism, while Clark's natural-born cyborgs are humans whose cognitive processes are inherently intertwined with external tools and technologies. In both cases, there is an acknowledgement that technology is not just a separate tool but an integral part of the human experience. This aspect is key for the last and crucial point that the two thinkers share, and we shall consider: identity. Haraway's concept of the cyborg challenges fixed and stable notions of identity, suggesting that identities are fluid and continuously constructed through interactions with technology and culture. Clark's notion of natural-born cyborgs similarly implies a dynamic relationship between humans and their technological extensions, leading to a fluid conception of cognitive identity.

While Haraway and Clark approach the concept of cyborgs from different disciplinary perspectives (Haraway from feminist theory and Clark from philosophy and cognitive science), their ideas converge in challenging traditional boundaries and envisioning a more nuanced and integrated relationship between humans and technology. Both perspectives contribute to a broader conversation about the nature of humanity in a technologically mediated world – and lead us to our next step in this journey: if minds (and bodies) are indeed fluctuating between the artificial and the natural world, the digital and the analytic dimension, the outside and inside of ourselves, what are we to think about *our* identity?

5.5 The Challenges of Brainchips to Our Identity – Hence to the Way We Understand Sport

After having considered the theoretical dimension, we shall now dwell on the more practical outcomes that the constant development and increasingly widespread use of BCIs and neural implants will have on our understanding of what are our "natural" identities. Without claiming this to be an all-encompassing list of the resulting key considerations, some points are particularly relevant for the present investigation.

To begin with, we should take into consideration the augmentation of cognitive abilities. Neural implants and BCIs could enable cognitive enhancements, potentially boosting memory, problem-solving abilities, and overall cognitive performance. This augmentation may lead to a redefinition of intelligence and what it means to be "smart" or "wise", challenging traditional notions of cognitive abilities and academic achievement. Moreover, improved memory recall and the ability to rapidly acquire new skills could change how we perceive learning and personal development. The integration of information directly into the brain could impact our sense of self as it relates to knowledge acquisition and mastery of skills. More specifically, if brainchips will allow for faster information processing and decision-making, individuals might experience a shift in their perception of time. Rapid access to information and quicker thought processes could alter our subjective experience of time and how we navigate the world. Our senses could also be altered through the integration of additional sensory modalities or enhancing existing ones. This could lead to an expanded perception of the world, challenging traditional notions of sensory experiences and personal reality.

In relation to this, we can imagine that BCIs might allow individuals to integrate ethical or moral frameworks directly into their decision-making processes (after all, that is what we are aiming at with the AI behind autonomous vehicles). This raises questions about who defines these ethical guidelines and how they might shape individual and collective identities. As a natural result of all these challenges and revolutionary changes, it is reasonable to foresee that the ability to modify or enhance aspects of our cognitive and sensory experiences through brainchips could give rise to existential questions about the nature of consciousness, personal identity, and what it means to be human. In terms of social and interpersonal dynamics, Brain-to-Brain communication technologies (possible through the use of BCIs in two or more individuals) will impact how we connect with others. Direct neural interfaces might influence the way we understand and empathize with each other, potentially challenging traditional notions of interpersonal relationships and communication. Moreover, the integration of external technology into the brain raises questions about individual autonomy. Striking a balance between the benefits of enhanced capabilities and the potential loss of personal agency is a critical consideration, as it is of understanding the risks our privacy is facing. If thoughts and neural activity become accessible or hackable, individuals may grapple with issues related to the boundaries between the private and public aspects of their identities.

There is little doubt that the development and implementation of brainchips have the potential to challenge our identities by reshaping cognitive abilities, altering perceptions, introducing ethical complexities, impacting social dynamics, and raising fundamental questions about what it means to be human. As these technologies advance, it will be crucial to consider the ethical, social, and philosophical implications to ensure responsible and thoughtful integration into society. More humbly perhaps, it would be useful to try and assess in which way such a revolution could impact the realm of sport.

5.5.1 In Which Way Brainchips Could Be Relevant for Sport?

The integration of brainchips or neural implants could have several implications for the world of sport, impacting both the performance of athletes and the overall landscape of sport competition. More specifically, we can imagine a number of ways in which these technologies could be relevant for many of the sport disciplines we engage in as amateur, professionals, or aficionados.

Improved Decision-Making. Brainchips may enhance an athlete's decision-making capabilities by providing quicker access to relevant information and facilitating rapid analysis of game situations. This could be particularly beneficial in fast-paced sport where split-second decisions matter.

Accelerated Learning. Neural implants could potentially accelerate the learning process, allowing athletes to acquire and master new skills more quickly. This could revolutionize training programmes and shorten the time required for athletes to reach peak performance.

Real-Time Performance Metrics. Brain chips could provide real-time data on an athlete's physiological and neurological states during training and competition. This information could be used to optimize training regimens, prevent injuries, and maximize performance.

Enhanced Communication. Brain-to-brain (a variant of BCIs) communication technologies might facilitate instantaneous communication between teammates, improving coordination and strategy during competitions. This could lead to more efficient teamwork and strategic decision-making.

Injury Prevention. Brainchip technology could be used to monitor an athlete's neurological health, helping identify signs of fatigue or stress that might lead to injuries. This proactive approach to health and safety could contribute to the well-being of athletes.

Reevaluation of Sporting Norms. Finally, given their impact on our notion of identity, the use of BCIs and neural implants may challenge traditional norms and definitions of athletic performance. This could lead to debates about what constitutes a fair advantage and how technology intersects with the essence of sportsmanship.

In addition, I can think of at least the following two spin-offs that could revolutionize sport as we know it even further. The first point is more connected to the commercial side of the sport industry, and it must do more with the fan engagement and entertainment. The integration of advanced technologies into sport could provide new and immersive experiences for fans. For example, brainchip-enabled athletes might participate in virtual reality simulations, allowing fans to experience the sport from the athlete's perspective. The second point is instead related more directly to the boundaries of sport and the nature of competitions. The introduction of brainchips might give rise to entirely new sport or competitions that leverage cognitive abilities in novel ways. This sport could attract a different audience and create unique challenges for participants. We shall get back to this issue later in the chapter.

While the potential benefits of brainchips technology in sport are intriguing, it is extremely important to approach its implementation with careful consideration of ethical, legal, and societal implications. Striking a balance between technological advancement and the preservation of the values inherent in sport will be crucial for the responsible integration of these innovations into the athletic realm. In order to do that, we will now move towards an analysis of the new boundaries that brainchips are set to create in our societies – underlining some of its most evident problems: who is going to assess what constitutes an unfair advantage in sport if everyone will use more and more frequently outside of a pitch? To do so, we will have to go back to the EMT.

5.6 Extended Mind Thesis and Neurotechnologies

Though intriguing and useful for expanding the discussion on EMT, due to space I will not engage with the discussion brought forward by Mirko Farina and Andrea Lavazza (2022) on the distinction between functionalist understandings, complementarity approaches and third-wave views. I will also not consider previous speculations brought forward on the implications of EMT for the conceptualization of AI as morally responsible agents. I will instead consider a work that fits very well the trajectory of this chapter. In a recent article (Tesink et al., 2024), the authors explore the implications of the EMT for the right to mental integrity. In line with what was explained earlier, the authors of the article stress that the EMT holds that the mind is not confined within the skull but extends into the environment through the use of external tools and devices, and there is an evident challenge to the traditional internalist view that the mind is entirely brain-based. Neurotechnologies, such as brain-computer interfaces (BCIs), blur the boundaries between the brain and external devices, suggesting that these technologies might become integral parts of our cognitive processes. With this premise in mind, they then move to engage with the concept of mental integrity.

5.6.1 *The Right to Mental Integrity*

First brought forward by Marcello Ienca and Roberto Andorno (2017), the right to mental integrity is a fundamental human right that aims to protect individuals from harm to their mental states. In their work, Ienca and Andorno highlight the significance of this right in the context of emerging neurotechnologies that have the potential to affect the brain and mind directly. This new right (or neuroright as it has come to be defined even in some legislations) encompasses several key aspects.

First of all, it aims to safeguard individuals from actions that can cause mental suffering, distress, or disorders. This includes protecting against psychological torture, coercion, and manipulation. Secondly, the neuroright emphasizes the importance of informed consent and autonomy in decisions related to mental interventions. Individuals should have control over any procedures or technologies that can alter their mental states. This is intertwined with another neuroright: the right to mental privacy – ensuring that individuals' thoughts, emotions, and other mental data are protected and not accessed or manipulated without their consent. By establishing their neurorights, Ienca and Andorno advocate for a comprehensive approach to protecting individuals' mental freedom in the face of advancements in neuroscience and neurotechnologies, ensuring that these innovations respect human dignity and autonomy.

Within the suggested new set of rights, the right to mental integrity is seen as crucial due to the increasing capabilities of neurotechnologies to manipulate mental states. However, defining what constitutes the mind (and thus what this right protects) is complex – especially in the light of the EMT, where our mind is suggested to be expandable or displaceable into a wider "body". Notably, the right to mental integrity is still evolving and is less established than the right to bodily integrity. Legal frameworks such as the European

Charter of Fundamental Rights acknowledge this right but do not provide clear definitions (Tesink et al., 2024). Scholars argue for the necessity of protecting mental integrity, especially against non-consensual neurotechnological interventions, which can alter mental states directly. Yet, it seems difficult to protect something, if we are not able to define its borders. The EMT adds this layer of complications into the equation of how we should act. And such unclarity, this is my claim, underlines very well what are the limits that will translate into sport and neurodoping.

5.6.2 *Mental Integrity, BCIs, and EMT*

As we will see in more detail in the next section, using brainchips like Neuralink in sport can be considered a form of neurodoping, where the traditional boundaries of physical and mental enhancement are redefined. The EMT implies that neural implants could come to be considered as part of an athlete's cognitive apparatus, blurring the lines between natural and artificial enhancement.

Ever more so than cases of prosthetic limbs such as that of Oscar Pistorius (Garasic, 2012), adopting brainchips for cognitive or motor enhancements in sport raises ethical concerns about mental integrity and fair play. If on the one hand, neural implants become integrated parts of the mind and identity, on the other hand distinguishing between an athlete's natural abilities and those augmented by technology becomes a very challenging process, complicating the classification of such devices as neurodoping. This could undermine the integrity of sport, where fair competition is based on natural human abilities. In addition, it is interesting to note that, following from Tesink et al.'s approach, brainchips themselves might be protected under the right to mental integrity if they are considered part of the extended mind. This raises ethical questions about infringing on an athlete's rights if their cognitive enhancements are deemed essential to their mental integrity. Conversely, it also raises the issue of whether allowing such enhancements undermines the mental integrity of competitors who do not use them.

5.7 BCIs and Doping

The integration of BCI implants could have several implications for the world of sport, impacting both the performance of athletes and the overall landscape of sport competition. Historically – and in a very schematic way – by doping we refer to the use of banned substances or methods to enhance athletic performance, and traditional anti-doping efforts have primarily focused on substances such as steroids, EPO and drugs (Murray, 2016). However, as technology advances, the definition of doping may need to expand to include enhancements facilitated by neural implants. Even if unable to cover the whole range of options, it would be useful to consider some of the possible ways in which brainchip technology could relate to doping in sport.

To begin with, the use of brainchips for cognitive enhancement could be viewed as a form of performance enhancement, similar to traditional doping practices. If athletes use neural implants to gain a competitive edge in decision-making, memory, or other cognitive functions, it raises questions about fairness and the spirit of fair play in sport. As ensuring a level playing field is a fundamental principle in sport, we must be aware that the use of brainchip technology could potentially create disparities between athletes who can afford or access these enhancements and those who cannot. Hence, regulators will need to address issues of equity and fairness to prevent the emergence of an uneven competitive landscape. Moreover, anti-doping efforts may need to incorporate new monitoring and testing protocols to detect the use of neural implants or cognitive-enhancing technologies. This could involve the development of methods to identify changes in brain function that result from external interventions.

Evidently, the possibility of gaining a competitive advantage through the use of brainchips may lead to a technological arms race among athletes, teams, and nations. This could create ideological challenges to the very notion of sport, as society might embrace the unsporting mentality of "anything goes as long as you win" at its very core. If neural implants become widespread, the standards of excellence in sport may shift from natural prowess and training dedication to technological enhancement, altering the fundamental nature of athletic competition and jeopardizing the spirit of sport at the centre of any competition. The spirit of sport embodies the principles of fair play, respect, and the celebration of human physical and mental abilities. It is rooted in the idea that sport is a domain where individuals can push the limits of their natural talents and hard work. Central to this concept is the notion of a level playing field, where no athlete has an undue advantage over another due to artificial enhancements (Loland & McNamee, 2016). Hence, in order to resist this ethical devolution, athletes, coaches, and sport organizations will need education and awareness programmes to understand the ethical implications of using BCIs. Clear communication about the boundaries of acceptable performance enhancement will be crucial to preserve the integrity of the spirit of sport.

Lastly, the World Anti-Doping Agency (WADA) and other governing bodies may need to adapt their regulations to explicitly address cognitive enhancements facilitated by technology. This process will likely involve collaboration with experts in neuroscience, bioethics, and technology to stay ahead of emerging challenges. Moreover, they will need to adapt their regulations to address the use of neural implants. Establishing clear guidelines on acceptable and unacceptable forms of cognitive enhancement will be essential to maintaining the integrity of sport competitions. As technology continues to advance, the intersection of sport and neurotechnologies will require ongoing dialogue, research, and regulatory efforts to ensure that sport remains a fair and equitable arena for competition. The ethical considerations surrounding cognitive enhancements in sport are complex, and a proactive approach is needed to address potential issues before they become widespread concerns.

5.8 Neuroenhancements and Health

The use of Transcranial Direct Current Stimulation (tDCS) as a tool for cognitive enhancement has sparked considerable interest across various domains, including sport. tDCS offers the potential to modulate neural activity and improve cognitive functions such as attention, memory, and decision-making. However, the introduction of tDCS into sport challenges traditional understandings of nature, as it allows athletes to potentially augment their cognitive abilities beyond the constraints of natural human capacities. While proponents argue that tDCS merely enhances existing cognitive functions without fundamentally altering human nature, critics contend that its use in sport blurs the distinction between natural and artificial means of performance enhancement, undermining the authenticity and integrity of athletic competition. A similar discussion, perhaps even more fervent, could stem from the debate on the ethical permissibility of BCIs in sport.

In 2018 I argued that certain neuroenhancement technologies, such as tDCS (Imperatori, Milbourn & Garasic, 2018), if proven safe and cost-effective, could potentially reduce rather than exacerbate unfairness in sport. Together with Laura Imperatori and Luke Milbourn, we suggested that such technologies might level the playing field by making advanced training and performance enhancement more accessible to a broader range of athletes. Though since then we received critiques (Pugh & Pugh, 2021) that have made me wonder how much I am still convinced of the position we brought forward at the time, I believe that at least some of the points still hold. Most notably, we introduced an important counterpoint to the prevailing view that tDCS inherently lead to unfair competition. If access to neural enhancements like tDCS is democratized and regulated to ensure safety, it could mitigate existing inequalities where wealthier athletes and teams have access to better training and medical resources. Transferring this reading of the technology to the current discussion, we could suggest that rather than outright banning BCIs, a nuanced approach focusing on equitable access and safety could align with ethical sportsmanship principles.

Appropriately, discussions on the use of tDCS and BCIs must take into consideration the risks that these technologies carry with them when it comes to fairness and equality. Some argue that accessibility and affordability of tDCS may exacerbate existing inequalities in sport, as elite athletes and affluent individuals may have greater access to tDCS technology and expertise, further widening the gap between the haves and the have-nots in sport. Additionally, the normalization of tDCS in sport may reinforce harmful stereotypes about the relationship between biology and athletic ability, perpetuating inequalities based on factors such as socio-economic status and access to technology. Similar reasoning can apply to brainchips. Neural implants could provide certain athletes with cognitive and physical enhancements that are unattainable through natural means or traditional training. This would create an uneven playing field, contradicting the principle of fairness that is central to the spirit of sport. Moreover, the cost and availability of neural implants may limit access to these technologies to only the wealthiest athletes or nations, exacerbating existing inequalities in sport.

Notwithstanding said similarities between the two cases, even the most optimistic interpretation of our previous work could not help seeing some substantial differences between the two scenarios – first and foremost in terms of health hazards connected to the technology in question. While tDCS is a completely non-invasive technique, brainchips are exactly the opposite, as they are rather invasive devices. Even if true for all recent technologies, the long-term health effects of neural implants are not yet fully understood. Potential risks include neurological damage and other medical complications, raising ethical concerns about the safety and well-being of users. Athletes might also feel pressured to adopt neural implants to remain competitive, potentially compromising their autonomy and well-being.

Ensuring that any neuroenhancement technology used in sport is thoroughly tested for long-term effects and approved by relevant medical and ethical bodies is thus paramount. This not only addresses health concerns but also supports the principle of doing no harm, which is central to both medical ethics and sport ethics. In addition, revisiting the spirit of sport, the notion of natural talent and effort remains a cornerstone. Surely, if neuroenhancements such as tDCS or drugs are regulated to promote safety and fairness, their use could be seen as analogous to advancements in sport nutrition, equipment, and training methodologies that have historically been accepted. Yet, brainchips do not appear to fall under the same category as the level of risks is substantially higher. The challenge lies in drawing clear ethical boundaries that preserve the essence of human athletic achievement while embracing beneficial innovations.

5.9 Conclusion

In conclusion, EMT has significant implications for understanding human cognition, suggesting that our mental capabilities are not limited to the neural confines of our brains but are dynamically interwoven with our environment. This perspective prompts a reconsideration of cognitive science, Artificial Intelligence, and even our everyday interactions with technology. Moreover, within the framework of EMT, the integration of BCI technology into cognitive processes has profound implications for our conceptualization of identity and the ethical landscape of neuroenhancement. By blurring the boundaries between internal cognition and external tools, brainchips challenge traditional notions of identity, autonomy, and self.

In the context of sport, the potential use of neural implants poses significant challenges to the spirit of athletic competition. While brainchips offer exciting possibilities for enhancing human capabilities, they also threaten to undermine the principles of fairness, equality, and the celebration of natural human talent that define the essence of sport. As neural implant technology continues to advance, it is imperative for the sport community to engage in thoughtful and proactive discussions about how to preserve the integrity and spirit of sport in the face of these new ethical dilemmas. If I am indeed my brainchip, what constitutes a breaking of the "natural limits"? What constitutes an "unfair advantage"? Within the sport realm, this opacity in understanding which boundaries stand where could easily lead us to implement – willingly or not – abundant cases of neurodoping. We need to be aware of the problem to begin with if we want to respond to it in effective and ethically sound ways. Something that we should aim at doing sooner rather than later, as addressing these challenges necessitates a sophisticated understanding of both ethical principles and the implications of emerging technologies.

References

Clark, A., & Chalmers, D. (1998). The extended mind. *Analysis, 58*(1), 7–19.

Clark, A., & Erickson, M. (2004). Natural-born cyborgs: Minds, technologies, and the future of human intelligence. *Canadian Journal of Sociology, 29*(3), 471–473.

Farina, M., & Lavazza, A. (2022). Mind embedded or extended: Transhumanist and posthumanist reflections in support of the extended mind thesis. *Synthese, 200*(6), 507.

Garasic, M. (2012). Human enhancement in the EU. *Australian and New Zealand Journal of European Studies, 4*(1), 31–41.

Haraway, D. (2006). A cyborg manifesto: Science, technology, and socialist-feminism in the late twentieth century. In Stryker, S., & Whittle, S. (Eds.). *The transgender studies reader* (pp. 103–118). Routledge.

Ienca, M., & Andorno, R. (2017). Towards new human rights in the age of neuroscience and neurotechnology. *Life Sciences, Society and Policy, 13*, 1–27.

Imperatori, L. S., Milbourn, L., & Garasic, M. D. (2018). Would the use of safe, cost-effective tDCS tackle rather than cause unfairness in sport?. *Journal of Cognitive Enhancement, 2*, 377–387.

Loland, S., & McNamee, M. J. (2016). Anti-doping, performance enhancement and 'the spirit of sport': A philosophical and ethical critique. In Ahmadi, N., Ljungqvist, A., & Svedsäter, G. (Eds.). *Doping and public health* (pp. 111–123). Routledge.

Murray, T. H. (2016). The ethics of doping from a public health perspective. In Ahmadi, N., Ljungqvist, A., & Svedsäter, G. (Eds.). *Doping and public health* (pp. 124–138). Routledge.

Pugh, J., & Pugh, C. (2021). Neurostimulation, doping, and the spirit of sport. *Neuroethics, 14*, 141–158.

Tesink, V., Douglas, T., Forsberg, L., Ligthart, S., & Meynen, G. (2024). Right to mental integrity and neurotechnologies: Implications of the extended mind thesis. *Journal of Medical Ethics, 50*, 656–663.

Chapter 6

The Ethics of Using BCI, CBI, and BBI to Enhance Performance in Sport

Francesca Minerva and Vittorio Grasso

6.1 Introduction

I need to focus. This set is crucial to winning this tennis tournament. My opponent is serving. I can see my coach beside the court giving me the thumbs-up, meaning that all the cameras and systems are operational. My opponent is now throwing the ball up to smash it into my side of the court. Suddenly I perceive a flickering dot out of the corner of my eye. I know what it means: cameras are filming my opponent from different angles and my coach has reviewed their footage using sophisticated machine learning algorithms capable of predicting which trajectory the ball will take. He now wants to tell me that the ball will hit the ground on my right side, thus he is sending my brain a signal from the implant in his scalp to the one in mine. I sprint to catch the ball and place it on the opposite side from where my opponent served. He is astonished: in fact, I ran before he touched the ball, and I returned his serve before he could move a muscle. I won the game, now it is my turn to serve. I am just one game away from victory. I feel focused. I am bouncing the ball, preparing to serve but, suddenly, I feel a tap on my left arm. Again, I know what it means: the implant is sending data from my EEG to some algorithms, and they are giving me haptic feedback because they have detected I am not focused enough to land my first serve. I need to concentrate and try again. I throw the ball and smash it. That was a striking first serve and I won the point. My opponent is puzzled by the percentage and number of first serves I have successfully landed today.

One might assume that this scene is an excerpt from a sci-fi book or movie. However, current research suggests that we are not far from developing technologies that could make the described scenario a reality. In our example, there is no verbal communication, but rather a mental connection between the coach, sitting beside the court, and the player on the field. While this type of communication might seem highly implausible to those who do not believe in magic, we already have such tools. BrainNet, introduced in 2019, is described as "the first non-invasive direct brain-to-brain interface for collaborative problem-solving" (Jiang et al., 2019). With BrainNet, Subject A can

DOI: 10.4324/9781003520290-7

send a message via electroencephalography (EEG) and, after some computation, Subjects B and C can receive the message through transcranial magnetic stimulation (TMS), allowing them to exchange information without talking, gesturing, or even looking at each other. It is only a matter of time until BBI technology can link together a much larger number of people, enabling, for instance, an entire football team to exchange simple coded messages among players.

In the second part of this hypothetical scenario, the player could receive feedback on his *concentration* status through haptic feedback. Although this also might sound quite far-fetched, studies suggest that the feedback, synchronized with specific cortical activity, could be immediately provided to users through haptics – i.e., a technology which could emulate tactile stimulation and let the user experience a "touch" response (Biswas & Visell, 2019) – whilst undergoing EEG scans involving motion, thus improving their *concentration* and cognitive abilities (Jeunet et al., 2019, p. 129).

Although these technologies have become more widely used only over the past few years, they have been developed for half a century. For instance, the Defense Advanced Research Projects Agency (DARPA) has promoted and funded research on BCI, CBI, and BBI through two main programmes, one aimed at restoring neural and/or behavioural function and one aimed at improving human training and performance (Miranda et al., 2015, pp. 52–67). After a few decades of research, it seems that BCI technologies hold promise not only for restoring the capacity of moving a limb in paralyzed patients, or to allow amputees to move their prosthetic limbs as effectively as they moved their own, but also for speeding up the learning process as well as acquiring new skills altogether. For instance, already in 2009, a technology called "Adaptive Peak Performance Trainer" (APPT) was developed and successfully used to improve the learning trajectory by a factor of 2.3 of subjects that were not familiar with a certain task (in this specific study, training with a rifle) (Miranda et al., 2015, p. 61).

These technologies are now even more advanced; they are smaller, and data transmission is faster, enabling their use in various domains of life, including sports. For instance, as we have previously argued, BCIs can be used to overcome disabilities and to gather new information on neurological disorders such as epilepsy or Parkinson's disease (Turconi et al., 2014). They can also be successfully implemented in our everyday life, for example, for giving a more immersive game experience (Plass-Oude Bos et al., 2010), as an input device to control some specific applications, or more generally to give insight into our mental well-being, for example, with Emotiv Contour software. Given the wide range of contexts in which these technologies can be used and the likelihood of decreasing costs over time, we can expect a significant increase in their use over the next few years.

Before discussing the ethical issues raised by the use of these technologies, we will first explain how they function and how they might be used – or abused – to enhance athletic performance.

6.2 What Are BCI, CBI, and BBI and How Do They Work?

A Brain-Computer Interface (BCI from now on) is a type of technology that allows to send and receive signals between the brain and an external device. BCIs are imaging tools that collect brain data, reorganize it coherently, and send it to a computer. It is also possible to send data back to the brain using a computer-to-brain interface: this technology is called CBI (Coin et al., 2020). Put it simply, BCIs and CBIs create a physical link between the brain and an external machine, thus enabling communication. We can also make a distinction between mere brain-machine interaction, mediated by BCI and CBI, and networks where there is a sender brain and a different receiver brain, thus being brain-to-brain interface (BBI), such as the one suggested in our first example that connected the coach's brain to the tennis player's brain. In sum, BBIs consist of a BCI and a CBI connected to each other through a computer. The BCI detects the neural signal from brain A and transfers it to the computer, which then processes it and delivers an output to brain B through a CBI (Hildt, 2019).

Since our goal is to discuss technologies that could enhance sport performance, we will focus solely on interfaces that can be eventually implanted in the skull as brain chips. Brain-to-computer techniques that require large pieces of equipment, such as magnetoencephalography (MEG), computed tomography (CT), positron emission tomography (PET), magnetic resonance imaging (MRI or fMRI), beside their size, have intrinsic ecological characteristics that could potentially hinder their successful implementation through miniaturization (Bertollo et al., 2020, pp. 666–667). One of the main reasons is that these machines require preparation before scan execution, such as the injection of a contrast agent, and also necessitate that the subject be situated inside the device, rather than the device adapting to the user's body. Instead, technologies like EEG and functional near-infrared spectroscopy (fNIRS) require less preparation, while still providing enough data to make gathering possible and effective. Regarding intervention (CBI), non-invasive neuromodulation techniques, i.e. technologies that do not require surgery, have high ecological scores, and some studies suggest that it is feasible to build and pack them together with the same hardware used for retrieval, managing to prevent strong interference (Sun et al., 2023), thus allowing seamless BCI and CBI communication. This type of technology includes transcranial direct/alternate current stimulation (tDCS or tACS), transcranial magnetic stimulation (TMS), or transcranial random noise stimulation (tRNS), each causing different and unique brain reactions, thus working in very different ways that could be implemented in various fields according to the effect one wants to achieve.

Technologies that work efficiently in combination and have a high ecological score could be successfully implemented in a sports context. Thus, they will be the focus of our analysis.

The interaction between the brain and the device can be effective in two ways, depending on whether the user adapts to the machine or vice versa. In the first case, the technology aims at teaching users how to self-regulate specific neural activity patterns, thus enhancing cognitive abilities (Jeunet et al., 2019, p. 126). In the second case, it is the machine which adapts to the user, and this is what makes BCI technologies so different from those which have been available for longer, such as Neurofeedback Training. Neurofeedback Training (NFT) has been proven effective in enhancing athletes' concentration capacities. For instance, in a study conducted by Pereira et al. within an Olympic shooting virtual reality (VR) environment, players successfully bolstered their shooting abilities using NFT (Pereira et al., 2018). Jeunet et al. demonstrated the feasibility of a BCI aimed at enhancing soccer goalkeepers' performance by improving their covert visual-spatial attention (CVSA) abilities (Jeunet, Tonin, et al., 2020), while Reis et al. suggested that anodal tDCS could be employed to improve motor learning (Reis et al., 2009).

Unlike NFT, BCI is often integrated with various machine learning (ML) algorithms that automatically detect patterns of brain activity that relate to specific mental tasks. In other words, with NFT, users need to find their own strategy to activate patterns and trigger the output device, whilst BCIs are more focused on interpreting brain activity and acting accordingly (Wyckoff & Birbaumer, 2014). For example, if the user is asked to move a cursor on a screen via EEG, with NFT the device is set to be triggered when a specific brain pattern is detected, and the user must find their own way to activate it. Instead, with a BCI approach, data retrieved through EEG is interpreted by algorithms that detect the user's attempt at moving the cursors, thus accommodating their brain's operating modes (Jeunet et al., 2019, p. 130). This does not mean that BCIs are always better than NFT; rather, these technologies serve different purposes and have different cost/benefit profiles, for instance, in time-to-feedback evaluation and bits-per-second score, i.e. precision performance (Pandarinath et al., 2017). In our hypothetical case at the beginning of the chapter, the player received feedback from an NFT device before serving, as he needed to modulate his brain activity to improve his chances of landing a first serve. There are various technologies that may be suitable for application in sports contexts, and in the next section, we will review these implementations.

6.3 BCI, CBI, and BBI, Possible Applications in Sports

6.3.1 *More Effective Training*

Optimal performance in sport extends beyond physical prowess, and it has been associated in pro athletes with better perception and anticipation skills, as well as faster and smarter decision-making processes (Yarrow et al., 2009). A profound understanding of the unique cognitive patterns of these processes in one's brain could lead to the emergence of what Eran Klein has identified as the *Neural Signature* (Klein, 2020, p. 334), thus both accommodating neural diversity and assisting elite athletes in training these unique abilities (Jeunet, Hauw, et al., 2020, p. 2). The idea here is that if we understood how to modulate brain activity to enhance physical or cognitive performance, we could develop technologies with enhancing effects comparable to those achievable through doping drugs (Davis, 2013).

At the beginning of this chapter, we suggested that BCI could be used to extend cognition during a competition; however, other technologies can support the training and enhance the overall performance in the long run (Davis, 2013). For instance, gathering *Neural Signature* from athletes during training could help improve their cognitive abilities during matches, as specific patterns could be detected and subsequently communicated to them. Nevertheless, it could also benefit their long-term training through self-neuromodulation that, as previously argued, could be used to enhance specific abilities such as motor learning or covert visual-spatial attention. Motor Imagery (MI) is pivotal in achieving this goal: trying to envision motion-related tasks triggers patterns similar to those activated by actual motor execution (Jeunet et al., 2019). Users could just think about moving their hand (MI) in order to interact and control an application or device. With Motor Imagery it is also possible to detect and measure sensorymotor rhythm (SMR), namely the brain wave associated with the idle state of a motor cortical region.

At the moment, all the devices we just mentioned need to be worn by users, which negatively impacts the overall ecology of their performance and precludes real-time usage during matches. Moreover, the vast majority of them must be operated in adequately equipped facilities. This means that they can be used to improve training, but they cannot be used as a form of illegal doping because, given the size, they would be detected immediately. However, new versions of these technologies are being developed, and they are much smaller in size and do not require specific facilities, potentially expanding the use of these tools to a much wider range of human activities. For instance, it is now conceivable to build implants that send data to a processing unit and then provide haptic feedback to the user based on computational output. In the future, both BCI and CBI could be integrated into the same implant, enabling bi-directional communication without affecting performance ecology. Additionally, companies such as Neuralink (and similar) seek a deeper connection between BCI and Artificial Intelligence, allowing for real-time task execution that would otherwise require seconds to be processed and executed, encompassing greater precision. Noland Arbaugh, the first quadriplegia-affected patient who joined the Neuralink PRIME Study clinical trial, successfully set a new record for BCI performance, achieving 8.0 BPS (Neuralink, n.d.), overcoming the previous highest score of 4.2 BPS (Pandarinath et al., 2017), and looking forward to beating Neuralink engineers that scored 10.0 BPS with a mouse (Neuralink, n.d.). In this case, the bits-per-second (BPS) achieved value represents the information throughput rate, i.e. the speed at which the user can successfully transmit commands through the interface, whether it is a mouse or a BCI. In the context of sports, this feature will prove pivotal, as anticipation skills and rapid thought-to-decision processes are fundamental in competitive environments.

6.3.2 Better Coordination and Nonverbal Communication

The use of these new and emerging technologies will represent a significant innovation in sports performance enhancement, differing quite dramatically from all tools available until now. For instance, drugs currently used and labelled as illegal doping can improve focus, increase resistance and stamina, and enhance overall bodily strength, thus providing an advantage over competitors who do not use these drugs. However, current doping drugs cannot offer the same wide range of interventions that BCI can provide.

One obvious field where BCIs can provide advantages not available through other "traditional" sport-enhancing tools is the capacity to coordinate instantly with the coach or other members of a team without having to talk or even look at each other. As we have seen, interfaces like BrainNet could be widely used in team sports, enabling team members to communicate with each other and with the coach during the game. This would allow the team to respond more promptly to unexpected situations. For example, if a team player feels unwell, they can inform their teammates that their performance might be affected, allowing the others to compensate before the opposing team exploits the situation. The coach (or an AI algorithm) could send a signal to a player to prompt them to focus or to communicate the need to cover a specific area of the field. The players and the coach would have to agree beforehand about the code used to communicate with each other, as BBIs (at least at the moment) do not allow communication with natural language – they are not mind-reading tools –, but they allow to exchange basic information. The player and the coach could agree beforehand that "stop" feels like a tap on the shoulder, or that "run faster" feels like a stroke on the back. Combining BCI with wearables would make detecting the use of these tools very difficult, much more difficult than detecting the use of drugs through a blood test.

6.4 Ethical Issues Raised by the Use of BCI, CBI, BBI in Sports

6.4.1 Fairness

One obvious issue arising whenever a new tool with enhanced powers is developed is fairness. Fairness plays a particularly important role in sport, especially at the elite level, where economic and social status rewards play a major role. As pointed out by Foddy and Savulescu, "Elite sport can be fair if 'fair' is interpreted to mean that 'the rules are applied equally'. It can never be fair if 'fair' is interpreted to mean 'level playing field'" (Foddy & Savulescu, 2006, p. 515).

If only some teams (in the case of team sports) or some players had access to this kind of technology, it seems quite obvious that the one using BCI would have an unfair advantage over the other side, something that would make the competition so unbalanced to make it pointless to play or even just to watch. Imagine a football match where a team uses a BBI network so that players on one side of the field can be aware of what is happening on the other side: they would have much higher chances of winning the match if the team they are playing against did not use such technology. The same applies also to individual sports: imagine a tennis match where only one player can receive immediate feedback about their level of concentration or even anticipate where the ball will land given the position of the opponent in the opposite field, such as in the example that opened the chapter. Or imagine a boxing match where only one boxer shares control of their limbs with the coach, allowing the coach to help them punch at the right moment and in the right spot, overriding the boxer's decision to throw a less effective punch. In all these scenarios, it is clear that the advantage of one team or player over the other would render the competition unfair. However, in a scenario where both teams or players used BCIs, CBIs, and BBIs, we would have a level playing field. The matches would likely differ significantly from their current form, as athletes would possess much better knowledge of events occurring at the back of the field, for instance, but this would not necessarily make the matches worse or better.

A different issue concerns the fairness of using these new technologies for training. During this phase, athletes undergo various procedures, in addition to pure physical training, to bolster their performance. BCIs could be used conjointly with other training techniques to enhance athlete cognitive abilities, for instance, improving SMR self-regulation skills (He et al., 2020), thus positively influencing the overall performance and their learning curve. Every athlete should use whichever training procedures suit them best and that they have access to, provided they are reasonably safe. For the competition to be fair, we would need to ensure that all athletes have access to this type of enhancement. Of course, equal opportunity does not imply equal outcome;

individual genetic differences would still play a role, as they currently do with doping drugs.

6.4.2 *Agency*

Using these new and emerging technologies in sports would allow the coach, or an external party, to provide the player with information and feedback, and more. The coach could interfere with the player's actions in two ways. First, by prompting them to perform specific actions at certain moments, such as punching at a particular spot or throwing a ball at a specific angle. Second, by actually controlling the player's movements. BCIs allow the control of muscles through implants that connect the brain and the muscle one wants to move (Chung et al., 2020). Such technologies are already being employed to move the muscles of people suffering from paralysis, but it would be possible to implant the BCI in A's brain and in, say, B's leg. In such a scenario, A would be able to move B's leg basically just thinking of moving B's leg. B could not oppose the leg's movement commanded by A, or would have to negotiate with them the movement, or would have to use a certain amount of will power to counteract the command to move the body from the other brain.

Imagine a match where B is the player and A is the coach. B is extremely tired, injured, and wants to stop the boxing match. However, A has control over B's arms, hands, and legs and keeps commanding B to keep punching. In such a scenario, B has a higher chance of winning the competition by virtue of not stopping when his brain tells him to stop. However, there are serious risks involved in using BCI to connect the brain of one individual to the body of another. The safety of the player would obviously be at risk because they would be forced to keep fighting when their body and brain would normally tell them to stop. A similar scenario could apply to less violent sports, with similarly negative outcomes. In general, allowing someone to remotely control another person's muscles could result in serious, or even fatal, injuries.

6.4.3 *Moral Responsibility*

Another significant ethical issue prompted by the use of BCIs to connect one person's brain to another's muscles is that of autonomy, and more crucially in this context, moral responsibility. Imagine a scenario where a football player fouls another player by kicking him in the leg or elbowing him in the face. Currently, the player is considered responsible for these prohibited actions, and if the referee notices the foul, the player is punished, sometimes even expelled for the remainder of the game and for subsequent games.

In a scenario where someone else can take control of the player's movements through BCI and BBI, things become more complicated. We would need to determine who was in control of the muscles of the arm or leg that were used to foul the other player. It might be difficult to identify who was responsible for a certain action when both parties deny making the decision to foul. Moreover, there might be an overlapping of inputs to the brain that results in the foul; in this case, neither party is morally responsible, as the foul is the result of interference between the two inputs. However, if a foul has occurred and a player is injured as a result, the referee needs to punish someone, at least if the rules remain the same. The fact that the foul was an unintended outcome of a coordination issue between the parties is unlikely to be considered a valid reason to avoid punishment. Yet, being punished for an action that nobody intended to take, or that someone else took by remotely controlling one's body, does not seem fair.

What complicates matters further is that if BCIs were secretly used as a form of enhancement during a match, the player would be held responsible for all actions that appear to be hers but are actually controlled remotely by someone else. In such a scenario, the blame would inevitably fall on the player, putting them in a difficult position where they must either take responsibility for something they did not intend to do or admit to using BCI technologies, which we assume will be banned as illegal forms of doping. Even worse, the BCI could be hacked, allowing someone to take control of the athlete's body with the intent to harm one of the players, injure the person they're controlling, or both. BCIs could also be used to decrease or remove inhibitions, letting the player act more aggressively or impulsively: at the moment, there are studies showing that it is possible to modulate inhibition and impulsivity through CBI techniques (Cheng et al., 2022; De Vidovich et al., 2016; Kuhn et al., 2024). In this case, the player would choose to foul the opponent, but this would not be an entirely free choice, given the fact that his impulses have been altered by the BCI, especially if the athlete had been forced to use the BCI.

In sum, BCIs that surrender control of one's body to another individual seem to pose greater risks than those that allow brain to brain communication. The former has the ability to override, and sometimes overcome, the player's autonomy, leading to potential stalemate situations where no one has clearly intended the action, or the act itself results from interference. In such cases, it appears that the foul has not been carried out by anyone but the machine. In fact, BCIs enable new forms of human-machine interaction. Although one could argue that we constantly work with computers, smartphones, and other technologies, and thus BCIs are merely another type of human-machine interaction or represent a higher degree of connection, these technologies pose completely new issues. Indeed, there seems to be a fundamental difference between human-machine interactions carried out with and without BCIs. In our everyday engagements with technologies, we are fully aware, proprioceptive, of what we are doing: when using a laptop, we know that we need to perform certain movements to turn it on or to type a sentence in a document. We act upon technology, and it responds, hopefully, in accordance with our actions. However, as argued by Pim Haselager (Haselager, 2013, pp. 406–408), the interaction operates very differently with BCIs: actually, we are not *acting* in the ordinary sense of the word, because very often, as shown previously, we are merely performing some MI task. Whereas, when we act with our body against the world, we have proprioception of our intentions, sensations, and feedback. Conversely, BCIs do not necessarily support all these kinds of input and output to complete their tasks. In this sense, we lack *brain proprioception* because we are not conscious of the interaction between our thoughts and BCI activity (Burwell et al., 2017, p. 337). Thus, while we are prone to make mistakes about our own agency – and we could be held liable and responsible for our actions –, it is not necessarily the same case for BCI, in the sense that we are not fully aware of the process that leads to the result, and we can therefore attribute causal role to the device itself – or other external agents manoeuvring it. In CBI too, it is not always possible to determine whether the input is perceived in an egosyntonic or egodystonic way, meaning that the individual's sense of agency could be questioned, and they could properly ask themselves, "Did I do that?" (Klein, 2020, p. 337). The distinction between these two types of self-awareness could play an important role when attributing responsibility, because the player might not be held fully liable for their actions. If the causal role is egosyntonic, the action itself is possibly so self-integrated that there is no such distinction between "the player's will" and the "BCI signal". Conversely, if the causal role is egodystonic, the player could reject the outcome of their body movements, in a way that could be similar to Tourette's syndrome.

6.4.4 *Changing the Nature of Sport*

One of the most common objections to the use of sport-enhancing tools, both pharmaceutical and technological, is that they could fundamentally alter the true nature of sport. The use of BCIs, CBIs, and BBIs in sports could change the nature of some of them in even more radical ways than doping drugs do. In particular, the possibility of remotely controlling an athlete's body to dramatically enhance their endurance and resilience is something that traditional sport enhancers cannot achieve on demand. While some drugs can boost an athlete's energy levels, focus, or strength, the athlete will eventually become so exhausted that they will stop running or be too tired to throw another ball. The use of BBI could, in theory, overcome this issue to the point where the athlete would resemble a remotely controlled car.

Even if we do not know the type of proprioception caused by CBI, another aspect that could be considered here is the relationship between the coach and their players, because these technologies have the ability to lead to a complete reification of the player's role. Although some authors, such as Nick Davis (Davis, 2013), suggested that all the effects of this type of technology could be referred to Neurodoping, thus making their implementation comparable to that of drugs and evaluated within common frameworks, there are important differences between drugs and CBI utilization. CBIs have the potential to interact live with players' brains, possibly supervening their will. Even in sports where the resultant performance is not primarily up to the player, such as Formula 1, the driver maintains overall autonomy and control over their actions. Doping doesn't seem to affect the athlete's autonomy, though the decision to use doping can be not entirely autonomous, for instance, because the athletes are pressured or tricked into taking these drugs. The direction that this technology could possibly take is one where players are in large part controlled by the coach or by an AI algorithm, like in a videogame, something that old types of doping could never do.

Although innovation is part of sports, and sports have evolved and changed over time, it seems to us that one fundamental element that has remained constant and represents a core pillar of athletic competition is the accountability of athletes for their actions and their status as autonomous agents, judged on their own performance. Removing such elements would dramatically alter the nature of sports, potentially transforming them into something fundamentally different.

6.4.5 Safety

One of the main problems with doping in sports is that it can cause health issues for the athletes who use such drugs. Steroids, for instance, can cause heart conditions, liver damage, infertility, and even premature death (Pärssinen & Seppälä, 2002). The short-term and long-term risks associated with the use of BCIs are less known, since such technologies are not widely used and studied. So far, we know that BCI can cause some discomfort in the area where they have been placed, but no serious adverse reaction has been reported. However, there are some quite serious potential side effects that could derive from the use of BCI, rather than from their application to the skin or skull.

One obvious concern is linked to potential malfunctioning of these tools: if the biofeedback is not accurate, the athlete might get injured or might feel distressed and anxious because there is, for instance, a discrepancy between what they intuitively perceive as a strenuous effort but which the tool erroneously reports as minimal effort.

The greatest risks are related to data breaches and privacy (Coin et al., 2020). The data collected by the microchip and transferred to a computer is highly sensitive, as these technologies track and record health, neurological, and behavioural information, often over extended periods. A data breach of this nature would expose a substantial volume of personal information about the athlete, potentially resulting in severe repercussions for their professional and personal lives. Additionally, since these technologies have the ability to detect and record different brain status or activations, meaning they are able, for instance, to detect the emotional state of the player. Issues arise when trying to determine who exactly could access those data and what type of risk is posed to players' privacy. If the recorded data can be read just by their own team, upon previous agreement and consent, they would be treated as other medical records that the team owns about their players. But one could imagine a situation in which the referee asks to access these data during a match, for instance, to check for a player's emotional state while they were committing a foul, thus gaining more information about their intentions. This particular scenario would expose the player's personal data to a third party, not necessarily upon prior consent, and their personal and private reaction could be possibly used against them. We are not suggesting that these data could not absolutely be gathered and delivered to the referee for this reason, but that they create potential privacy issues, since they could be used to reconstruct personal psychological profiles, leading – as it has been argued before – to potential repercussions on private lives.

Among the three technologies discussed in this chapter, BBI presents the highest level of risk. Allowing external control over an athlete's body or interference with their movements can lead to significant harm. For instance, compelling an athlete to persist in a movement when they wish to stop, or to remain in a match against their will, can result in severe physical injuries. Psychologically, the loss of control over one's own body can be highly confusing, distressing and traumatic. There are no studies, to our knowledge, testing the long-term psychological effects of the use of BBI to allow one person to control another person's body. However, given that we normally prefer not to be restrained and controlled (for instance, people do not want to go to prison), we imagine that BBI involving this kind of external control would probably be perceived, at the very least, as unpleasant.

6.5 Conclusions: How Should These Technologies Be Regulated in the Context of Sport?

Regulating these new performance-enhancing technologies in sports will be particularly challenging due to the increasing difficulty of detection. Neuralink, for instance, is currently the size of a coin, but as technology advances, the size of Neuralink and similar chips will become even smaller and thus very hard to detect. Moreover, these chips are implanted in the body (e.g., on the skull), which would require quite invasive testing of the athletes. Currently, the use of illegal doping substances can be detected through blood or urine tests, which are somewhat invasive but not dangerous. However, detecting very small chips in the body would necessitate the use of X-rays or MRI, which are not harmful when used sporadically but may pose health risks if used repeatedly. Therefore, regularly testing athletes to detect microchips might not be feasible at present. While it is possible that less invasive and safe testing methods may be developed in the future, this is not currently the case. Thus, there is a problem with regulating the use of these technologies that stems directly from their technological features, namely their difficulty to detect and the potentially harmful nature of detection methods.

Besides these practical issues, we should consider whether banning BCI, CBI, and BBI is the right thing to do from a moral perspective. It is important to distinguish between the use of BCI, CBI, and BBI for training purposes versus their use during a match, and among different kinds of uses during the match itself.

Regarding training, it appears that the use of these technologies is generally safe and can significantly enhance athletes' training routines. For instance, BCI can provide immediate and accurate neurofeedback, CBI can offer valuable insights into the athlete's strengths and weaknesses during training, and BBI can help prevent injuries and support rehabilitation exercises. Overall, using these tools for training is likely to become common practice and does not pose major health risks to athletes, particularly when compared to some performance-enhancing drugs. Additionally, research on BCIs in sports contexts could yield insights and neural signatures beneficial for other research areas. For example, data collected from elite athletes could be utilized in healthcare for the recovery and rehabilitation of patients with neurodegenerative diseases, stroke survivors, or individuals recovering from car accidents.

A separate issue is the use of such tools during a competition, as these technologies could alter the nature of the sport being played. As Foddy and Savulescu have pointed out, changes in equipment, training, and the use of drugs have long been part of sports, and they have not caused any significant loss in public enjoyment (Foddy & Savulescu, 2006). However, there is a point where changes could become so radical that they raise questions about what it means to play a certain sport and how we should fairly assess performance. We need to determine if BCI, CBI, and BBI could bring about this kind of dramatic change if used during a match

In the chapter-opening example, we imagined an athlete playing a tennis match using CBI, thereby receiving simple nonverbal messages from the coach and real-time feedback from AI regarding their level of concentration during crucial moments of the match. Although advantageous, this additional feedback does not seem to significantly distort the nature of the sport. Therefore, if all athletes were allowed to use such tools, it appears there would be no reason to prohibit the use of CBI and BCI in sports.

We believe there are compelling reasons to ban the use of BBI for remotely controlling an athlete's body. More research is needed to understand the long-term physical and psychological effects of its use. Moreover, it seems to us that employing this tool in sports could fundamentally alter the nature of competition by introducing elements that are incompatible with the current spirit of sports, where agency, autonomy, and the moral responsibility and accountability of the athlete for their actions are considered essential components of competition.

References and Bibliography

Bertollo, M., Doppelmayr, M., & Robazza, C. (2020). Using brain technologies in practice. In G. Tenenbaum & R. C. Eklund (Eds.), *Handbook of sport psychology* (1st ed., pp. 666–693). Wiley. https://doi.org/10.1002/9781119568124.ch32

Biswas, S., & Visell, Y. (2019). Emerging material technologies for haptics. *Advanced Materials Technologies, 4*(4), 1900042. https://doi.org/10.1002/admt.201900042

Burwell, S., Sample, M., & Racine, E. (2017). Ethical aspects of brain computer interfaces: A scoping review. *BMC Medical Ethics, 18*(1), 60. https://doi.org/10.1186/s12910-017-0220-y

Cheng, J., Li, P., Tang, Y., Zhang, C., Lin, L., Gao, J., & Wang, Z. (2022). Transcranial direct current stimulation improve symptoms and modulates cortical inhibition in obsessive-compulsive disorder: A TMS-EEG study. *Journal of Affective Disorders, 298*, 558–564. https://doi.org/10.1016/j.jad.2021.11.043

Chung, E., Lee, B.-H., & Hwang, S. (2020). Therapeutic effects of brain-computer interface-controlled functional electrical stimulation training on balance and gait performance for stroke: A pilot randomized controlled trial. *Medicine, 99*(51), e22612. https://doi.org/10.1097/MD.0000000000022612

Coin, A., Mulder, M., & Dubljević, V. (2020). Ethical aspects of BCI technology: What is the state of the art? *Philosophies, 5*(4), 31. https://doi.org/10.3390/philosophies5040031

Davis, N. J. (2013). Neurodoping: Brain stimulation as a performance-enhancing measure. *Sports Medicine, 43*(8), 649–653. https://doi.org/10.1007/s40279-013-0027-z

De Vidovich, G. Z., Muffatti, R., Monaco, J., Caramia, N., Broglia, D., Caverzasi, E., Barale, F., & D'Angelo, E. (2016). Repetitive TMS on left cerebellum affects impulsivity in borderline personality disorder: A pilot study. *Frontiers in Human Neuroscience, 10*. https://doi.org/10.3389/fnhum.2016.00582

Foddy, B., & Savulescu, J. (2006). Ethics of performance enhancement in sport: Drugs and gene doping. In R. E. Ashcroft, A. Dawson, H. Draper, & J. R. McMillan (Eds.), *Principles of health care ethics* (1st ed., pp. 511–519). Wiley. https://doi.org/10.1002/9780470510544.ch70

Haselager, P. (2013). Did i do that? Brain–computer interfacing and the sense of agency. *Minds and Machines, 23*(3), 405–418. https://doi.org/10.1007/s11023-012-9298-7

He, B., Yuan, H., Meng, J., & Gao, S. (2020). Brain–computer interfaces. In B. He (Ed.), *Neural Engineering* (pp. 131–183). Springer International Publishing. https://doi.org/10.1007/978-3-030-43395-6

Hildt, E. (2019). Multi-person brain-to-brain interfaces: Ethical issues. *Frontiers in Neuroscience, 13*, 1177. https://doi.org/10.3389/fnins.2019.01177

Jeunet, C., Glize, B., McGonigal, A., Batail, J.-M., & Micoulaud-Franchi, J.-A. (2019). Using EEG-based brain computer interface and neurofeedback targeting sensorimotor rhythms to improve motor skills: Theoretical background, applications and prospects. *Neurophysiologie Clinique, 49*(2), 125–136. https://doi.org/10.1016/j.neucli.2018.10.068

Jeunet, C., Hauw, D., & Millán, J. D. R. (2020). Sport psychology: Technologies ahead. *Frontiers in Sports and Active Living, 2*, 10. https://doi.org/10.3389/fspor.2020.00010

Jeunet, C., Tonin, L., Albert, L., Chavarriaga, R., Bideau, B., Argelaguet, F., Millán, J. D. R., Lécuyer, A., & Kulpa, R. (2020). Uncovering EEG correlates of covert attention in soccer goalkeepers: Towards innovative sport training procedures. *Scientific Reports, 10*(1), 1705. https://doi.org/10.1038/s41598-020-58533-2

Jiang, L., Stocco, A., Losey, D. M., Abernethy, J. A., Prat, C. S., & Rao, R. P. N. (2019). BrainNet: A multi-person brain-to-brain interface for direct collaboration between brains. *Scientific Reports, 9*(1), 6115. https://doi.org/10.1038/s41598-019-41895-7

Klein, E. (2020). Ethics and the emergence of brain-computer interface medicine. In *Handbook of clinical neurology* (Vol. 168, pp. 329–339). Elsevier. https://doi.org/10.1016/B978-0-444-63934-9.00024-X

Kuhn, L., Choy, O., Keller, L., Habel, U., & Wagels, L. (2024). Prefrontal tDCS modulates risk-taking in male violent offenders. *Scientific Reports, 14*(1), 10087. https://doi.org/10.1038/s41598-024-60795-z

Miranda, R. A., Casebeer, W. D., Hein, A. M., Judy, J. W., Krotkov, E. P., Laabs, T. L., Manzo, J. E., Pankratz, K. G., Pratt, G. A., Sanchez, J. C., Weber, D. J., Wheeler, T. L., & Ling, G. S. F. (2015). DARPA-funded efforts in the development of novel brain–computer interface technologies. *Journal of Neuroscience Methods, 244*, 52–67. https://doi.org/10.1016/j.jneumeth.2014.07.019

Neuralink. (n.d.). *PRIME study progress update—User experience*. https://neuralink.com/blog/prime-study-progress-update-user-experience/

Pandarinath, C., Nuyujukian, P., Blabe, C. H., Sorice, B. L., Saab, J., Willett, F. R., Hochberg, L. R., Shenoy, K. V., & Henderson, J. M. (2017). High performance communication by people with paralysis using an intracortical brain-computer interface. *eLife, 6*, e18554. https://doi.org/10.7554/eLife.18554

Pärssinen, M., & Seppälä, T. (2002). Steroid Use and Long-Term Health Risks in Former Athletes: *Sports Medicine, 32*(2), 83–94. https://doi.org/10.2165/00007256-200232020-00001

Pereira, M., Argelaguet, F., Millán, J. D. R., & Lécuyer, A. (2018). Novice shooters with lower pre-shooting alpha power have better performance during competition in a virtual reality scenario. *Frontiers in Psychology, 9*, 527. https://doi.org/10.3389/fpsyg.2018.00527

Plass-Oude Bos, D., Reuderink, B., Van De Laar, B., Gürkök, H., Mühl, C., Poel, M., Nijholt, A., & Heylen, D. (2010). Brain-computer interfacing and games. In D. S. Tan & A. Nijholt (Eds.), *Brain-computer interfaces* (pp. 149–178). Springer London. https://doi.org/10.1007/978-1-84996-272-8_10

Reis, J., Schambra, H. M., Cohen, L. G., Buch, E. R., Fritsch, B., Zarahn, E., Celnik, P. A., & Krakauer, J. W. (2009). Noninvasive cortical stimulation enhances motor skill acquisition over multiple days through an effect on consolidation. *Proceedings of the National Academy of Sciences, 106*(5), 1590–1595. https://doi.org/10.1073/pnas.0805413106

Sun, Y., Shen, A., Du, C., Sun, J., Chen, X., & Gao, X. (2023). A real-time non-implantation bi-directional brain–computer interface solution without stimulation artifacts. *IEEE Transactions on Neural Systems and Rehabilitation Engineering, 31*, 3566–3575. https://doi.org/10.1109/TNSRE.2023.3311750

Turconi, M. M., Mezzarobba, S., Franco, G., Busan, P., Fornasa, E., Jarmolowska, J., Accardo, A., & Battaglini, P. P. (2014). BCI-Based Neuro-Rehabilitation Treatment for Parkinson's Disease: Cases Report. In P. Bernardis, C. Fantoni, & W. Gerbino

(A c. Di), *Proceedings of the Trieste Symposium on Perception and Cognition* (Vol. 1). Edizioni Università di Trieste.

Wyckoff, S., & Birbaumer, N. (2014). Neurofeedback and brain–computer interfaces. In D. I. Mostofsky (Ed.), *The handbook of behavioral medicine* (1st ed., pp. 275–312). Wiley. https://doi.org/10.1002/9781118453940.ch15

Yarrow, K., Brown, P., & Krakauer, J. W. (2009). Inside the brain of an elite athlete: The neural processes that support high achievement in sports. *Nature Reviews Neuroscience, 10*(8), 585–596. https://doi.org/10.1038/nrn2672

Chapter 7

Assistive Technologies, Brain-Computer Interfaces and the Radical Cyborgization of Athletes

Between Performance Optimization and Enhancement

Francesco Bianchini and Silvia Camporesi

7.1 Introduction

The question of the participation of athletes with assistive technology in the able-bodied category is fascinating and complex and deserves to be investigated to understand how it is constructed in relation to the question of unfair advantage and of the perceived unfairness of the participation of athletes with a disability in the able-bodied category. In the first part of this chapter we trace the stories of three high-profile cases of athletes competing with assistive technologies that have made it to the Court for Arbitration of Sport (CAS 2008: Oscar Pistorius; 2020: Blake Leeper; 2021: Markus Rehm). In the second part of this chapter, we outline the technological advances in terms of brain-computer interfaces (BCI) and the impact that they could have in the near future on sports in terms of performance optimization and enhancement and on Paralympics classification.

7.2 The Tension of Assistive Technology in Sport: From Disability to Super-ability

There is no general rule that prevents Paralympic athletes from participating in Olympic events. As a matter of fact, the list of athletes with disabilities who have competed in events alongside able-bodied athletes is extensive. This includes the Italian archery champion Paola Fantato, who participated in the 1996 Atlanta Olympics. Fantato was the second archer in a wheelchair to compete at the Olympics, following New Zealander Neroli Fairhall in Los Angeles in 1984. Another example is the visually impaired American marathon runner Maria Runyan, who competed in the 2000 Sydney Olympics, reaching the finals and finishing eighth in the 1,500 m. South African swimmer Natalie Du Toit, who has a single amputation, also competed in the 10 km swim at the 2008 Beijing Olympics, finishing 16th (Smith & Thomas, 2016).

DOI: 10.4324/9781003520290-8

Although these athletes have various types of impairments, all of them share something: they start at a disadvantage. They do not need to resort to assistive technology in order to compete (if we don't count the wheelchair for the archers, which is not seen as part of the activity itself of the sport, but more of an assistive technology for moving around).

In 2008, for the first time, the Court for Arbitration of Sport based in Lausanne (sometimes referred to as the "Supreme Court" for international sports disputes) dealt with the case of an athlete employing assistive technology to compete, appealing against the international track and field sports governing body (known at that time as IAAF) to be able to compete in able-bodied events. This is the case of the South African runner and double-amputee Oscar Pistorius, born with a congenital condition that left him without fibula bones in his legs. At the age of 11 months, his legs were amputated below the knees. For running purposes, Pistorius used a prosthetic known as the "Cheetah Flex-Foot," produced by the Icelandic-based company Össur HF. Although this type of prosthetic had been used by many athletes with single or double transtibial (below-the-knee amputation) and transfemoral (above-the-knee amputation) since 1997, Pistorius was the first athlete to run with this type of prosthetic and reach speeds comparable to those of athletes running without assistive technology. At the 2004 Athens Paralympic Games, Pistorius won the gold medal in the 200 meters with a time of 21.97 seconds. In the same year, Pistorius began competing in events organized by the IAAF in South Africa, alongside non-disabled athletes. He won an "open competition" in the 100 m with a time of 11.51 seconds. In March 2007, Pistorius finished second at the South African Athletics Championships in the 400 m event with a time of 46.56 seconds. He thus began to attract the attention of members of athletic federations, who followed him with a mix of curiosity and growing concern. On March 26, 2007, the World Athletics (WA) Council introduced an amendment to Rule 144.2 with the aim of regulating the use of technical devices:

> For the purposes of this Rule, "assistance" is defined as, and therefore not permitted: the use of any technical device that incorporates springs, wheels, or any other element that provides the user with an advantage over another athlete who does not use such a device. Where there is no sufficient evidence of a metabolic advantage in favor of a disabled athlete—a double amputee using a prosthetic—due to the fact that the disabled athlete uses the same amount of oxygen as able-bodied athletes at a sub-maximal running speed, and no evidence that the biomechanical effects of using this particular prosthetic device provide the athlete with an advantage over other athletes who do not use such a device, the disabled athlete cannot be excluded from competing in IAAF-sanctioned international events with able-bodied athletes.

The first and most important point about this rule is that the burden of proof rests entirely on the athlete, who must demonstrate that they do not gain a competitive advantage from any type of assistive technology that includes springs, blades, wheels, etc. The second point is that if this burden of proof is successfully met, WA must allow the athlete using assistive technology to compete with able-bodied athletes. On the basis of this rule, on January 14, 2008, World Athletics declared that Oscar was ineligible to compete in WA-organized events, including the 2008 Beijing Olympic Games. WA explained that the use of prosthetics violated Rule 144.2.

Pistorius filed an appeal to the Court for Arbitration of Sport shortly thereafter. On May 26, 2008, CAS issued a verdict asserting Oscar Pistorius's eligibility to compete against Olympic athletes. The justification for this decision was that the WA "had not sufficiently demonstrated the assertion of an unfair advantage." On this basis, and because of the way that rule 144.2 was formulated, Pistorius was allowed to participate in the Olympics and other non-Paralympic events. However, it is important to emphasize that the CAS arbitrators were firm in stating that the decision had no validity for other athletes with double amputations, nor for Oscar wearing different prostheses (CAS 2008/A/1480 14 Pistorius v/ IAAF). Hence, although his decision by CAS was hailed as a victory for Oscar Pistorius, it was not a victory in general for the participation of athletes with assistive technology in able-bodied events. As a matter of fact, it was a very partial one, with narrow margins that left the door open for a possible WA appeal based on new tests. It also closed the door to hopes for other athletes with prosthetic limbs, making each appeal a completely separate case.

Following the CAS Award, Pistorius was allowed to participate at the Daegu World Athletics Championships in South Korea in 2011, and at the Olympics in London in 2012 in the 400 m and the 4 x 400 m relay. His participation at the London Olympics was seen by many as a watershed moment event for the realization of the Paralympic ideals of fairness, equality, and inclusivity (Swartz et al., 2016, p. 3). However, that promise remained unfulfilled: no other athletes with assistive technologies have competed in high-profile able-bodied events since then. The reason is twofold: first, as we have seen, the award reached by CAS in May 2008 on the eligibility of Oscar Pistorius to compete with able-bodied athletes could not be applied to any other athletes with similar assistive technologies, and second, in 2016 World Athletics introduced a new rule which *de facto* excluded the participation of athletes with assistive technologies from able-bodied events, unless they had successfully demonstrated the absence of advantage deriving from the prostheses.

The new rule, which Roger J. Pielke, at that time Director of the Sports Governance Centre at the University of Colorado in Boulder, named the "Rehm Rule" due to its timing, states that athletes with a prosthetic limb (specifically, any type of "mechanical aid") cannot participate in WA events "unless the athlete can establish on the balance of probabilities that the use of a mechanical assistive device does not provide them with a net competitive advantage over an athlete not using such mechanical aid" (Pielke, 2016). As argued by Norman and Moola (2011), WA has deployed a "strategy of containment" in which the burden of proof is set on the athlete requiring assistive technology to compete. To this athlete it is requested to demonstrate that assistive technology does not generate an unfair advantage over able-bodied athletes. The body of comparison, henceforth, is always the able-bodied athlete. It is not surprising, henceforth, that in the two most recent cases (Leeper in 2020, Rehm in 2021), the question of assistive technology has been ruled by CAS in favor of the World Athletics (WA) federation. It is this most recent rule that effectively closed the door to the participation of Paralympic athletes in the Olympic Games since 2012 (Viret, 2020).

Markus Rehm, German Paralympic record holder in the long jump since 2014, who jumps further than the current Olympic long-jumper gold medalist, has an acquired impairment: at the age of 14, due to an accident during wakeboarding training, his right leg was amputated below the knee. In 2014, Rehm achieved a jump of 8.24 m at the German Regional Championships in Ulm, the first athlete with assistive technology to beat able-bodied athletes in the long jump. The following year, at the Paralympic WA Championships in Doha, Rehm jumped 8.40 m. Despite being more than 30 cm shorter than his current personal best (8.72 m jumped in Rhede Germany in June 2023), this distance would have earned him the gold medal at the 2012 London Olympics, ahead of British athlete Greg Rutherford, who secured first place with an 8.37 m jump (Guardian Sport, 2015). This sets Rehm apart from Oscar Pistorius, who, with his best time in the 400 m, never posed an "actual threat" to the Olympic podium (he finished sixteenth, crossing the finish line last, in the London 2012 semifinals) (Adelson, 2015).

Blake Leeper is an American Paralympic athlete born on August 31, 1989, with a professional track and field career dating back to 2009. Leeper was born with a congenital condition very similar to that of Oscar Pistorius: fibular hemimelia, which resulted in the absence of most of his calf muscles, tibia bones, and feet at birth, hence he runs with double transtibial prostheses. On June 4, 2018, Blake Leeper participated in a WA-approved event in Prague, and completed the 400 m race in a time of 44.42 seconds, meeting the Olympic qualification standard by 0.48 seconds for the first time in his career. On February 27, 2020, Leeper appealed to CAS to compete in the Olympics in Tokyo. On the one hand, Mr. Leeper argued in court that placing the burden of proof (to demonstrate a lack of advantage) on the athlete should be considered discriminatory because: (a) it applies only to athletes who require mechanical support to compete; and (b) it is impossible for any amputee athlete to compete in a competition without such mechanical support (the problem here with assistive technology as essential for performance but also enhancing performance, as noted by Brendan Burkett, 2010). On the other hand, WA's legal presentation reaffirmed the precautionary principle expressed earlier: WA claimed to have the right to require Mr. Leeper to demonstrate, as a condition for being exempted from the ban on mechanical aids, that his performance in the 400 m are obtained solely through his natural athletic ability and not from the artificial advantage derived from his specially designed assistive prostheses:

> The IAAF claims that it has the right to place the burden of proof on Mr. Leeper. In particular, the ban on mechanical aids exists to protect the integrity of the sport, to ensure that the result of the athletics sport is determined by natural talent and effort, rather than technology. As a basic principle, it is fair to require that a person seeking an exception to the rule prove that the sought exception is not a threat to integrity.
>
> (CAS, 2020)

However, this request is tautologically impossible to fulfill, as the athletic ability of an athlete requiring assistive technology cannot be separated from technology, which is essential for performance. According to Baker from Arizona State University (Baker, 2016) the requirement of comparing the performance of athletes with assistive technologies with the performance with able-bodied athletes mode of comparison disproportionately limits the capabilities of athletes who require assistive technology, while imposing no limits on the capabilities of those who do not, and as such, it is unfair. For example, when looking at Usain Bolt, no one has ever claimed that there is a limit to human capabilities in the 100 m, set at 9.72 seconds, a record held by Asafa Powell for the same distance. Powell's record was shattered by Bolt with his incredible time of 9.58 seconds at the 2009 World Championships in Berlin (Baker, 2016). Able-bodied human possibilities are not constrained by an upper limit imposed from thereof. If the possibilities for able-bodied humans are not restricted to their upper limit, and there is always the possibility that a new athlete emerges and surpasses what was once thought to be an insurmountable limit, why shouldn't the same be the case for athletes who require assistive technology to compete? Baker's reflection underscores the need for a fair and open approach when evaluating athletes' capabilities, regardless of the use of assistive technology.

In practice, hence, the precautionary principle becomes a clause that prohibits the participation of athletes who compete with technological support in the same category as athletes who compete without such technology. Here, American science and technology scholar Raymond Fouché's statement about Pistorius being a "condenser" (author's expression) of all our technoscientific hopes and fears seems to fit perfectly. The tension between the desire to protect the integrity of sport and the desire to be inclusive towards athletes with disabilities is always resolved in favor of the former by regulatory bodies, through a containment strategy that imposes limits on bodies that deviate from the established norm.

The verdict issued by the CAS on October 23, 2020, dismissing Leeper's appeal revolves around the key issue of the burden of proof and answers the question of whether the provision that places the burden of proof on the athlete to establish the absence of a clear competitive advantage is valid and legal. In the ruling, issued in October 2020, the jury reached partly conflicting statements. On the one hand, it recognized that placing the burden of proof on the athlete to prove the absence of an advantage resulted in effectively a prohibition to their participation. And since the Olympics are, at least in principle, pro-inclusion in their original Olympic spirit, the CAS jury recommended changing the WA rules, placing the burden of proof back on the sport governing body. On the other hand, the jury acknowledged the "legitimate" purpose of WA to protect the integrity of the sport from technologies that could provide an unfair advantage to athletes, and undermine the meaning of the practice itself.

The limits of human nature always seem surmountable once they have been surpassed. Every Olympics sees the breaking of additional world records. The bar is raised higher and higher for human capacities. However, for Paralympic athletes, this limit appears insurmountable. The bar is set externally and is always based on the able-bodied human norm. What this amounts to in practice is that the capabilities of athletes needing assistive technology are not questioned, as long as their performances do not start being too close to the existing, and necessarily contingent upper human limit determined based on an athlete without assistive technology. This use of the upper human limit has been exemplified in the case of Markus Rehm, whose current long jump record of 8.72 m would have earned him gold medals at the last three Olympics, including Paris, which was won by the Greek Miltiadis Tentoglou with 8.48 m. The world record in the long jump belongs to Mike Powell, who jumped nearly 9 m in 1991 at the Tokyo Olympics, while currently, gold medals in the long jump are won with much "modest" measurements around 8.40 m. A record that has since remained unchallenged. The Norwegian philosopher Sigmund Loland refers to this as the "stagnation of records" (Loland, 2006).

We find ourselves in a paradox of Catch-22, where it is difficult, if not impossible, to escape, because the benchmark is invariably the able-bodied human. Every time technology proposes something close to the limits of human capability, there arises the suspicion of an unfair advantage. American technology scholar Rayvon Fouché, author of the 2017 book *Game Changer: The Technoscientific Revolution in Sports,* captures beautifully this tension:

> What makes [the case of Pistorius, and we could add, that of Markus Rehm] so compelling for spectators, intriguing for scientists, and problematic for sports regulatory bodies is that it represents all our techno-scientific hopes and fears condensed into one individual. In rosier scenarios, techno-science allows humanity to transcend the limits of human bodies and the natural world, highlighting human creativity, ingenuity, and brilliance. In darker scenarios, unrestrained technoscience undermines the body and

the natural world, revealing the shortsightedness, arrogance, and hubris of our species.

(Fouché, 2017, p. 124)

The only way sports has attempted to address such issues is by using a comparison with existing able-bodied human capabilities. This seems to us a narrow way to proceed, a "strategy of containment" that sports governing bodies have devised to exclude the participation of athletes who are seen as increasingly posing a threat to the un-rivalled primacy of the able-bodied athletes. What could be an alternative mode of comparison? Instead of imposing the norm of Olympic athletes as a limit for Paralympic athletes, one could consider using an exceptional type of benchmark and view the cyborg, the union of technology and flesh, as the benchmark for mixed performances; and think of how AI could be applied to simulate the performance of a given athlete competing with assistive technologies, with the same athlete competing without assistive technology. We will address this question in Section 7.5 after presenting the most recent advances in the field of bionics and biomechanical engineering applied to neuro-prostheses.

7.3 A Glimpse into the Near Future of Assistive Technologies Applied to Sport

The applications of AI to bionics promise to meet the currently unmet clinical need of restoring cutaneous sensation in a neuro-prosthetic system after amputation. In particular, brain co-processors, devices that combine decoding and encoding in a unified framework using AI, are cognitive artifacts (Fasoli, 2022), whose applications go beyond restoring motor function through neuro-prosthesis, as they allow for the creation of de novo functions (Rao et al., 2020; Qi et al., 2023).

The concept of cognitive artifacts is integral to the extensive and ongoing debate about the extended mind, which began with a seminal paper by Clark and Chalmers in 1998 (Clark & Chalmers, 1998). While it is not possible to trace all stages of this debate here, we will concentrate on aspects pertinent to evaluating sports performances by athletes using assistive technologies. Notably, this particular area has not been extensively explored in the literature. In the context of sports disciplines, especially individual sports, the focus has primarily been on mechanical assistive technologies rather than software-related aspects. However, the rapid expansion and impact of artificial intelligence (AI) technologies in recent years present an opportunity to discuss this topic. This shift also suggests a new perspective on the current or soon-to-be-realized potential assistance that technologies can offer in sports.

In a nutshell, the notion of the Extended Mind suggests that artifacts that are external to the mind and skull can become part of a subject's cognitive activities, effectively integrating into the cognitive process (Clark & Chalmers,

1998). Over the years, it has been proposed as binding for extension that if the instrument extending cognition is removed, the cognitive process that was created by integrating the mind/brain system with the tool is also lost (Rupert, 2009; Heinrichs, 2017). This underscores the highly integrated nature that a tool must possess to extend cognition and be classified as a cognitive artifact. Such cognitive artifacts are not typically found in the sporting world. From an inverse perspective, it is challenging to identify artifacts in sports disciplines that can be considered cognitive. However, in a broad sense, some tools can be labeled as cognitive artifacts. For example, in shooting sports, certain types of glasses enter the action and perception loop (Chalmers, 2019), which is central to these specialties, thereby extending cognitive performance and potentially improving results.

A different discussion arises when considering AI. In recent years, we have explored the possibility of AI cognitive artifacts, evaluating how AI systems can extend certain cognitive functions by integrating with human systems. Hernandez-Orallo and Volt (2019), for instance, analyzed various cases where AI systems extend cognition. They highlighted that a key characteristic for an AI system to be considered an "AI extender" is the lack of autonomy. Their examples span many fields, including navigation, memory, attention, and decision-making. However, there are still a few examples of AI being used extensively in sports, though it may only be a matter of time before this technology becomes integrated into various sports. For instance, in car racing, AI is already used to predictively simulate racing strategies based on extensive real-time data. Recent years have seen efforts to refine these techniques (Patil et al., 2023). It is conceivable that AI systems could increasingly be used in real time to provide information for drivers, effectively athletes, to influence their strategies and performance. This differs from external help provided by coaches or engineers, on the contrary, involving a tool with a cognitive impact that modifies, if not necessarily improves, performance.[1]

Many sports could potentially benefit from these AI predictive tools. In these contexts, the tool does not enhance the athlete's physical abilities (as in some running disciplines) but instead intentionally alters their cognitive performance during the sporting event. This raises several questions. To what extent are these tools acceptable or considered legitimate according to the rules of the sport? At what point do they provide an unfair advantage through their cognitive impact? Can it be considered unfair if everyone has access to these technologies? And if everyone *can* use them, does that mean everyone *should* use them to avoid being disadvantaged? Is it acceptable to mandate the use of certain technologies in a sporting context, which is also governed by ethical standards and respect for human rights?

Another important aspect to consider when using AI systems to extend human capabilities is their autonomy. Hernandez-Orallo and Volt (2019) emphasize that the absence of autonomy in AI systems is essential for them to truly extend human capabilities; otherwise, it is more accurately described as collaboration. However, the issue is more complex because a certain degree of autonomy is inherent in AI systems. Autonomy is part of their definition as active, rather than passive, tools in executing various tasks. One of the goals of AI is to develop systems capable of autonomously performing functions considered intelligent, or in more contemporary terms, cognitive. This foundational aspect of contemporary AI can significantly impact its applications in the sports field, as we will explore further.

Autonomy has long been a key concept in AI, especially with recent advancements. The notion of autonomy has become increasingly central as AI systems draw inspiration from biological systems, where autonomy is a fundamental characteristic (Steels, 1995). We can hypothesize that the concept of autonomy has helped bridge AI and biological systems, providing a common basis for systems analysis. The evolution of AI systems based on machine learning and neural networks, up to generative AI, has strengthened this integration, raising ethical and regulatory questions regarding autonomy (Chia et al., 2023). In line with these developments, the same issue of cognitive extension has been broadened to also include Brain-Computer Interaction (BCI) devices, as devices that extend cognition to all intents and purposes, even if regardless of an informational connotation of the interaction (Heinrichs, 2021). Combining these elements, an intriguing conceptual framework emerges in relation to sports disciplines. Cognitive artifacts that extend cognition through AI systems, exhibiting a significant degree of autonomy, even at the neuronal level, open up numerous possibilities and risks that have yet to be fully assessed. One approach to addressing these issues is by exploring the concept of the cyborg as applied to sports. In order to do so, we introduce the Cybathlon, which has been referred to as a place to experiment with "capability hybridization" between humans and technology (Richard & Andrieu, 2019), as we discuss below.

The Cybathlon, held for the first time in Zurich in 2016, in Graz in 2020, and for the second time in Kloten, in Switzerland in October 2024, aims to drive the development of user-center assistive technologies by "providing a benchmarking platform in an out of laboratory setting" (Jaeger et al., 2023, p. 448). In its 2024 edition, the Cybathlon consists of eight events where athletes (called "pilots") compete with the help of assistive technologies in tasks representing their actual daily life challenges: brain-computer interface races, functional electric stimulation bike races, arms and legs motorized prostheses, exoskeletons, and powered wheelchairs. The applications of BCIs to Cybathlon have been manifold and synergistic as the Cybathlon has enabled the further development of BCIs (Jaeger et al., 2023). There are eligibility criteria for competing in the Cybathlon. These serve two purposes as laid out by Jaeger et al. (2023): (a) guarantee a level-playing field among participants and (b) ensure that participation is safe for the pilot.

One of the primary applications of Cybathlon is in Brain-Computer Interface (BCI) technology, exemplified by the Brain-Computer Interface Race. In this competition, athletes control their avatars in a virtual running race using BCI tools. These tools translate neural impulses, collected through non-invasive methods such as functional near-infrared spectroscopy, functional magnetic resonance imaging, or electroencephalography (Huang et al., 2013), into virtual movements of the avatar. The extracted signals are decoded using machine learning algorithms, which is the most intriguing aspect of this process. These algorithms, based on AI techniques, offer possibilities beyond merely controlling an external device with neural impulses. Machine learning algorithms adapt to the behavior of the human user, who, in turn, learns to refine their neural skills. This creates a dual co-evolution of the human user and algorithm system, as demonstrated by established techniques and methodologies (McFarland, Wolpaw, 2018).

This type of BCI can be considered a cognitive extension through AI (machine learning) tools, leading to progressive and adaptive improvement in user performance. In the case of Cybathlon, the application in sports serves not only for competition but also to enhance tools for controlling and implementing movement in the everyday lives of users who need them. It is not difficult to envision similar applications in the sports field, where BCI systems and machine learning methodologies can help model and perfect performances. These applications may not necessarily push athletes' performance beyond limits but could optimize performance within plausible ranges by modulating, for example, the biophysical system and the potential devices that are used in performing a sport. In this context, AI extensions could be used to rebalance and eliminate differences that are not accepted in competitions. Swartz et al. (2016) distinguish two ways in which fairness, equity, and inclusivity are understood in the context of the Paralympic movement, with the first one being actualized with the application of "technologies to the body in order to optimize the function of individual athletes who are appropriately assisted and classified" (Swartz et al., 2016, p. 3), and the second being a much broader global aim to contribute to a better world for people with disabilities. In this sense, AI extensions could be seen in line with the former actualization of fairness, equity, and inclusivity in the Paralympics.

According to the Cybathlon 2024 Races and Rules book (the most recent competition), each team's pilot must meet the eligibility criteria for their discipline, and has to undergo a medical check conducted with a Cybathlon medical examiner aimed to establish "the pilot's eligibility based on written medical documentation" prior to the event (Cybathlon 2024 Medical Check). While the eligibility criteria emphasize the inclusion of pilots with varying levels of ability, they are in place to ensure fairness across all of the disciplines, so that no teams hold an immediate advantage. In this respect, they are similar to the functional assessment that determines the minimum impairment criteria for the Paralympics. This also helps to guarantee that a competitive spirit remains to drive the innovation needed to create much better devices.

For the 2024 edition of the Cybathlon, implanted BCI systems has been eligible to participate for the first time (Cybathlon 2024 Races and Rules). The eight events in which pilots have competed at the 2024 Cybathlon are: (1) Brain-Computer Interface Race (BCI); (2) Functional Electrical Stimulation Bike Race (FES); (3) Arm Prosthesis Race (ARM); (4) Leg Prosthesis Race (LEG); (5) Exoskeleton Race (EXO); (6) Wheelchair Race (WHL); (7) Vision Assistance Race (VIS); (8) Assistance Robot Race. For the purposes of technical eligibility in the BCI Race, "any mobile technology that allows to measure brain activity is permitted for participation. Electroencephalography (EEG), electrocorticography (ECOG), microelectrode arrays, near infrared spectroscopy (fNIRS), or magnetoencephalography (MEG) are allowed, but also any other signal acquisition method provided it primarily measures brain activity" (Cybathlon 24 Races and Rules). In addition, during any race at the Cybathlon "It is not allowed to intentionally use eye or muscle activity to control the BCI." In the criteria for pilots any devices that are implanted in the pilot's body must be "medically stable for six months prior to the event, and pilots must reach the legal age in their home country by the first day of the event" (Cybathlon 2024 Races and Rules). The use of BCI systems, and consequently invasive technologies, instead of using eyes or muscles for control, demonstrates an evolution in this competition toward a further cyborgization of the pilot. This could foreshadow similar developments, both in terms of possibilities and implications, in standard, Olympic, or Paralympic sports disciplines.

The Cybathlon offers the possibility to experiment with the functionalities of the body, which go beyond mere restoration to previous functions or augmentation of existing functions. On this note, Richard and Andrieu (2019) argue that the Cybathlon is not a space of reiteration of transhuman cyborg, but a place to experiment with "capability hybridization" between flesh and technology aimed at deconstructing the normative ableist framework. Athletes competing at the Cybathlon encompass the "radical cyborg," an alternative embodiment that questions the ableist figure and is more closely reminiscent of Haraway's cyborg, which by definition acts as a form of resistance to pre-established categories. Its symbiotic relationship with technology undoes human nature by embodying technology in a way that enables the activation or creation of previously undisclosed bodily capabilities and does not merely "enhance" or "augment" existing human function, but creates radically new ones. By so doing, Richard and Andrieu are in line with Hugh Herr's vision of augmenting human capabilities in a way that is not necessarily quantitatively (more of the same function), but it is radically creative. Hugh Herr is a biophysicist, double amputee, and former professional rock climber, who for decades has been pioneering new ways of connecting the human nervous system bidirectionally with synthetic computation (Herr et al., 2003; "Augmented," 2022). In the field of bionics and biomechanical engineering, some of the most advanced applications of brain co-processors are being developed by Hugh Herr's laboratory at MIT, in Cambridge, USA

(Srinivasan & Herr, 2022). Herr's group has already developed an ankle-foot prosthesis for enhanced rock climbing (Rogers et al., 2020), and his research aims include the "augmentation" of human capabilities for a variety of functions which go beyond our species' typical functioning. The explicit goal of Herr's research is the achievement of the cyborg status (Lopez Frias, 2017, 2018), in which the athlete feels embodied into the cognitive artifact, as if it were their flesh and bone (Pielli & Zlatev, 2020).

As previously mentioned, within sports, the concept of the cyborg and the embodiment of cognitive artifacts are part of the broader trend concerning the relationship between AI and sports. From an embodiment perspective, one of the most exploited areas in sports is robotics, which operates in a bidirectional manner. On the one hand, robotic applications in sports have led to various robotic competitions, the most well-known being RoboCup Soccer (Kitano et al., 1997). In these competitions, robots compete against each other, usually in teams, with one of the objectives being the continuous improvement of the robotic technologies used to achieve victory in the tournament. On the other hand, and of greater interest for our purposes, are the recent developments of training systems based on robotic exoskeletons. These exoskeletons are utilized in human neuromuscular rehabilitation. AI machine learning technologies, together with techniques as electroencephalography and electromyography, allow the exoskeleton to adapt to the patient's intentions by decoding neural signals. This enables the patient to feel as though they are performing the movement themselves, even if it is actually executed by the exoskeleton. These non-invasive brain-computer interface (BCI) technologies align with the expanded notion of extended cognition discussed earlier and facilitate effective training in sports activities. As Kirchner highlights, "the combination of user intention recognition and mental state with the Exoskeleton driven muscular activation is a perfect basis for athlete training" (Kirchner, 2023, p. 95), creating a personalized experience for the athlete. A key aspect of this application is that the combined system of the nervous system, anatomical structure, robotic artifact, and AI algorithm functions as a single unit, regardless of the individual involved. This could be a patient undergoing rehabilitation, a person with neuro-deficit physiological or physical conditions, or an athlete without particular conditions.

Regardless of their level of invasiveness, BCI technologies can dynamically and adaptively change human behavior (Peksa & Mamchur, 2023). This dynamic capability, which can be implemented in real time, allows BCI technologies to be increasingly used for rehabilitation purposes. However, this dynamic capability also raises issues related to the alteration of personality or subjectivity, particularly in cases involving neuroenhancement (Ferretti & Ienca, 2018). Therefore, any use of these technologies must address the ethical challenges stemming from epistemic problems associated with extending cognitive activity through AI – specifically, machine learning algorithms that interpret neural signals and operate at a neural level in individuals.

The autonomy of AI does not cause humans to relinquish their performance or ability to act, but instead creates a different system. Positively, there are numerous cases where the intervention or action of BCI tools aids in recovering cognitive functions, such as Deep Brain Stimulation, which is used to restore compromised cognitive abilities in diseases like Parkinson's (Heinricks, 2021) and is increasingly being tested also in severe cases of eating disorders such as anorexia nervosa (Shaffer et al., 2023). The autonomous, real-time neural interaction facilitated by these instruments can return individuals to a healthy state, generating a cognitive effect. Similar examples include epileptic patients. While the benefits of BCI technologies in these cases are substantial, the risk of compromising individual integrity is also significant (Tesink et al., 2024).

The algorithmic AI techniques used in BCIs for controlling robotic artifacts vary, but they share a common feature: they are adaptive and capable of optimizing performance based on selected parameters. This raises interesting questions about their implications for the world of sports and various sporting disciplines, including those involving individuals who compete using artificial artifacts or in conditions not always considered physiologically admissible. Some key questions arise: Can AI technologies help level the playing field for athletes in a competition through BCI and/or robotic applications? For example, consider fencing, which consists of events where reaction times are crucial. If BCI and AI technologies could not only improve reaction times but also eliminate differences between athletes using prosthetic devices and those who do not, would these technologies be acceptable for creating a common competitive ground? Or could they at least be used to evaluate and quantify differences among athletes based on data produced during athletic performances? What would sports federations think of such tools? Could or should they incorporate them in line with the principles of equity and inclusion? These questions pertain to the present or near future. The future may present even greater challenges as human-machine integration advances, potentially leading to new forms of cyborg athletes.

Siegel and Morris (2020, p. 73) point out how robotics and automation will lead to the creation of new sports and predict that by 2040, humans and machines "may merge through actuator-driven augmentations or assistive technologies enhancing strength, speed, stamina, and reaction times." We believe that the increasing "radical cyborgization" of humans will pose a challenge for Paralympics classification.

7.4 Radical Cyborgization and Challenges for Classification

In the Paralympics, athletes are grouped by the degree of activity limitation resulting from their impairment(s). Classification in the Paralympics follows the three criteria:

1. Does the athlete have an eligible impairment for this sport?
2. Does the athlete's eligible impairment meet the minimum disability criteria of the sport?
3. Which sport class describes the athlete's activity limitation most accurately?

By "eligible impairment," it is understood as one of ten impairments identified in the "Policy on Eligible Impairments in the Paralympic Movement." A panel of three "classifiers," which usually includes a medical doctor and a sport technician, evaluates each athlete. The classifiers work with specific guidelines (a "functional classification system") which are designed to "classify individual sporting participants by their ability to undertake certain physical tasks" (ibid., p. 137). The physical tasks are general ones that are intended to provide an operational measure of function or ability. In addition, each sport's Paralympic classification rules describe how severe an eligible impairment must be, related to the sport context, for an athlete to be considered eligible. These criteria are referred to as "minimum disability criteria." Examples of minimum disability criteria could be maximum height for short stature, or the degree of amputation of a particular limb. In order to achieve standardization, athletes are always assessed before competition and sometimes during competition. Athletes can be assessed multiple times in their careers, as their impairment may change. This means that athletes may elect to change the category in which they can compete or may be forced to do so. Minor quantitative differences can mean moving from the best in class of one category to the worst in class of another. As stated by the International Paralympic Classification, the rationale for a sport class is one of ensuring fair equality of opportunity within a given category: "A sport class groups athletes with a similar activity limitation together for competition, so that they can compete equitably" (Eligible Impairment Types). Thus, classification – which is the central ethical problem of Paralympic sport according to Howe and Jones (2006) – attempts to cater for impairment and sporting contexts in order to generate fair classifications within and between disability groupings.

A question will arise of whether the further developments in cyborgization, including BCIs and exoskeletons, will be included in the Paralympics, or will continue to be included in the parallel event of the Cybathlon. This will depend in part on whether the technology is considered performance-assistive or performance-enhancing. As highlighted above, it is plausible to speculate that BCI systems and machine learning methodologies could help optimize performances. Although these applications may not necessarily push athletes' performance beyond limits, but could optimize performance within plausible ranges by modulating, for example, the biophysical system and the potential devices that are used in performing a sport. At what point does a technology that optimizes performance become an unfair technological advantage?

We believe that, in the future, the use of BCI and neuroprosthetic technologies could play a decisive role in enabling more accurate and fair classifications for athletes who use assistive technologies in specific sporting disciplines. This will be achieved through AI machine learning algorithms, once their potential for performance standardization is recognized. While these technologies are often discussed in the context of neurorehabilitation, with significant benefits that extend beyond sports, they are also considered for neuroenhancement. Neuroenhancement could potentially offer advantages beyond natural human capabilities, raising concerns about fairness. However, this issue is not yet fully clarified. In many sports, advancements in equipment or clothing technology can create advantages that are accessible to all. This was, for example, the case of the Speedo LZR swimsuits in 2008. Similarly, BCI technology with AI algorithms could become a universally available enhancement, making it comparable to other accessible technologies.

It is plausible to speculate that the debate about the introduction of BCI technology with AI algorithms into sport could follow a similar pathway to the debate that ensued following the introduction of Speedo LZR Swimsuits, which we briefly rehearse here. These full-body suits, leaving only the hands and feet uncovered, were unique in the world of international swimming competition suits: they represented a new application of polyurethane that allowed the suit, and thus the body, to reach unprecedented levels of hydrodynamic efficiency. The Speedo LZR suit, which was immediately imitated by more than 20 companies right after its debut in 2008, represented an unprecedented leap in technology as it increased buoyancy by up to 8% while significantly reducing hydrodynamic resistance (Foster et al., 2012). One telling fact: in the first 17 months that LZR suits were made available to professional swimmers, more than 130 world records were broken. Reactions to the series of records being shattered like dominoes were not long in coming. In Italy, the Italian national team coach, Alberto Castagnetti, was one of the first to express strong criticism of the LZR suits. In April 2008, Castagnetti referred to the new LZR full-body suits as a form of "technological doping":

> We are heading down a very dangerous path. We are setting aside the purely competitive aspects of the sport to make room for external factors. Swimming has always been based on technique, but now other aspects are coming into play. We are talking about technological doping, which is therefore contrary to the spirit of sport.
>
> (Eurosport, 2008)

Similar voices came from other coaches, including Bob Bowman, coach to the multiple American Olympic champion Michael Phelps, who was one of the first to suggest that all records obtained with LZR should have a separate ranking. In July 2009, the International Swimming Federation (now, World

Aquatics) voted on the American proposal to ban polyurethane competition suits, with the rule to take effect on January 1, 2010. The reasons put forward by the International Swimming Federations for banning this type of suit were as follows: they posed a threat to the integrity of the sport; and they had produced "unnatural" explosions in performance that had completely upended the sport's record books in less than a decade, thereby undermining the very meaning of records. According to FINA, these LZR suits had dangerously impacted the narratives of human athletic achievement and therefore had to be removed to restore the primacy of the natural human body. The proposal to ban polyurethane full-body suits in competition, advanced by the American swimming federation in 2009 was approved with 180 nations voting in favor of banning the Speedo suits and only 7 voting against. Although some experts at that time suggested distinguishing the records set by swimmers wearing polyurethane suits from other records, it was ultimately decided not to differentiate or nullify the records (MacDonald, 2017). This remains to date a contentious issue, with proposals to restore the previous world records obtained without the aid of the technology (Gao et al., 2020).

Putting aside for the moment this debate and the inevitable challenges associated with it, we could consider the use of neuroprosthetic AI and BCI-AI systems as an equalizing factor in sports. Currently, athletes using assistive technologies bear the burden of proving that they do not gain an unfair advantage. This responsibility often falls on the athletes or their federations because they are the ones requesting an exception. As we have previously stressed, this creates a paradox, as it is impossible to evaluate an athlete's performance with and without assistive technologies when these technologies are essential for competition, as seen in sports like athletics, fencing, or basketball.

To address this issue extensively, we can explore two fundamental approaches. First, AI can be used in a simulative way to create a virtual environment that reconstructs the various possibilities an athlete experiences with prosthetic technology during performance, establishing their average physiological standard. This allows for the calibration of assistive technologies based on factors such as size, length, elasticity, and flexibility, tailored to the specific sporting discipline. In this virtual environment, parameters can be adjusted until the optimal solution is found, aligning with the athlete's physiological values. Once determined, these parameters can be transferred to the prosthesis. With a reasonable degree of certainty, it can then be argued that any variation in the athlete's performance, whether better or worse, is attributable to the athlete rather than the technology.

A second approach involves using BCI technologies equipped with AI systems to rebalance physiological systems that have hormonal or metabolic imbalances not caused by external substances. This method, which seems relatively straightforward given the existing BCI technologies previously discussed, may present ethical challenges rather than practical ones. However, it could serve as a valuable tool for evaluating, possibly through predictive simulations, the physiological aspects of individuals whose physical parameters are at the limits of what is permitted.

Once this type of predictive analysis is accepted in sports, two paths emerge:

1. **Acceptance of Limit Values**: It could be accepted that an athlete has physiological values at the limits compared to the average, and they are considered in compliance, potentially eliminating some forms of doping.
2. **Intervention with BCI Technologies**: Alternatively, invasive BCI technologies, enhanced by AI, could be used to rebalance physical, neural, or hormonal parameters in real time during sports competitions, ensuring they remain within fair limits.

Whether these approaches are acceptable is a matter for ethical evaluation. When evaluating the role of technology in sports, Murray presents three possibilities for technologies in relation to an ethical standard (Murray, 2009, pp. 157–159):

i. A technology could be "ethically desirable" if it reduces the impact of factors other than natural talents and their enhancement, thereby reducing unequal access to legitimate means of improving performance. An example of an ethically desirable technology defined in this way is the hypoxic chamber, as it equalizes the initial conditions for athletes who, due to geography or economic conditions, cannot access high altitudes for training.

ii. A technology could be "ethically permissible" if, for example, it is ethically neutral in relation to the connection between talent, virtue, and performance. For instance, disparities in access to coaches and sports equipment are widespread and depend on geographic and birth conditions. Typically, the differential access athletes have due to their geographic and economic conditions in relation to different levels of coaches or sports equipment is considered a tolerable inequality that does not require intervention.

iii. Finally, a technology could be "ethically undesirable" if it undermines the meaning of sport by significantly interfering with the relationship between natural talents, their virtuous enhancement, and athletic success. Examples of ethically undesirable technologies, according to Murray, include technological doping and genetic doping.

Although not yet fully realized, these BCI technologies appear close to becoming a reality. In which category they would fall remains a matter of debate, which will need to be necessarily sports-contextual. While improper or distorted uses are always conceivable, though not justifiable, we can consider these technologies from an ethical standpoint as either equalizers or, at the very least, permissible according to Murray's categorization. The key distinction lies in their level of integration with the human being and the degree of autonomy in the processes they can implement – two aspects that require careful evaluation. Nonetheless, neurocyborgs of this type could transform the meaning of sport, especially if we are unprepared to understand their limits and actual possibilities in the sporting field.

Finally, there is a third possibility in line with the evolution of cyborgization, which we propose to properly frame the conceptual system of reference. This involves conducting sports competitions with exoskeletons that equalize all participants, regardless of their physical condition. These exoskeletons would function as robots internally piloted by human beings, similar to those depicted in Japanese anime. In such a scenario, the competition would become almost entirely a mental discipline, akin to a chess game. This approach demonstrates that it is not possible to completely detach from the embodied nature of the athlete. It highlights that the balance and fairness these technologies can help achieve should not come at the expense of the athlete's physicality.

7.5 Conclusions

In the first part of this chapter we have traced the histories of three high-profile cases of athletes competing with assistive technologies for whom the suspicion of unfair advantage has been raised: Oscar Pistorius, Markus Rehm, and Blake Leeper and we have shown how World Athletics has adopted strategies of containment revolving around an impossible burden of proof to exclude them from competing with Olympic Athletes. In the second part of this chapter, we have outlined the technological advances in terms of brain-computer-interfaces (BCI) and the impact that they could have in the near future on sports in terms of performance optimization and enhancement, and on Paralympics classification. Across both parts of this work, we have argued that imposing the norm of able-bodied Olympic athletes on athletes requiring assistive technologies to compete is problematic and fundamentally unfair, and that sports federations should instead view the cyborg, the combination of technology and flesh, as the benchmark for mixed performances. Finally, we have suggested that the use of AI could be applied to resolve the vexed question of the eligibility of athletes with assistive technology to compete in able-bodied events.

Note

1 In a certain sense this may recall a statement contained in Turing's article which presents the idea of a test to attest intelligence or thinking capabilities in digital machines by imitation of interactive linguistic behavior : "We do not wish

to penalise the machine for its inability to shine in beauty competitions, nor to penalise a man for losing in a race against an aeroplane" (Turing, 1950, p. 442).

References

Adelson, E. (2015, August 5). The disabled athlete who's too able. Yahoo Sports. https://sports.yahoo.com/the-disabled-athlete-who-s--too--able-125741818.html

Baker, D. A. (2016). The "Second Place" problem: Assistive technology in sports and (Re) constructing normal. *Science and Engineering Ethics, 22*(1), 93–110.

Burkett, B. (2010). Technology in Paralympic sport: Performance enhancement or essential for performance? British Journal of Sports Medicine, 44(3), 215–220. https://doi.org/10.1136/bjsm.2009.060798

CAS 2021/A/8167 Markus Rehm v. International Olympic Committee (IOC) & World Athletics (WA), award of September 1, 2021 (operative part of 23 July 2021)-.

CAS 2020/A/6807 Blake Leeper v. International Association of Athletics Federations. https://www.tas-cas.org/fileadmin/user_upload/Award__6807___for_publication_.pdf

CAS 2008/A/1480 Pistorius v/ IAAF, award of May 16, 2008. https://jurisprudence.tas-cas.org/Shared%20Documents/1480.pdf

Chalmers, D. (2019). Extended cognition and extended consciousness. In M. Colombo, E. Irvine, & M. Stapleton (Eds.), *Andy Clark and his critics* (pp. 9–21). Oxford University Press.

Chia, H., Beck, D., Paterson, J. M., & Savulescu, J. (2023). Autonomous AI: What does autonomy mean in relation to persons or machines? *Law, Innovation and Technology, 15*(2), 390–410. https://doi.org/10.1080/17579961.2023.2245679

Clark, A., & Chalmers, D. (1998). The extended mind. *Analysis, 58*(1), 7–19.

Cybathlon. (2024). Medical check. https://cybathlon.ethz.ch/en/events/edition/cybathlon-2024/team-registration/medcheck (retrieved August 6, 2024).

Cybathlon. (2024). Races and rules. https://cybathlon.ethz.ch/documents/races-and-rules/CYBATHLON%202024/CYBATHLON_RacesAndRules_2024.pdf (retrieved August 6, 2024).

Eligible Impairment Types in the Paralympic Movement. https://www.paralympic.org/classification#:~:text=A%20Sport%20Class,same%20Eligible%20Impairment (retrieved August 7, 2024).

Eurosport, Nuoto. (2008, April 4). https://www.eurosport.it/motogp/nuoto_sto1535779/story.shtml (retrieved August 12, 2024).

Fasoli, M. (2022). Cognitive artifacts between cognitive sciences and the philosophy of technology. In Terrone, E., Tripodi, V. (eds), *Being and Value in Technology* (pp. 45-59). Palgrave Macmillan. https://doi.org/10.1007/978-3-030-88793-3_3 ,

Ferretti, A., & Ienca, M. (2018). Enhanced cognition, enhanced self? On neuroenhancement and subjectivity. *Journal of Cognitive Enhancement, 2*, 348–355.

Foster, L., James, D., & Haake, S. (2012). Influence of full body swimsuits on competitive performance. *Procedia Engineering, 34*, 712–717.

Fouché, R. (2017). *Game changer: The technoscientific revolution in sports*. JHU Press.

Gao, Z., Li, Y., & Wang, Z. (2020). Restoring the real world records in Men's swimming without high-tech swimsuits. *Journal of Quantitative Analysis in Sports, 16*(4), 291–300.

Herr, H., Whiteley, G. P., & Childress, D. (2003). Cyborg technology--biomimetic orthotic and prosthetic technology. *Biologically Inspired Intelligent Robots,* 103–143.

Heinrichs, J.-H. (2017). Against strong ethical parity: Situated cognition theses and transcranial brain stimulation. *Frontiers in Human Neuroscience, 11*(171), 1–13.

Heinrichs, J.-H. (2021). Neuroethics, cognitive technologies and the extended mind perspective. *Neuroethics, 14*(1), 59–72. https://doi.org/10.1007/s12152-018-9365-8

Hernández-Orallo, J., & Vold. K. (2019). AI extenders: The ethical and societal implications of humans cognitively extended by AI. In *Proceedings of the 2019 AAAI/ACM conference on AI, ethics, and society (AIES '19). Association for computing machinery* (pp. 507–513). New York. https://doi.org/10.1145/3306618.3314238

Howe, P. D., & Jones, C. (2006). Classification of disabled athletes: (Dis) empowering the Paralympic practice community. *Sociology of Sport Journal, 23*(1), 29–46.

Hwang, H-J., Kim, S., Choi, S., & Im, C-H. (2013). EEG-based brain-computer interfaces. A thorough literature survey. *International Journal of Human Computer Interaction, 29,* 814–826.

Jaeger, L., Baptista, R. D. S., Basla, C., Capsi-Morales, P., Kim, Y. K., Nakajima, S., ... & Sigrist, R. (2023). How the CYBATHLON competition has advanced assistive technologies. *Annual Review of Control, Robotics, and Autonomous Systems, 6*(1), 447–476.

Kessel, A. (2012, August 5). London 2012: Greg Rutherford strikes gold after 17 hamstring tears. The Guardian. https://www.theguardian.com/sport/2012/aug/05/london-2012-greg-rutherford-gold

Kirchner, F. (2023). Robotics and AI: How technology may change the way we shape our bodies and what this does to the mind. InSchmidt, S. L. (Ed.) *21st century sports: How technologies will change sports in the digital age* (pp. 87–104). Springer International Publishing.

Kitano, H., Asada, M., Kuniyoshi, Y., Noda, I., Osawa, E., & Matsubara, H. (1997). RoboCup: A challenge problem for AI. *AI Magazine, 18*(1), 73. https://doi.org/10.1609/aimag.v18i1.1276

Loland, S. (2006). Olympic sport and the ideal of sustainable development. *Journal of the Philosophy of Sport,* 33(2), 144–156.

Lopez Frias, F. J. (2017). The defining components of the cyborg: Cyborg-athletes, fictional or real?. In *Sport and play in a digital world* (pp. 97–111). Routledge.

Lopez Frias, F. J. (2018). Walking into the cyborg gym: Two conceptions of the cyborg athlete. Teknokultura, 15(1), 105–117.

Lima, V. M. (2022). Transhumanism and the phenomenology of cyborg senses. *The Routledge Handbook of Digital Consumption.*

MacDonald, R. (2017). Doping on a hanger: Regulatory lessons from the FINA elimination of the polyurethane swimsuit applied to the international anti-doping paradigm. *Columbia Journal of Law & Social Problems, 51,* 275.

McFarland D. J., & Wolpaw, J. R. (2018). Brain-computer interface use is a skill that user and system acquire together. *PLOS Biology, 16*(7), e2006719. https://doi.org/10.1371/journal.pbio.2006719

Murray, T. H. (2009). In search of an ethics of sport: Genetic hierarchies, handicappers general, and embodied excellence. In T. H. Murray, K. Maschke, & A. A. Wasunna (Eds.), *Performance-enhancing technologies in sports* (pp. 225–238.). Johns Hopkins University Press

Norman, M. E., & Moola, F. (2011). 'Bladerunner or boundary runner'?: Oscar Pistorius, cyborg transgressions and strategies of containment. *Sport in Society, 14*(9), 1265–1279.

Patil, A., Jain, N., Agrahari, R., Hossari, M., Orlandi, F., & Dev, S. (2023). A data-driven analysis of formula 1 car races outcome. In L. Longo, & R. O'Reilly (Eds.), Artificial intelligence and cognitive science. AICS 2022. Communications in computer and information science, vol 1662. Springer. https://doi.org/10.1007/978-3-031-26438-2_11

Peksa, J., & Mamchur, D. (2023). State-of-the-art on brain-computer interface technology. *Sensors, 23*(13), 6001. https://doi.org/10.3390/s23136001

Pielli, L., & Zlatev, J. (2020). The cyborg body: Potentials and limits of a body with prosthetic limbs. *Cognitive Semiotics, 13*(2), 20202033.

Pielke, R. J. (2016). Get ready for the coming wave of technologically enhanced athletes. *The Guardian,* August 3, 2016. https://www.theguardian.com/science/political-science/2016/aug/03/get-ready-for-the-coming-wave-of-technologically-enhanced-athletes

Pielke, R. J. (2020). The blade runner and the burden of proof. *The Honest Broker Blog,* November 2, 2020. https://rogerpielkejr.substack.com/p/the-blade-runner-and-the-burden-of

Purdue, D. E., & Howe, P. D. (2013). Who's in and who is out? Legitimate bodies within the Paralympic Games. *Sociology of Sport Journal, 30*(1), 24–40.

Qi, Y., Sun, Y., Liu, Q., Zhang, Q., Cai, H., Zheng, Q.. (2023). The intersection of artificial intelligence and brain for high-performance neuroprosthesis and cyborg systems. *Frontiers in Neuroscience*, 17, 1133002.

Richard, R., & Andrieu, B. (2019). The Cybathlon experience: Beyond transhumanism to capability hybridization. *Journal of the Philosophy of Sport, 46*(1), 49–62.

Rogers, E. A., Carney, M. E., Yeon, S. H., Clites, T. R., Solav, D., & Herr, H. M. (2021). An ankle-foot prosthesis for rock climbing augmentation. IEEE Transactions on Neural Systems and Rehabilitation Engineering, 29, 41–51. https://doi.org/10.1109/TNSRE.2020.3033474

Romanska, M. (2024). The bionic body: Disability, technology and posthumanism. *Body, Space & Technology, 23*(1).

Rupert, R. (2009). *Cognitive systems and the extended mind.* Oxford University Press, 1–17.https://doi.org/10.16995/bst.11480

Shaffer, A., Naik, A., Bederson, M., Arnold, P. M., & Hassaneen, W. (2023). Efficacy of deep brain stimulation for the treatment of anorexia nervosa: A systematic review and network meta-analysis of patient-level data. *Neurosurgical Focus, 54*(2), E5.

Shu, T., Herrera-Arcos, G., Taylor, C. R., & Herr, H. M. (2024). Mechanoneural interfaces for bionic integration. *Nature Reviews Bioengineering*, 2, 374–391.

Siegel, J., & Morris, D. (2020). Robotics, automation, and the future of sports. *21st century sports: How technologies will change sports in the digital age*, 53–72.

Smith, A., & Thomas, N. (2016). The politics and policy of inclusion and technology in Paralympic sport: beyond Pistorius. In The'Olympic and Paralympic' Effect on Public Policy (pp. 97-110). Routledge.

Steels, L. (1995). When are robots intelligent autonomous agents. *Robotics and Autonomous Systems, 15*, 3–9.

Srinivasan, S., & Herr, H. M. (2022). A cutaneous mechanoneural interface for neuroprosthetic feedback. Nature Biomedical Engineering, 6(6), 731–740.

Swartz, L., Bantjes, J., Rall, D., Ferreira, S., Blauwet, C., & Derman, W. (2016). "A more equitable society": The politics of global fairness in Paralympic sport. *PloS One, 11*(12), e0167481.

Tesink, V., Douglas, T., Forsberg, L., Ligthart, S., Meynen, G. (2024). Right to mental integrity and neurotechnologies: Implications of the extended mind thesis. *Journal of Medical Ethics. 50*(10), 656-663. https://doi.org/10.1136/jme-2023-109645

Turing, A. M. (1950). Computing machinery and intelligence. *Mind, 59*, 433–460. (reprinted in J. Copeland (Ed.), *The essential Turing* (pp. 441–464), Oxford University Press, 2004).

Viret, M. (2022). CAS 2020/A/6807, Blake Leeper v. IAAF, award of October 23, 2020. In A. Duval & A. Rigozzi (Eds.), *Yearbook of international sports arbitration 2018–2020. Yearbook of international sports arbitration*. T.M.C. Asser Press. https://doi.org/10.1007/15757_2022_45

World Para Athletics Classification Rules and Regulations (2023). https://www.paralympic.org/sites/default/files/2024-07/2023_02_17%20WPA%20Classification%20Rules%20and%20Regulations_Edition%20February%202023_Final%20%282%29.pdf

Chapter 8

The Ethical-Educational Aspects of Neurodoping

Barbora Badurova and Daniela Kováčová

8.1 Introduction

Neurodoping is a relatively new area of improvement in sports. In this context, it can be broadly understood as a certain brain stimulation to improve athletic performance. This brain stimulation has to be external and artificial and not generated by the brain itself, thanks to natural internal neuroplasticity, as there can be some changes in the brain occurring naturally, thanks to training, nutrition, health issues, etc. (Mohammadi, 2016). However, of course, the ambiguity of the understanding of what is, for instance, artificial and natural (Siipi, 2008) and internal and external can be open for discussion; we will leave it here for intuitive understanding. Also, as other chapters of the book suggest, the problem of cyborgization makes it sometimes difficult to draw a clear line between internal and external neuroenhancement.

Neurodoping brain enhancers are usually in the form of chemical substances – drugs (such as Ritaline) or neurological stimulation that uses mostly the so-called transcranial magnetic stimulation (TMS), transcranial current stimulation (TCS), or transcranial direct-current stimulation (tDCS). In the literature, this distinction is captured in terms of the narrow and broader concepts of neurodoping. Authors such as Thomas S. Petersen and Kasper Lippert-Rasmussen (2021) conceptualize neurodoping more broadly. According to their opinion, neurodoping also includes brain-boosting drugs such as Ritalin and Modafinil. K. Park, a representative of a narrow understanding of neurodoping, points out that a narrower view of neurodoping as tDCS is similar in its implications: "they are similar to the effects of brain-boosting drugs such as modafinil, methylphenidate, and dextroamphetamine. These drugs are used illicitly and off-label to chemically enhance athletic performance and can influence the moment that decides victory or defeat within top competitions" (Park, 2017, p. 2).

In this chapter, we will focus primarily on TCS, and we will not consider the neurodoping based on chemical substances. Transcranial Current Stimulations (TCSs) "are non-invasive brain stimulation techniques which

DOI: 10.4324/9781003520290-9

modulate cortical excitability and spontaneous brain activity by the application of weak electric currents through the scalp, in a safe, economic, and well-tolerated manner" (Annarumma et al., 2018). At the same time, there exist invasive methods of brain enhancement, but we will not focus on them here. But some other parts of the book also deal with them.

Similar to other forms of (neuro)doping, TCS has also been used for medical purposes for treating, for instance, depression (Brunon et al., 2016). At the same time, just like other types of doping, this also can open up the question of access to it (if classified as doping), as some may use it for medical reasons. We will focus, however, primarily on the neurodoping in relation to sport and not that much on the other areas of use, although sometimes they may overlap. In the following chapter, we will first sketch the benefits and risks of neurodoping, then point out the problem of detection, and then consider the educational context of the issue.

The neurodoping has the potential to help athletes achieve to a greater extent the ideal of the sporting imperative and the Olympic motto: Citius, Altius, Fortius – Faster, Higher, Stronger; however, it is not that clear whether it is always desirable as it also has its dark side, as it can, for example, put many athletes at a disadvantage and potentially undermine the idea of sport as a fair play. Moreover, this type of doping is even more difficult to detect, so the call for fair detection and punishment by the authorities does not seem to be sufficient. We will deal with these issues in the following lines.

8.2 The Benefits of Neurodoping

It is self-evident that the motivation to use neurodoping is based on the expectation of certain benefits. In this section, we will not make any distinction between "neurodoping" with morally negative connotations and more neutral "neurostimulation" or "neuroenhancement" but prefer to use the term "neurodoping." So, what are the benefits of neurodoping? It seems that neurodoping brings, among others, especially these advantages to athletes:

- Quicker acquisition of skills and the retention of such skills, which is useful as it makes learning and training quicker and more efficient so it has the potential to save time (Park & Girginov, 2017).
- The reaction time is shorter, which may be beneficial in most sports to take advantage of competitors (Park & Girginov, 2017).
- Also, mental stamina enhancement can be useful in sports such as chess (Shaw, 2021).
- Motivation enhancement is another advantage of neurodoping, which can increase the willingness to train harder and longer and to feel more energy (Bowman-Smart, 2021).

- Suppression of tremor is another significant benefit for athletes (Carrio Sampedro & Pérez Triviño, 2017; Park & Girginov, 2017).
- Another enticing advantage is that there are also often cited minimal side effects for the user (Park & Girginov, 2017).

However, it is worth noting that in order to achieve these benefits, it requires regular training. Similar to other doping means, neurodoping offers improvement but not miraculous results, that is, it will not make a top-level athlete from an untrained individual without any additional effort or good genetic predisposition (Carrio Sampedro & Pérez Triviño, 2017; Park & Girginov, 2017). These immediate benefits, of course, potentially lead to other possible benefits such as winning, becoming rich, becoming famous, popular, etc., which may influence the motivation for using it. The benefits may consequently also have an impact on the other people around the athlete using neurodoping.

It may be interesting to mention that some authors point out that there are actually no significant effects of neurodoping in improving exercise performance (Holgado, Vadillo, & Sanabria, 2019). For the sake of the text, we will not doubt the effect of neurodoping on performance enhancement as we are focusing on the moral aspects of such enhancement, which, if not now, have the potential to open up similar discussions in the future.

8.3 The Dark Side of Neurodoping

Unfortunately, although the side effects of neurodoping are often presented as minimal, there are still certain risks and potential negative effects of it (for discussion on risks of doping in a broader sense, see, e.g., MacGregor & McNamee, 2011). The dangers of neurodoping can be grouped into two categories – negative impact on those who use it and negative impact on those who don't use it.

The neurodoping, despite the optimistic hopes of some proponents, also poses some potentially negative impact on the users since the outcome is still experimental and therefore the long-term risks are still unclear (Park & Girginov, 2017). It can cause health risks for athletes (or possibly even amateur users), which can cause harm to a smaller or greater extent – one of the mentioned risks is lowering the IQ of the user (Park & Girginov, 2017). Moreover, the procedure is costly and results are not certain so it also poses financial risks (Park & Girginov, 2017).

On the moral side, there are other questionable things related to neurodoping and the aim, and why it is used. For instance, the goal can be to achieve better results, win, entertain others, make money, or become famous. But the question is whether the athletes should do it at any cost. And there is an open question – is it good? This may be related to the concept of virtue ethics, which we will mention later in the chapter. The possible motivation behind using neurodoping – I want to get better, I want to outperform others, I want to win, I want to try it – should then also be examined from a moral point of view. The possibility of using and developing new forms of neurodoping raises controversy over the possibility of irreversible changes in human behavior with macrosocial consequences, e.g., in the form of even increased pressure to perform.

If we consider the risks and potential negative outcomes for others, not just the athletes, we can consider several impacts. It is often mentioned that the negative outcome of neurodoping is also related to the impact on those who don't use it, namely, in creating unequal or unfair competition. And that the neurodoping violates the spirit of sport, for instance, appeals to naturalness often take place, just like fairness or justice. As it has been critically discussed by Petersen and Lippert-Rasmussen (2021), it is often pointed out that "legalizing neuro-doping will result in some enjoying an unfair advantage over others" (Petersen & Lippert-Rasmussen, 2021). From a financial point of view and the point of view of labor, there is also a problem of "the unfair health care costs imposed on everyone as a result of athletes' use of neuro-doping" (Petersen & Lippert-Rasmussen, 2021).

However, these concepts that are often mentioned in relation to the disadvantages of neurodoping are quite ambiguous and can often lead to different conclusions. At first sight, it may look obvious that neurodoping, similar to other types of doping, is clearly undermining the concept of fairness. Nevertheless, for instance, Tännsjö (2021) interestingly points out that neurodoping can actually help to make sports more fair in helping to overcome the natural disadvantages of some individuals (Tännsjö, 2021). Similarly, as stated by Verner Møller and Ask Vest Christiansen (2021) "neuro-doping cannot be considered a threat to the integrity of sport," and moreover, they suggest that "neuro-stimulation techniques become an effective performance-enhancing mean in sport" (Møller & Christiansen, 2021).

It is worth mentioning that the discussion on the issue of fairness in relation to neurodoping is very fruitful, and thus it points to the complexity of the problem. Arguments invoking fairness range from equality of conditions (Park & Girginov, 2017) to equality of opportunity (Lenk, 2007), operating on the assumption that neurodoping will fundamentally undermine this equality, thereby establishing unfair conditions and opportunities that will systematically favor, for example, athletes from richer countries. Consequently, the neurodoping should be banned. The question remains, however, whether the concept of fairness with which the given arguments work is defensible in the light of the development of contemporary sport beyond the issue of neurodoping, as also pointed out by the above-mentioned pair of authors. The discussion about the similar issues as sketched above opens the problem of the aim of the sport as such.

8.4 The Problem of Detection

Following the problem with the risks and possible negative impact of neurodoping, there is another catch – the problem of detection. Traditionally, there are mostly two ways used in order to detect certain banned substances classified as doping – blood tests and urine tests. (Anti-Doping, 2024a; Ponzetto et al., 2016; Faiss et al., 2019).

However, as neurodoping is of a slightly different nature, unlike many other forms of doping, it cannot be so easily detected by these means and by the sample of biological fluids. Moreover, in the current state of neurodoping the possibilities of detection are minimal. However, some authors also deal with the possibility that it may be more available in the future by the use of artificial intelligence (Petersen et al., 2024).

Nowadays, there is also the possibility of using Magnetic Resonance Spectroscopy (MRS), "which is a technique that can detect alterations of concentrations of related metabolites and neurotransmitters—that may possess the ability to detect neuro-doping" (Park & Girginov, 2017, p. 5). However, the likelihood of using the technique regularly is minimal due to its extremely high costs, which can be around $1 million per year, which is 10% of WADA's annual budget for doping (Park & Girginov, 2017).

Due to the high costs and insufficient reliability, the problem of detection using even the above-mentioned techniques remains open as their reliability is still not sufficient. As pointed out by Park and Girginov (2017, p. 6): "All of this makes tDCS look to athletes—who want to get around the anti-doping policy—like perhaps the ideal source of performance enhancement." But as we have mentioned, it is not ideal in the sense of lacking potential risks.

Therefore, in order to prevent neurodoping from causing harm, we have to use other ways. One of the options is (ethics) education that we will deal with in the following part. The issue also opens questions for alternative ways of regulation – not just external but also internal, and the approach to the issue can be strengthening of the own responsibility of a moral agent.

8.5 Education as a Part of the Solution

As sketched above neurodoping, although having many possible advantages, poses also some risks and not just for the user but also for others. The external regulation and punishment of it by the authorities such as WADA is for many reasons problematic as it practically cannot be detected and thus enforced. Therefore, the approach to the issue can be to strengthen the own responsibility of moral agents through education. This, however, can complement other forms of regulation. The education can target the athletes and other stakeholders to discourage or at least inform and de-incentivize neurodoping rather than just punish it. We have already sketched the answer to the question of why to teach neurodoping issues above. Now we will try to answer other related questions – How to teach neurodoping issues? And to whom? Education in the ethical aspects of neurodoping is presented as an area with the potential to enhance individual responsibility and the ability to make sound moral judgments. We will attempt to highlight the importance of virtue ethics as a theoretical starting point, framing an ethical-educational approach to the issue of neurodoping.

It is well known that WADA represents a respected organization for the regulation of doping and it also organizes anti-doping education (Anti-Doping, 2024b; Cléret, 2011). The legal framework constitutes the regulation of doping based on law. However, there is still room for ethical considerations that may even to a greater or smaller extent differ from the legal ones. There is then the question of what kind of approach to education to adopt. Should it be more traditional anti-doping education? Should education related to neurodoping be focused only on the prevention of doping, that is, in the sense of anti-doping education, or are there other possibilities? The risks and benefits of neurodoping mentioned in the previous part of the text as well as the fruitful discussion about them show that the problem is multidimensional. It is not that easy to make a clear verdict and to, for instance, ban the neurodoping in sport. As it is possible to see in the other chapters of the book, the moral evaluation of neurodoping is complex. Along with the problem of various types of sports and variations of neurodoping, there is a variety of situations so the guidelines have to consider the multitude of possible applications. The negative impact on health can probably be quite straightforwardly understood as wrong, some of the other impacts can be more questionable in determining their moral value. Moreover, the problem is evolving, and the discussion about finding the best solution is still relevant. Therefore, it is questionable whether training only in legal rules and regulations would be sufficient.

Similarly, anti-doping education in general was thematized, for instance, by Petróczi and Boardley (2022), who suggest that anti-doping should be understood as a wicked problem. They claim, however, that "Wicked problems, such as doping, cannot be solved but they can be tamed" (Petróczi and Boardley, 2022, p. 12). And they suggest an educational model as a solution (Petróczi and Boardley, 2022). But if someone makes the conscious decision to dope, knowledge will have, according to Woolf (2020, Conclusion), no impact: "However, a baseline level of information is not only desirable, it is mandated by both WADA and the Charter of Athletes Rights. Furthermore [...] it is necessary for developing mental models." We propose that educational programs anchored in a virtue ethics approach can be an effective tool for the development of these mental models.

We also perceive the problem of neurodoping as complex, as presented by the authors above. Therefore, we assume that education focused on the promotion of critical thinking is relevant to ethics education in relation to neurodoping. The moral nature is complicated, and mere indoctrination is often not persuasive or motivational for learners (Woolf, 2020; Houlihan,

2008). If the education is focused only on indoctrination and mechanical understanding of legal rules and teaching prevention of doping, it doesn't take into account the complexity of the issue of doping and its various forms, and the evolving nature of the problem. On the other hand, if it is too much focused on its own attitudes to doping of students without considering the legal framework, it is also not very useful for the practical application.

8.5.1 *Virtue Ethics in Neurodoping Education*

We assume that the mentioned approach to education can benefit from virtue ethics and is fully compatible with the desirable development of virtues. One of the advantages is that virtue ethics considers not only the individual but also the wider community framework, which is significant from the point of view of the ethical analysis of the neurodoping. The virtue ethics education in relation to the neurodoping ideally takes into account the cognitive, affective, and conative dimensions of education. The approach considers the outcomes and reasons but also the emotional part of the actions. Since a truly virtuous person acts based on the right reasons and at the same time has the correct feelings. Actions that only resemble virtuous actions from outside solely based on the consequences are not fully virtuous if there is no correct reason and feelings. For example, in order to be able to call someone honest, the person has to speak the truth but not regardless of the reason. Speaking truth merely because of fear of being caught or to impress someone doesn't count as truly virtuous based on virtue ethics (Baďurová, 2018, p. 68). Virtue ethics is also interesting in relation to sports in the sense of ethical perfectionism where the goal of sport is physical improvement and from the point of view of virtue ethics, it is moral perfection. Čović (2021, p. 11) points out that already the ancient Greeks "used sport to promote and nurture virtues and proper humanistic values."

In the following text, we will try to outline the problematic nature of neurodoping in terms of mostly four neuralgic points of this theoretical approach – the concept of virtue, the concept of moral integrity, the broader social framework, and the impact of moral role models (not just) for younger generations. In general, virtue ethics emphasizes the development of an agent's good character through virtue-oriented action. The cardinal virtues include: wisdom, courage, justice, and moderation. Despite the existence of various catalogues of virtues, these four are found in each of them. Thus, from the perspective of virtue ethics, we ask whether neurodoping facilitates the development of an actor's good character through the reinforcement of virtues or, conversely, leads to the promotion of non-virtuous action.

If we dwell on the virtues mentioned above, we can think as follows. Wisdom (phronesis) could potentially be improved by the use of neurodoping. If we view it as a set of abilities oriented toward solving certain tasks in order to achieve desirable results through cognitive abilities, then neurodoping could lead to its enhancement. Although as we could see when we mentioned the risks, neurodoping in sport can paradoxically lead to decreased IQ as it is one of the potential side effects of the technology (Park & Girginov, 2017). Wisdom as a virtue, however, appears to us to be something different; it is a cultivated, developed, and continuously present character trait rather than a faculty realized separately over time. In this case, the use of neurodoping could in turn lead to its weakening in the sense of relying on external means instead of working on personal development. This is somewhat more evident with the virtue of temperance (sophrosyne).

The desire for immediate improvement behind neurodoping is inconsistent with the concept of the virtue of moderation, not least because of the omission of possible consequences. This is also problematic in the case of the virtue of justice (dikaiosyne). We may ask, is it fair that better results will be achieved by those who possess certain capabilities, often regardless of their own efforts? But the question is also whether this objection raised against neurodoping is not actually an objection against the already existing state of affairs too. Similarly, in the case of the virtue of courage (andreia). We may ask whether the use of neurodoping is not rather a way of avoiding this virtue. Is it not a shorthand orienting us toward partial performance rather than continuous work on oneself? Some authors point out the necessity of the aspect of effort in order to be able to judge athletic achievements as praiseworthy (Erler, 2021)

Another concept in the virtue ethics perspective that can help us in the ethical analysis of neurodoping is the concept of moral integrity. Virtue ethics emphasize moral integrity in the sense of living authentically in accordance with the virtues. However, if we achieve partial results through ethically questionable means, our moral integrity and the authenticity of our performances and achievements are questionable. As it is possible to see in many aspects, the virtues mentioned above are compatible with anti-doping values education by WADA (Anti-Doping, 2024b).

As we have already mentioned, virtue ethics also takes into account the broader social dimension of the phenomena under study. From what has already been mentioned, it follows that neurodoping has the potential to actively modify social norms and structures, given the possibility of reinforcing inequality or injustice in society. This would reduce the degree of social cohesion and trust in key social institutions such as the education system and others.

It is equally important to reflect on the impact and importance of moral role models (not just) for younger generations. It is suggested that the acceptance of neurodoping may change the perception of the younger generation of the role of ethics and virtue in human life. Thus, it is clear that from the perspective of virtue ethics, the neurodoping is highly controversial. However, the justified conclusion may not be the complete ethical unacceptability of this technology, but rather its strict regulation and monitoring.

8.5.2 *Neurodoping Ethics Education*

Ethics education oriented on virtues can play a crucial role in this regard in relation to the regulation. Education has the potential to provide athletes and coaches with tools and perspectives through which they can identify, evaluate, and resolve ethical problems and dilemmas they encounter in their professional activities, which may be related specifically to neurodoping. Consequently, education and training in ethics appear to be both a tool for solving currently occurring problems and a tool for prevention and education in ethics also within professional sports.

As we have mentioned, the advantage of ethics education in this regard is to raise awareness of ethical dilemmas both at the individual and societal levels. For these purposes, we can work with the method of case studies enriched with an element of discussion or debate (Velema et al., 2023; Klimková, 2015) with the ambition of promoting the development of critical thinking. The critical thinking of individuals is also crucial in the process of ethical decision-making, as it enables us to better weigh and evaluate the various alternatives and the risks involved. Moreover, we can also consider the positive consequences of the development of critical thinking in terms of the stabilization of democratic processes both at the societal level and in individual social institutions such as sports (Kováčová et al., 2022). Moreover, this approach opens the possibility of informing participants about the different types of risks associated with neurodoping, thus fulfilling the ambition of prevention. Education in ethics anchored in the theoretical approach of virtue ethics also facilitates the development of participants' personal virtues, and we can point out the importance of moral role models.

We believe that ethics education programs should be primarily oriented toward youth athletes and their coaches and assistants. This is also reflected in the design of these programs, as Woolf (2020) points out when she notes that guidelines for the design of anti-doping prevention programs have come from other fields that examined behavioral prevention-based interventions, particularly among youth. These educational programs should begin early, be multi-faceted, involve multiple sessions coupled with periodic reinforcement, be peer-led, provide alternatives to drug/doping, and focus on the motivation and character development of the individual, not just as an athlete. However, educational programs should not bypass the adults and wider public either. For this purpose, however, they must be designed slightly differently or appropriately to the age and specification of the group.

Within the various didactic approaches and methods, we would like to highlight the experiential learning approach and specifically its form of game-based learning. This approach we consider to be particularly effective in ethics anti-doping education. Experiential learning is sometimes referred to as "learning through experience," "action-based learning," or "learning by doing." It can be defined as follows:

> Experiential education is a broad term referring to educational approaches that emphasize first-hand participation by learners in a diverse range of activities typically occurring outside of a classroom, but usually under pedagogical supervision. Experiential education generally espouses a constructivist epistemology focusing on interactions between the individual, the task(s), and the learning environment. Constructivist models of experiential education emphasize the learning process and promote reflection on that process, with a view to abstraction and future experiences. Experiential education differs from vocational training and community organizing in its prioritization of subject area mastery, social-emotional growth, communication and teamwork skills, and self-awareness as key outcomes of interest.
>
> (Allison & Seaman, 2017, p. 1)

Thus, we can conclude that experiential learning is the opposite of learning that involves only the mind. The main ambition of this educational strategy is to exert a stronger influence on the attitudes, behavior, and actions of the individual through the experience gained. The key steps in experiential learning form a spiral of – experiencing, reflecting, thinking, acting.

The emphasis on the cultivation of the agent's agency makes this didactic method an appropriate strategy for a didactic approach to the design and implementation of anti-doping education programs. The game-based learning, as a form of experiential learning, is also one of the student-oriented didactic methods that are demonstrably more effective in the educational process than frontal teaching methods. As the name suggests, it focuses on incorporating games into learning. Game-based learning seems to have several advantages – motivational, it supports player engagement and adaptivity, and moreover, it offers room for graceful failure (Plass, Homer, & Kinzer, 2015). It is worth noting that concepts like gamification and playful design are similar to game-based learning. They all promote playfulness and fun as advantages leading to higher motivation and efficiency of learning (Strahovnik et al., 2023). Game-based learning involves using games that are specifically designed to achieve educational goals. It aims to blend academic content with engaging gameplay, helping players understand, remember, and apply what they've learned to real-life situations. (Aberšek, 2016, p. 557). These are some aspects that we can keep in mind when deciding which game to use when and for which group of students. What is the age composition of the group? Do we want to primarily promote the cooperation of the students? Do we want them to make them remember certain things? Do we want to stimulate their creativity? Do we want to reinforce their attitudes, e.g., on doping issues? The game can be a good tool to acquire and consolidate experiences that are crucial for future moral and ethical decision-making. Artificial intelligence (AI) also finds its use in the process of education, which may also be transferred to anti-doping education (see, e.g., Titko and Studená, 2023).

8.6 Conclusion

By appealing to courage, wisdom, justice, and moderation, we strengthen personal moral and ethical integrity. In doing so, we emphasize the authenticity of individual action. In addition, by appealing to fairness, we can reduce the pressure that often leads to the use of neurodoping as a competitive advantage. Comprehensively, this education leads to the promotion of values such as honesty, integrity, and fairness. In this way, we can cultivate the values and attitudes of professional sports through this type of education and also strengthen and create ethical norms regulating the conduct attached to it and shape the various control mechanisms in the form of either codes of ethics, commissions, etc. Ethics education can thus provide us with a framework for understanding the diverse ethical aspects and issues tied to such a complex phenomenon as neurodoping.

It may be objected that there are other ways to reduce the harm caused by neurodoping. For instance, it is also possible to improve the method of neurotechnology so doping will not cause harm. However, as was sketched above, some of the harms are more complex, and it is not clear whether it would be possible to diminish them fully. For instance, the physical harm to the user can be possibly diminished, but the other forms of harm are more questionable. To avoid harming others because of inequal access to this type of doping can be diminished by making it available for all athletes. Also, there is a possibility of using different categories of sports – with or without doping, which would, however, still require an honest approach of the users and stakeholders. We also see many of the other solutions as complementary with our proposed educational approach. However, the approaches above seem to be, at the moment, far from the real-life application.

Another problem can be perceived in the proposed approach to education based on virtue ethics, since the possible disadvantage of the virtue ethics approach to neurodoping education is that virtues are not simply a set of basic moral rules that one can learn and straightforwardly apply to every situation to act virtuously. Instead, they require experience, sensitivity, well-developed practical reasoning, and the ability to grasp the complexity of various situations, a skill that often takes considerable time to cultivate (Athanassoulis, 2018; Baďurová, 2018). However, as we have proposed above, the virtue ethics approach can and should be paired with the more traditional approach to anti-doping education, informing about current anti-doping policy and legislation, which offers more strict guidelines, but at the same time enriched by theemphasis on the promotion of critical thinking of students. The need for critical thinking education has been thematized, for instance, by Ćurko et al. (2022) as they see it relevant, especially in the contemporary digital era. In this regard, the PLATO's EU Philosophical Learning Applied to Online Surroundings in the EU project (http://platos-eu.org/), which highlights the benefits of philosophical learning for both individual character development and community well-being, can be an inspiration for us.

As we have mentioned, the problem with educational activities is individuals who consciously choose to engage in unethical or otherwise unacceptable behaviors and actions due to cognitive dissonance, akrasia, or other reasons (Woolf, 2020; Houlihan, 2008). There we can focus more on the external motivation to act in accordance with legal rules and avoid punishment. An interesting approach is one of Persson and Savulescu (2012), who propose neuroenhancement for treating unethical behavior. We are, however, more reserved to this approach so far due to the experimental nature and unpredictable impact. The educational approach mentioned above should also be concretized by teaching manuals and tested by empirical studies in practice to be able to see the effect on the society (similarly to, for instance, Hurst et al., 2023).

References

Aberšek, B. (2016). Schola Ludus. *Journal of Baltic Science Education, 15*(5), ISSN 1648–3898, 556–558.

Allison, P., & Seaman, J. (2017). Experiential education. In M. Peters (Eds.), *Encyclopedia of educational philosophy and theory*. Springer. https://doi.org/10.1007/978-981-287-532-7_449-1

Annarumma, L., D'Atri, A., Alfonsi, V., & De Gennaro, L. (2018). The efficacy of transcranial current stimulation techniques to modulate resting-atate EEG, to affect vigilance and to promote sleepiness. *Brain Sciences, 8*(7), 137. https://doi.org/10.3390/brainsci8070137

Anti-Doping. (2024a). Anti-doping process. https://www.wada-ama.org/en/athletes-support-personnel/anti-doping-process

Anti-Doping. (2024b). Anti-doping education. https://www.wada-ama.org/en/athletes-support-personnel/anti-doping-education

Athanassoulis, N. (2018). *Virtue ethics*. Internet Encyclopedia of Philosophy. https://www.iep.utm.edu/virtue/#H1

Baďurová, B. (2018). The potential of virtue ethics in ethical education in Slovakia. *METODIČKI OGLEDI, 25*, 2, 67–68

Bowman-Smart, H., Savulescu, J. . (2021). The ethics of motivational neuro-doping in sport: Praiseworthiness and prizeworthiness. *Neuroethics, 14*(Suppl 2), 205–215. https://doi.org/10.1007/s12152-020-09445-5

Brunoni, A. R., Moffa, A. H., Fregni, F., Palm, U., Padberg, F., Blumberger, D. M., Daskalakis, Z. J., Bennabi, D., Haffen, E., Alonzo, A., & Loo, C. K. (2016). Transcranial direct current stimulation for acute major depressive episodes: Meta-analysis of individual patient data. *The British Journal of Psychiatry: The Journal of Mental Science, 208*(6), 522–531. https://doi.org/10.1192/bjp.bp.115.164715

Carrio Sampedro, A., & Pérez Triviño, J. L. (2017). On the compatibility of brain enhancement and the internal values of sport. *Sport, Ethics and Philosophy, 11*(3), 307–322. https://doi.org/10.1080/17511321.2017.1320687

Cléret, L. (2011). The role of anti-doping education in delivering WADA's mission. *International Journal of Sport Policy and Politics, 3*(2), 271–277. https://doi.org/10.1080/19406940.2011.577084

Čović, B. (2021). On contemporary sport as a humanistic value through a bioethical approach. *Pannoniana, V*(I), 9–30.

Ćurko, B., Kovačević, A., & Pavlic, M. (2022). Combining critical thinking with digital skills in european context: An example of project "PLATO'S EU", ICERI2022 Proceedings, pp. 2403–2407.

Erler, A. (2021). Neuro-doping and the value of effort in endurance sports. *Neuroethics, 14*(Suppl 2), 191–203. https://doi.org/10.1007/s12152-020-09450-8

Faiss, R., Saugy, J., & Saugy, M. (2019). Fighting doping in elite sports: Blood for all tests!. *Frontiers in Sports and Active Living, 1*, 30. https://doi.org/10.3389/fspor.2019.00030

Holgado, D., Vadillo, M. A., & Sanabria, D. (2019, April). "Brain-doping," is it a real threat? *Frontiers in Physiology, 10*, Article 483.

Houlihan, B. (2008). Detection and education in anti-doping policy: A review of current issues and an assessment of future prospects. *Hitotsubashi Journal of Arts and Sciences*, 49.

Hurst, P., King, A., Massey, K., Kavussanu, M., & Ring, C. (2023). A national anti-doping education programme reduces doping susceptibility in British athletes. *Psychology of Sport and Exercise, 69.* https://doi.org/10.1016/j.psychsport.2023.102512

Klimková, A. (2015). *Prípadovosť - komunikácia - ekologická etika*. Univerzita Pavla Jozefa Šafárika.

Kováčová, D., Baďurová, B., & Strahovník, V. (2022). Could the universities and philosophy help us create a more democratic society? ICERI2022 Proceedings, pp. 2440–2445.

Lenk, C. (2007). Is enhancement in sport really unfair? Arguments on the concept of competition and equality of opportunities. *Sport, Ethics and Philosophy, 1*(2), 218–228. https://doi.org/10.1080/17511320701425157

MacGregor, O., & McNamee, M. (2011). Harm, risk, and doping analogies: A counter-response to Kious. *Theoretical Medicine and Bioethics, 32*(3), 201–210. https://doi.org/10.1007/s11017-011-9178-9

Mohammadi, A. (2016). Induction of neuroplasticity by transcranial direct current stimulation. *Journal of Biomedical Physics & Engineering,* 6(4), 205–208.

Møller, V., & Christiansen, A. V. (2021). Neuro-doping – A serious threat to the integrity of sport?. *Neuroethics, 14*(Suppl 2), 159–168. https://doi.org/10.1007/s12152-020-09446-4

Park, K., & Girginov, V. (2017). Neuro-doping: The rise of another loophole to get around anti-doping policies. *Cogent Social Sciences, 3*(1). https://doi.org/10.1080/23311886.2017.1360462

Persson, I., & Savulescu, J. (2012). *Unfit for the future: The need for moral enhancement.* Oxford University Press

Petersen, T., Holmen, S., & Ryberg, J. (2024). AI, doping and ethics: On why increasing the effectiveness of detecting doping fraud in sport may be morally wrong. *Journal of Medical Ethics*. Online first 2024, February 21. https://doi.org/10.1136/jme-2023-109721

Petersen, T. S., & Lippert-Rasmussen, K. (2021). Neuro-doping and fairness. *Neuroethics, 14*(Suppl 2), 179–190. https://doi.org/10.1007/s12152-020-09447-3
Petróczi, A., & Boardley, I. D. (2022). The meaning of "clean" in anti-doping education and decision making: Moving toward integrity and conceptual clarity. *Frontiers in Sports and Active Living, 4*, 869704. https://doi.org/10.3389/fspor.2022.869704
Plass, J. L., Homer, B. D., Kinzer, C. H. K. (2015). Foundations of game-based learning. *Educational Psychologist, 50*(4), 258–283. https://doi.org/10.1080/00461520.2015.1122533
Ponzetto, F., Giraud, S., Leuenberger, N., Boccard, J., Nicoli, R., Baume, N., Rudaz, S., & Saugy, M. (2016). Methods for doping detection. *Frontiers of Hormone Research, 47*, 153–167. https://doi.org/10.1159/000445177
Shaw, E. (2021). Neurodoping in chess to enhance mental stamina. *Neuroethics, 14*(Suppl 2), 217–230. https://doi.org/10.1007/s12152-020-09456-2
Siipi, H. (2008). Dimensions of naturalness. *Ethics and the Environment, 13*(1), 71–103. http://www.jstor.org/stable/40339149
Strahovnik, V., Jeglič, U., Miklavčič, J., Weilguny, M., Kovacova, D., Badurova, B., Ćurko, B., & Škifić, F. (2023). *Manual cultivating resilient and responsive persons: A teacher's manual for utilizing philosophical methods for and in digital world.* Belianum.
Tännsjö, T. (2021). Neuro-Doping as a means to avert fascistoid ideology in elite sport. *Neuroethics, 14*(Suppl 2), 169–178. https://doi.org/10.1007/s12152-020-09443-7
Titko, M., & Studená, J. (2023). Problematic moments of implementing virtual reality in the educational process: Climate change education example. ICERI2023 Proceedings, pp. 2251–2257.
Velema, F., van den Berg, D., Kienstra, N. (eds.) (2023). *Debating ethical dilemmas in the classroom.* ISVW Uitgevers
Woolf, J. R. (2020). An examination of anti-doping education initiatives from an educational perspective: Insights and recommendations for improved educational design. *Performance Enhancement & Health*, 8(2–3). https://doi.org/10.1016/j.peh.2020.100178

Chapter 9

You Need Guidance?

On the Benefits and Challenges of Ethical Guidelines on AI Used to Detect (Neuro-) doping Fraud in Sport

Thomas Søbirk Petersen

9.1 Introduction

The use of artificial intelligence (AI) in sport is already prevalent, and it is easy to predict that its use will increase over the next decades. AI is used in sport for a variety of reasons. For example, an AI system can collect and analyse huge amounts of data (e.g., data concerning endurance, technique, tactics, health, genetics, sleep and diet), that can be used to improve training, competition and restitution, and to prevent injury (Carrio Sampedro, 2021). However, and more relevant for this chapter, promising studies have shown that using AI systems to handle big datasets can increase the efficiency and reliability of detecting doping fraud[1] compared to the current use of non-AI tools (Saar University, 2022 and Rahman et al. 2022). By the term doping, I understand the more than 300 substances and methods that are listed on the World Anti-Doping Agency's prohibited list (WADA, 2023, and Petersen 2021a). Some of these substances may enhance the athlete's attention span (e.g., Ritalin), or reduce physical symptoms of nervousness (beta blockers) (WADA, 2021). It has been standard to label these kinds of drugs for neuroenhancement or "neuro-doping". Neuro-doping has been contrasted to "physical doping" which includes, for example, the use of steroids in order to improve muscle mass and speed or the use of EPO or blood-doping to improve endurance (Petersen, 2021).

However, the use of AI to increase the detection rate of doping fraud in sport also raises some ethical challenges. First, the data collected and handled by an AI system has the potential to be misused. For example, data fed into the AI system may be incorrect and the output may be incorrectly analysed or interpreted, which potentially may result in innocent athletes being punished. Moreover, information about certain minority groups of athletes may be overrepresented in the data that is fed into the AI system, which may put people from minority groups at greater risk of being caught in doping fraud than the majority of athletes. Further, the collection of personal data concerning diet, health and whereabouts may, if not protected properly, violate the privacy of athletes.

DOI: 10.4324/9781003520290-10

To minimise the risk of AI being used in a way that is morally problematic, one instrument being employed is to introduce a set of ethical guidelines for the use of AI.[2] One clear example of this strategy is the *Ethics Guidelines for Trustworthy AI* (European Commission, 2019). According to these guidelines, the use of AI should comply with ethical principles such as accuracy, respect for autonomy and privacy, prevention of harm, non-discrimination and transparency. However, as some scholars and the EU Commission have pointed out, there are challenges to the use of such guidelines. For example, values such as the above-mentioned may be in conflict with one another. Imagine, for example, that the supportive use of AI for the detection of doping fraud turns out to be more accurate or robust (e.g., that it delivers fewer false positives and fewer false negatives) compared to those who try to detect doping fraud by *not* using AI as a supporting tool. Imagine also that, at the same time, it is clear that it is not transparent concerning precisely which features (e.g., race, religion, income, whereabouts and ethnicity) are fed into the algorithm, nor how these features are weighed in order to produce an evaluation of the risk that an athlete has committed doping fraud. Imagine, furthermore, that the company or organisation that has produced the algorithm wants to keep details about which features are fed into the algorithm as a trade secret in order to safeguard its profitability – because, if there is transparency on this point, the company will be unlikely to spend time developing and selling a more accurate algorithmic tool. Finally, imagine there exists no better alternative, meaning that access to a more transparent and at least just as accurate an algorithm to detect people committing fraud is not available. In such a case – let us call it *the accuracy vs transparency case* – there is a conflict between accuracy and transparency, in the sense that you cannot comply with one without violating the other.[3] The aim of this chapter is to articulate and critically discuss different answers to the following question: When it comes to implementing ethical guidelines for the use of AI in detecting doping fraud, what are the benefits and what are the challenges (e.g., what to do when the guidelines contain conflicting values)?

In order to prepare the ground for answering these questions, in Section 9.2 I will justify why it is worth spending time discussing these ethical guidelines. I will clarify some of the advantages and disadvantages of using ethical guidelines through an ethical analysis of the use of AI in sport. First, I will argue for the view that the implementation and use of ethical guidelines is morally important for several reasons. Second, I will specify how we should handle possible disadvantages of using ethical guidelines, such as the risk of using them as mere window-dressing. In Section 9.3, I will first differentiate between the kinds of value conflicts that ethical guidelines can invoke. Finally, in Section 9.4, I will critically discuss four different strategies to resolve such conflicts when faced with what I call *genuine value conflicts*. The strategies I will discuss are *metaethical cognitivism, the ranking strategy, value monism* and what I call *the acceptance of conflict view*. I will defend the last view, showing that although the first three views are more satisfying from a theoretical point of view, they are less satisfying than the final view when it comes to real-life decision-making. Section 9.5 summarises and concludes.

9.2 On the Advantages and Disadvantages of Using Ethical Guidelines

There are several advantages of using ethical guidelines in the moral evaluation of AI in the realm of sport. Ethical guidelines incorporate moral values such as accuracy, respect for autonomy and privacy, harm prevention, non-discrimination and transparency. In what follows, I will focus on the following two points: (a) identifying *what values to comply with* when it comes to the use of AI, and (b) providing material for *critical moral reasoning* concerning the use of AI.

One first step in a thoughtful moral evaluation of the use of AI in sport is to be clear about which values political decision-makers, AI-ethicists, the World Anti-Doping Agency (WADA) and the general public believe are important to take into account in order to estimate the moral status of the use of AI to detect doping in sport. Values expressed in ethics guidelines concerning the use of AI can thus direct our attention towards the relevant values. Indeed, few scholars, organisations or politicians would say that we should not care about values like accuracy, autonomy, harm prevention, non-discrimination and transparency. Rather, some researchers have stated: "This list of criteria [in ethical guidelines for the use of AI/machine learning] ... serves as a small sample of what an increasingly computerized society should be thinking about" (Bostrom & Yudkowsky, 2014). However, the mere existence and knowledge of these values does little in itself to bring about critical reasoning on AI.

This brings us to the second step, which involves directing our attention to such guidelines, so that we can be equipped with ammunition for the critical reasoning necessary for the moral evaluation of a certain use of AI. Consulting such guidelines and trying to estimate to what extent a specific use of AI complies with these guidelines can make us stop, think and discuss whether this use is morally acceptable, morally unacceptable or morally obligatory. As, for example, Morley et al. (2019, p. 3) have argued, such guidelines can be used as normative constraints for "the 'dos and don'ts' of algorithmic use in society". Therefore, the move from (1) identification of important values to (2) moral, critical discussion about these values, is important if we want to harvest the possible benefits of AI and minimise the possibility of initiating "ethical misuse or scandals" in the wake of AI use in the world of sport.

However, before I present different kinds of conflict problems in Section 9.3 and discuss different strategies to resolve genuine value conflicts in Section 9.4, we can begin by challenging the existence and use of ethical guidelines in some obvious ways. First, there is the challenge that the mere existence of such guidelines will lead to, for example, *ethics shopping* or alternatively to *ethical whitewashing*. Ethics shopping is, roughly speaking, the practice of picking and choosing ethical principles from among a variety of such principles in order to justify one's behaviour *a posteriori*, "instead of implementing or improving new behaviours by benchmarking them against public, ethical standards [e.g. ethical guidelines concerning AI]" (Floridi, 2019, p. 186). Ethical whitewashing (or *ethical window-dressing*) is, roughly speaking, the practice of making "misleading claims ... or implementing superficial measures" in order to defend one's practice and thereby make it appear more ethical than it is in reality (Floridi, 2019, p. 186).

Although these are serious challenges, I will not deal with these and related issues in any detail since several scholars within the fields of; for example, Computer Ethics and Business Ethics have already tried to answer how we should handle these types of challenges to which ethical guidelines are subject (see, e.g., Bowie, 2017 and Floridi, 2019). Concerning *ethics shopping,* the solution, according to Floridi, is to establish a shared, clear, authoritative and publicly accepted standard of what counts as morally good AI (Floridi, 2019, p. 187). A big improvement in this direction is the European Commission's *Ethics Guidelines for Trustworthy AI*, with which anyone in the EU ideally ought to comply with (European Commission, 2019).[4] The main solutions to ethical whitewashing are, according to Floridi (2019), among other scholars, transparency and education. Transparency means providing clear evidence that the development and use of AI does not violate values such as accuracy, non-discrimination and respect for privacy. A further strategy for minimising ethical whitewashing is educating the public and politicians, and having established professional ethical boards to deal with monitoring whether the values in the guidelines are actually implemented in the development and use of AI. However, even if ethical guidelines do not result in ethics shopping and do not (only) function as window-dressing, problems remain.

Apart from the above-mentioned criticism, the traditional philosophical criticism of ethical guidelines builds on the premise that the values are described in very vague terms, and furthermore, can be in conflict with one another. Moreover, insofar as this is true, such guidelines may therefore not provide much support for us when it comes to action-guiding. If it turns out that guidelines cannot really guide us, they are not of much use in the ethical evaluation of the use of AI in sport. In the next section, I will briefly elaborate on the problems of conceptual vagueness and conflicting values. This work is important in order to set the stage for Section 9.4, in which a critical discussion of several answers and solutions to the challenges of conflicting values will be the subject of inquiry.

9.3 The Challenges of Conflicting Values

In what follows, I suggest that we differentiate between three kinds of possible value conflicts when we want to apply ethical guidelines in the ethical evaluation of the use of AI in sport. These three kinds of conflict I shall call *conceptual conflicts*, *internal conflicts* and *external conflicts*. Let me present them, and make it clear why I will primarily discuss different kinds of answers to how we can solve the latter two kinds of conflicts.

A conflict can arise within one single value. The existence of such a conflict – which we can call a conceptual conflict – is due to different kinds of interpretations of the single value in question. As an example, take the value "respect for autonomy". If we want to know whether, for example, the use of AI to detect doping fraud is violating the autonomy of athletes, we need to know what we mean by the term "autonomy". One way to clarify what is meant by autonomy is to underline that it involves some kind of informed consent. However, there can be different notions of what is meant by informed consent. For example, how much information should be given to the athletes in order for them to accept that their personal information can be used in the detection of doping fraud? Should the information be given orally or in writing or both? Should the consent be given orally or in writing or both? In the philosophical literature, there are several examples of how different interpretations of the same value (such as autonomy or transparency) entailed in these ethical guidelines can lead to conflicts in estimating their meaning (for the former see Pugh, 2020, for the latter see, e.g., Ryberg, 2022). The existence of these types of conflicts makes it difficult to know in advance whether the use of AI is sufficiently transparent or non-discriminatory, for instance.

One obvious solution to this conceptual conflict is to try to specify what understanding of, for example, "autonomy" or "transparency" one adheres to. Nevertheless, this is not as easy as it may sound. This is because there are different interpretations of each value and because, from an epistemic point of view, it may be difficult to know how, for example, a producer or a user of AI understands the term "autonomy". However, with a specification of a value such as respect for autonomy, we at least know where to look in order to know if a user of AI complies with such a value or not.

We shall now turn our attention to the two other kinds of conflict, which I call internal and external conflicts. Unlike conceptual conflicts, these two kinds of conflict arise not within one value, but between different kinds of values. Let us begin with examples of internal conflicts. Imagine a case where AI will improve the detection of doping fraud , but will at the same time violate respect for autonomy, because what is fed into the algorithm is personal data about, e.g., health and genetics that the athletes have not given consent to. Such a conflict may be easily resolved, most obviously by making athletes consent to the use of their personal data. However, what if this is impossible for practical reasons (e.g., because of time or money), or if for their own moral reasons people do not wish to consent? If this is the case, we have a genuine conflict. A conflict where we cannot satisfy one value (e.g. preventing harm) by using AI to detect doping fraud, without violating another value (autonomy).

We need to know what to do in such cases. We need to know whether it makes sense to say that a specific use of AI complies successfully with the values embedded in the relevant ethical guidelines in cases where we "cannot have it all", so to speak (such as the case just mentioned as well as the accuracy vs transparency case mentioned in the introduction).

Furthermore, other kinds of conflict, let us call them external conflicts, can occur if there is a conflict between some of the values listed in the ethical guidelines and other values that are *not* listed in the guidelines. An example of this might be if the values of transparency and autonomy are satisfied in the development and use of AI to detect doping in sport, but somehow its use has negative consequences for the well-being of most citizens, and the value "maximise well-being of those who are affect by AI measures" is not part of the guidelines.[5]

Therefore, if we accept that both internal and external value conflicts do exist, it is of practical importance to know how we should deal with this if we want to apply ethical guidelines in the moral evaluation of the use of AI in sport. One could argue here that if there is a conflict between certain values in the application of AI, then it should not be used. But the problem with this kind of reasoning is that if we do not allow for any conflict between the values in ethical guidelines for AI, then we should probably never use AI at all (whether in sport or otherwise). However, few would accept this stance, as AI can be of tremendous help within the realm of sport. In what follows, I will only focus on examples of internal conflicts because external conflicts can easily be translated into internal conflicts when those who have worked out the guidelines can accept that a value that is not presented in their guidelines should in fact be incorporated. At least, this is my own experience after working on several ethical councils for the state or for private organisations.

9.4 Strategies for Dealing with Value Conflicts

So, what are we to do when there are conflicting values in ethical guidelines for the use of AI in detecting doping fraud? This question can be interpreted as a more concrete version of a traditional and general question within normative ethics that arises for all ethical theories that accommodate the existence of more than one intrinsic value. I shall therefore draw from some of this literature on this subject to answer our more concrete question. In what follows, I will present and critically discuss four different kinds of strategies:

metaethical cognitivism, the ranking view, value monism and *the acceptance of conflict view*.

However, before we move on to the investigation of these four strategies, we shall keep in mind that when we talk about conflicts between values, we are referring to what we could call *genuine conflicts* rather than *superficial conflicts* between values. Genuine conflicts between values are those that, unlike superficial conflicts, cannot be solved by a deeper understanding or specification of the values in question. One example of a genuine conflict between values might be the conflict between accuracy and transparency mentioned in the introduction. A conflict of values leads us to perform incompatible actions, where each value obligates us to do something we can do, but where we cannot fulfil both values because if we fulfil one, we cannot fulfil the other.[6] On the other hand, a superficial conflict between values is an alleged conflict between values that evaporates when we specify the contents of the values in question. As an example of how a conflict between values could be a superficial conflict, we can again use the case mentioned in the introduction, the accuracy vs transparency case. In this case, one could argue that there is actually no conflict between accuracy and transparency, because one believes that satisfying the value of transparency, for example, does not mean that everything in the algorithm should be explainable to the public or the athletes.[7] Therefore, not being able to tell the public or athletes everything that is going on in the AI system used to detect doping fraud is not really a break of transparency – at least, if we accept that lack of total transparency is morally right if it means we can detect or prevent doping fraud. When superficial conflicts between relevant values are resolved in the moral evaluation of a certain implementation or use of AI, we can say that this kind of implementation or use successfully complies with the ethical guidelines in question.

Therefore, if the conflict does not evaporate under the light of a specification or interpretation of the value in question, we have a genuine conflict. However, with the distinction between superficial and genuine conflicts in place, how can and should we handle a genuine conflict between values? In what follows I shall, as already stated, present and discuss four different strategies.

Long dissatisfied with the existence of value conflicts, philosophers have defended strategies by which we can, at least in theory, resolve all or some value conflicts (Parfit, 2011). One obvious answer to how one can solve moral conflicts, at least in theory, is to adhere to what is called *metaethical cognitivism*, according to which moral views and moral principles/theories can be true or false.[8] Imagine we have an alleged moral conflict between two people: say, one arguing in favour of using AI to detect doping fraud because of increased fairness, and the other arguing against such use because of privacy issues or respect for autonomy. When this is the case, such a conflict can, according to metaethical cognitivism, be solved by appealing to the true morality of the matter in question. However, to discuss whether cognitivism is plausible or not in any depth would take far more space than we can allow in a chapter on how to deal with conflicting values within ethical guidelines for AI. Furthermore, even if cognitivism were true, and could theoretically solve value conflicts by appealing to the true morality, that would not eradicate the existence of conflicting values in practice. Cognitivism would not be able to solve value conflicts between people in organisations such as WADA who have to make decisions. The reason for this is that not everyone would know about or accept cognitivism as true and/or because people would still, as a matter of fact, disagree about which version of cognitivism is the right one. In sum, an appeal to moral truth will not eradicate the existence of conflicting values in practice – it will just add new conflicts to the decision-making.

A second strategy to resolve conflicting values is to insist on a hierarchy among the values applied. This is *the ranking view*. One possible way in which a hierarchy could resolve moral conflicts between values would be to rank these values according to their moral importance. Such a ranking could be done in numerous ways; for example, in the manner of John Rawls (1999), who stated that the satisfaction of one set of basic rights or values (such as freedom of religion, freedom of speech, the right to property, the right to vote, etc.) may never to be violated for the sake of some other values (such as those expressed in his "principle of fair equality of opportunities" or the "difference principle"). However, in the literature on the ethics of AI, I have not come across any scholar or organisation developing and describing in any detail a hierarchy among values such as accountability, confidentiality, non-discrimination, autonomy and transparency. When they try, such ordering has unacceptable implications or is in tension with other ways of presenting the moral values at play in the guidelines. Take, for instance, the statement made by the EU Commission in its ethics guidelines for AI: "Certain fundamental rights and correlated principles are absolute and cannot be subject to a balancing exercise, e.g. human dignity" (EU, 2019, p. 13). There are at least two challenges with this possible ranking. First, it implies that a light manipulation (a small lie and thereby a violation of dignity) of a rich person in order to make her donate 0.01% of her fortune to save the life of 1,000 children (including your own child) is morally wrong. This cannot be right. Second, the quotation above seems to be in tension with the following quotation from the same source: "Without imposing a hierarchy, we list the principle that mirrors the order of appearance of the *fundamental rights* upon which they are based in the EU Charter" (EU, 2019, p. 11).

These critical comments are not made to rule out the ranking view, but simply to point out that the one suggested by the EU does not represent a detailed and well-justified ranking.

However, since we are not yet satisfied with the metaethical cognitivism strategy or the ranking view, a third possible strategy to use when faced with conflicting values is value monism.[9] An example of a monism could be the value theory adopted by adherents of utilitarianism. If you are a utilitarian, moral conflicts can always be resolved, at least in theory. Simply choose the act, for example, the use of AI, which maximises well-being. Alternatively, if you do not know or are in doubt about what the consequences of the use of a specific AI could be, then choose the use of AI that we have good reason to *expect* will maximise well-being, even though it might violate one of the moral values such as transparency or respect for autonomy. By this view, if you simply make these choices, you will have succeeded in satisfying the ethical guidelines for the use of AI.

However, although value monism, at least in theory, can solve conflicts between values (because according to monism there is only one value), it can also be challenged. First, one could argue that monistic theories such as utilitarianism do themselves give rise to value conflicts, as there exists a degree of pluralism about what well-being is and how to measure well-being. The sheer number of different versions of theories of well-being – for example, hedonistic theories, desire-based theories and objective-list-theories – clearly indicates a conflict between different understandings of the notion of well-being. However, although this kind of conflict about how to specify the value of well-being only amounts to a conceptual conflict and not a moral (and internal) conflict between the value of well-being and other values such as transparency, it is still a potential conflict for decision-makers.[10]

Second, a further challenge to value monism is that it does not (contrary to theories that allow for a plurality of values) make room for the complexity of our moral conflicts and experiences. Some philosophers (e.g., Beauchamp & Childress, 2013) claim that it is an advantage that a pluralism of values reflects our moral reality. In addition, several empirical studies support the idea that universally, people often adhere to several different values instead of just one (see, e.g., Haidt, 2012). If this is true, and the universal public or an organisation such as WADA only takes seriously ethical guidelines that entail the values that it adheres to, it is important that there is not too big a distance between WADA's values and the ethical guidelines. There are, however, some challenges to this kind of criticism. First, although our current moral framework may be a good place to begin, when we try to justify how we ought to act, history has often shown us that our morality has been wrong in several cases, for example, with regard to slavery, discrimination and the sexual harassment of women. Second, adhering to a monistic value, such as maximising well-being or human flourishing, does not mean that we should throw out all other values. Other values such as respect for autonomy, privacy, transparency and non-discrimination can serve as important instrumental values for the realisation of the ultimate aim, which could be to maximise well-being. If this were the strategy, there would not necessarily be any distance between a utilitarian decision-maker and the public's adherence to several values in the evaluation of AI. However, although this strategy works as a solution to the discrepancy between monism and people's many values, it does not solve the challenge of what decision-makers should do when values are in conflict. The problem of conflicting values has simply been shifted from intrinsic values to instrumental values.

A third challenge against monism is that although monism, like utilitarianism, does not accept the existence of moral conflicts, as they can be solved in theory (e.g., by choosing the act that we can expect will maximise well-being), there will from a practical standpoint probably still be grounds for much moral conflict. This could be either because adherents of utilitarianism disagree about whether, say, increasing the detection rate of doping fraud will maximise well-being or not. Alternatively, and if you are in favour of deontology, some deontologists believe, for example, that we must never violate autonomy or respect for privacy, even if such violations would maximise well-being.

Therefore, while value monism may look promising from a theoretical viewpoint, as it is simpler and more coherent than value pluralism, the acceptance of this view still involves many possible conflicts for decision-makers who have to deal with the ethics of AI in practice. Such conflicts are not only about issues that are conceptual (e.g., what do we mean by "well-being" or "autonomy") or empirical (e.g., will this particular use of AI increase human well-being) but also about moral conflicts. And not only can these moral conflicts arise if value monism accepts a plurality of values as instrumental, but also because what we morally believe to be right or wrong depends on conceptual and empirical issues too.

Dissatisfied with these traditional philosophical attempts to resolve value conflicts, the last strategy I will present and discuss is simply to accept that such conflicts may exist and that they may be irresolvable. This means that successful compliance with ethical guidelines may involve such conflicting values, including cases where it is uncertain whether an implementation of an AI measure X is *morally better (or worse)* than an alternative AI measure Y. In what follows, I have in mind WADA's attempt to improve the detection rate of doping fraud by the use of AI. Imagine that the implementation of an AI measure X to detect doping fraud will violate the autonomy of 10 people but will reduce harm to 1,000 people. Moreover, while the implementation of AI measure Y to detect doping fraud does not involve any violation of autonomy, it will harm 100 people. In such a case, it is uncertain which of the two AI measures, from a moral point of view, is the best to implement. This observation or way of reasoning is reflected, for example, in the work of bioethicists Tom L. Beauchamp and James F. Childress, who formulate their view as follows: "[Value] conflicts sometimes produce irresolvable moral dilemmas. When forced to a choice, we may "resolve" the situation by choosing one option over another, but we may still believe that neither option is morally preferable" (Beauchamp & Childress, 2013, p. 12). Therefore, in the context of our investigation, irresolvable conflict can occur when none of the uses of AI discussed are preferable (all options are equally morally bad) *or* when different uses are equally morally right.

Another example of a philosopher who accepts that moral conflicts can be irresolvable is Rosalind Hursthouse, who writes: "It is true both that a virtuous agent would do A, and that a virtuous agent would do B … both A and B are, in the circumstances, right" (Hursthouse, 2013, p. 650). In sum, irresolvable moral conflicts can arise in situations where none of the possible decisions are morally preferable (this is the position of Beauchamp and Childress) or when several different decisions may all be morally right (this is the view of Hursthouse). Apart from these differences, we should accept that both adhere to versions of the acceptance of conflict view.[11]

However, there are some obvious challenges to this kind of view. The first challenge is epistemic. How do we know which conflicts are irresolvable? What if one group of people say that, from a moral point of view, we should not accept the use of AI to detect doping fraud because respect for autonomy weighs more than harm reduction, and another group of people reaches the opposite moral conclusion? Is such a conflict between these two groups of people irresolvable or not? Defenders of the view that certain value conflicts are irresolvable do not say much about how we can know or differentiate between irresolvable conflicts and resolvable conflicts. What Hursthouse does say, however, is that if we accept the existence of irresolvable moral conflicts, this should not be taken as a counsel of despair or used as an excuse for moral laziness. Adding to this, Hursthouse writes: "It will always be necessary to think very hard before accepting the idea that a particular moral decision does not have one right issue" (2013, p. 650). But again, this does not take us much further in discovering whether we are confronted with an irresolvable conflict or not. For what does it mean to think hard about a moral question? Although each of us has some idea of what it means, our notions of what this act involves may differ considerably. For instance, considerations about what kinds of facts are relevant in the moral evaluation of the implementation of AI in sport could easily be a new point of disagreement. For example, a disagreement about whether we have taken into account a suitable number of empirical considerations or research studies, or whether we have explained central concepts in a satisfying way. In addition, when has one thought hard enough about a moral question? After one hour? After having studied ten ethical papers or reports about different answers to the given question? It is difficult to say anything precise about this, but that may not be necessary. For ideally, when it comes to the moral evaluation of whether or not we should use AI in a specific domain, the society we live in has already gone through a transparent democratic deliberative process. A process in which all the parties affected by the technology have been heard and all the values mentioned in the introduction have been discussed among scholars, in public as well as among decision-makers. This rough description should satisfy the notion of "thinking hard". As mentioned this is an ideal, and if it does not resemble what happens in practice, this is what ought to happen.

A second challenge, which is of a practical nature, is the following: if an irresolvable value conflict has been detected, then what? We cannot just settle with the view that we "agree that there is a conflict when it comes to an ethical evaluation of ... [AI] , as some policy is needed. So, what to do? Should we just toss a coin?"[12] Alternatively, should we, as mentioned above, consult a democratic process where the ethical view of scholars, politicians and those directly affected by the use of AI, guide our use of AI? The Canadian philosopher Will Kymlicka seems to accept this option when he reasons about the conflict between different moral values and principles in the context of assisted reproduction:

> Some potential conflicts between principles cannot be eliminated ... In these circumstances, the Commissioners will have to balance the competing values as best they can, giving due weight to each. This is similar to the process of balancing values that judges are often confronted with. In both contexts we have a rough sense of when the process is being carried out impartially, and when someone is unduly biased towards particular interests.
>
> (Kymlicka, 1993, p. 15)

While this kind of answer begins to clarify what we should do in cases of irresolvable conflict, it raises at least one challenge. This challenge is practical in nature. What does Kymlicka mean by, for example, "balancing" or "giving due weight"? Kymlicka does make some effort to clarify these concepts, for instance by writing that we should "ensure ... that all recommendations are checked against a comprehensive list of stakeholders and principles" (Kymlicka, 1993, p. 26). Although this does make us a little wiser, there are still some challenges remaining. What, for example, does it mean to let decision-makers who are considering the use of AI "check" a recommendation against values like autonomy and harm reduction? Is it enough to show that you have considered all relevant stakeholders and values by arguing why and how a specific use of AI does *not* violate a value like transparency but *does* violate the value of harm reduction? Anyway, what Kymlicka suggests is better than ethical reasoning not guided by ethical principles or guidelines, and goes very much in hand with some of the advantages of having ethical guidelines, as mentioned in Section 9.2.[13]

This section has found that metaethical cognitivism, the ranking view and value monism do not seem to offer us much guidance when conflicts between values arise (as all three involve value conflicts and other kinds of conflicts themselves) in ethical guidelines. Instead of these possible solutions to the conflicting values problem, we should settle on "the acceptance of conflict view". Although this view does also face some practical problems, it at least accepts that value conflicts need not be explained away and does also offer some guidance about how to deal with such real conflicts in a democracy.[14]

9.5 Conclusion

I hope to have shown that although there are some advantages to using ethical guidelines in the moral evaluation of the use of AI to improve the detection rate of doping fraud, there are also some challenges when using such guidelines. One important challenge is that there can be conflicts between the values embedded in the ethical guidelines for AI. In dealing with this challenge, we should first of all be clear about what kind of challenge we are referring to in order to be able to handle the conflict. Is it, for example, a conceptual challenge, or is it an internal conflict among the values expressed in the ethical guidelines, or an external conflict between values that are written vs not written into the guidelines? Is the conflict superficial or genuine? Then, if we are confronted with a genuine conflict, we can use different strategies. First, one theoretical suggestion on how to solve such conflicts would be to refer to metaethical cognitivism. However, it was argued that this approach would not eradicate the existence of value conflicts in practice, as far as everyone would know about or accept cognitivism as true. Second, the ranking view, although a possible strategy for solving moral conflicts between the values represented in ethical guidelines for AI, has not been adequately worked out by any scholars or governments in any detail, and it was further made clear that signs of a ranking view in the EU ethics guidelines for AI implies conflicting values too. Thirdly, we discussed value monism as a strategy that, at least from a pure theoretical point of view, could solve value conflict. However, when analysing the workings of value monism, it was revealed that it entailed different kinds of conflicts that we could not expect to be solved by those making decisions on the moral use of AI in sport. Finally, in light of the challenges for the former three strategies, "the acceptance of conflict view" was presented as a better "solution" to value conflicts. Although this view also faces both epistemic and practical problems, we found some reasonable answers to these. Therefore, what we can learn from the above discussions is that "the acceptance of conflict view" seems to be the least problematic strategy for real-life decision-making on how to use ethical guidelines for AI in doping detection in sport.

Notes

1 In what follows, I will use the words "doping fraud" to include (a) the intentional use of doping among athletes, (b) the manipulation of doping testing, (c) the possession, distribution and unauthorised selling of substances on WADA's prohibited list and (d) the manipulation of the so-called "whereabouts" of athletes. However, for stylistic reasons, I will primarily refer simply to (a).

2 According to Larsson (2021), more than 80 recommendations/guidelines about the ethics of AI have been published by public and private institutions within the last decade.
3 This case is inspired by Ryberg and Petersen (2022).
4 A further step towards harmonisation and therefore against ethics shopping is also found in Section 2.4 of the *Ethics Guidelines for Trustworthy AI* 2019 (European Commission, 2019), where it is mentioned that the EU wants to work in favour of building an international consensus on the ethics of AI.
5 The case mentioned here is constructed purely to illustrate a logical possibility. In fact, in the introduction to the EU Commission paper on trustworthy AI, they do mention that the use of AI should "improve welfare" (EU Commission, 2019, p. 6). However, they do not mention it as a distinct value, and they do not mention it in maximising terms.
6 See, e.g., Tännsjö (2011) for a specification of a value conflict close to my description.
7 This way of reasoning about a possible solution to an alleged conflict between different moral values is inspired by Hursthouse (2013).
8 See, e.g., Parfit (2011) for the view that cognitivism can solve moral conflicts and Rowland (2021) for a critical discussion of this view.
9 See, e.g., Mason (2023) for a splendid overview of arguments both for and against value monism as well as value pluralism.
10 The same types of problems can arise with monistic versions by deontologists who believe that a certain kind of conduct should not be violated (e.g., not harming or risking harm to innocent humans), as there are conflicts about what counts as harm and what counts as a morally problematic risk of harm to others.
11 A view similar to the "accepting the existence of irresolvable conflicts" view is also presented and argued for by, e.g., Williams (1981) and Stocker (1992).
12 Hursthouse (2013, p. 652) writes explicitly that tossing a coin is not the morally appropriate way to solve a moral conflict: "Would the virtuous agent toss a coin? Of course not." But why should a virtuous person not want to toss a coin? At least we can imagine situations where it would be the right thing to do, even for a virtuous person. If we are in need of a choice and if both choices are morally right, then it should not matter which one we choose. Moreover, there may be situations where it may be far more important that we *make a choice* than *how* we make it. Even though one finds it morally problematic to toss a coin in order to solve a moral problem, it may be more morally problematic to delay a choice from being made or not to make a choice at all. A virtuous agent should, for example, not delay a choice being made between alternative X or Y if both alternatives, all else being equal, would promote well-being to the same extent, but for different groups of otherwise identical individuals.
13 Elaborations of this kind of procedural justice we can find in the work of, e.g., Habermas (2004) and Nussbaum (2007).
14 For a further discussion of how to deal with such conflicts through, for example, compromise, see, e.g., Rowland (2021, Chap. 8).

References

Beauchamp, T. L., & Childress, J. F. (2013). *Principles of biomedical ethics* (7th ed.). Oxford University Press.

Bostrom, N., & Yudkowsky, E. (2014). The ethics of artificial intelligence. In K. Frankish & W. M. Ramsey (Eds.), *The Cambridge handbook of artificial intelligence* (pp. 316–334). Cambridge University Press.

Bowie, N. E. (2017). *Business ethics: A Kantian perspective*. Cambridge University Press.
Carrio Sampedro, A. (2021). The case of AI in sport: Some ethical concerns at play. *Diagoras: International Academic Journal on Olympic Studies, 5*, 18–29.
European Commission. (2019). *Ethics guidelines for trustworthy AI*. European Commission. Retrieved July 3, 2024, from https://digital-strategy.ec.europa.eu/en/library/ethics-guidelines-trustworthy-ai
Floridi, L. (2019). Translating principles into practices of digital ethics: Five risks of being unethical. *Philosophy & Technology, 32*(2), 185–193.
Habermas, J. (2004). Discourse ethics. In H.J. Gensler, E.W. Spurgin and J.C. Swindal (Eds.) *Ethics: Contemporary readings* (pp. 46–153). Routledge.
Haidt, J. (2012). *The righteous mind*. Penguin Books.
Hursthouse, R. (2013). Normative virtue ethics. In R. Shafer-Landau (Ed.), *Ethical theory: An anthology* (2nd ed., pp. 645–652). Wiley Blackwell.
Kymlicka, W. (1993). Moral philosophy and public policy: The case of NRTs. *Bioethics, 7*(1), 1–26.
Larsson, S. (2021). AI in the EU: Ethical guidelines as a governance tool. In A. Bakardjieva Engelbrekt, K. Leijon, A. Michalski, & L. Oxelheim (Eds.), The European union and the technology shift (pp. 85–110). (Palgrave Macmillan). Springer Nature. https://doi.org/10.1007/978-3-030-63672-2_4
Mason, E. (2023). Value pluralism. In E. N. Zalta (Ed.), *The Stanford encyclopedia of philosophy* (2023 Edition). https://plato.stanford.edu/entries/value-pluralism/#TheoVirt
Morley, J., Floridi, L., Kinsey, L., & Elhalal, A. (2019). From what to how: An overview of AI ethics tools, methods and research to translate principles into practices. *arXiv preprint* arxiv.org/abs/1905.06876.
Nussbaum, M. C. (2007). Capabilities as fundamental entitlements: Sen and social justice. In A. Kaufman (Ed.) *Capabilities equality* (pp. 54–80). Routledge.
Parfit, D. (2011). *On what matters* (Vol. 1). Oxford University Press.
Petersen, T. S. (2021). Sport, neuro-doping and ethics. *Neuroethics, 14*(Suppl 2), 137–140.
Petersen, T. S. (2021a) Doping in sport. A Defense. Routledge.
Pugh, J. (2020). *Autonomy, rationality, and contemporary bioethics* (p. 298). Oxford University Press.
Rahman, M. R., Bejder, J., Bonne, T. C., Andersen, A. B., Huertas, J. R., Aikin, R., ... & Maaß, W. (2022). AI-based approach for improving the detection of blood doping in sports. *arXiv preprint arXiv:2203.00001*.
Rawls, J. (1999) *Theory of Justice*. Revised edition. Oxford University Press.
Rowland, R. (2021) *Moral disagreement*. Routledge.
Ryberg, J. (2022). Sentencing and algorithmic transparency. *Sentencing and Artificial Intelligence*, 13–33.
Ryberg, J., & Petersen, T. S. (2022). Sentencing and the conflict between algorithmic accuracy and transparency. *Sentencing and Artificial Intelligence*, 57–73.
Saar University. (2022). How artificial intelligence can help in the fight against Doping. News Release. Retrieved February 10, 2022, from https://www.eurekalert.org/news-releases/943116
Stocker, M. (1992). Plural and Conflicting Values. Cambridge, Clarandon Press. –
Tännsjö, T. (2011). Sophie's choice. In W. E. Jones & S. Vice (Eds.), *Ethics at the cinema*. Oxford University Press.

WADA. (2021). World Anti-DopingCode. Retrieved June 28, 2024, from https://www.wada-ama.org/sites/default/files/resources/files/2021_wada_code.pdf
WADA. (2023) Prohibited list. Retrieved July 5, 2024, from chrome-extension://efaidnbmnnnibpcajpcglclefindmkaj/https://www.wada-ama.org/sites/default/files/2023-09/2024list_en_final_22_september_2023.pdf
Williams, J. (1981). *Moral luck*. Cambridge University Press.

Chapter 10

Neuroenhancement

The Challenge of Perfect Performance

Andrea Lavazza

10.1 Introduction

Sport is one of the most widespread human activities, capable of generating emotions and involvement both in those who practice it and in those who watch it (Vamplew, 2021). It is a phenomenon closely tied to the realm of the body and its efficiency, yet it also contains a significant cultural element. On the one hand, basic sports practices originate from human activities essential for survival (running, jumping, throwing, hitting, wrestling, skillfully handling tools). On the other hand, sport has evolved into a form of personal achievement that has lost touch with the evolutionary origins of its initial components. Sport mirrors the social dynamics of various historical phases and contexts in which the playful practice often becomes professional, encompassing an ever-wider range of disciplines. In many cultures, sport is a central aspect of many people's lives (mostly as spectators), as evidenced by the fact that media outlets often have a dedicated sports section more readily than sections for environment, health, science, or technology (Bellamy, 2009).

It is therefore unsurprising that the focus, investments, specialization, and competition among a growing number of athletes have driven sports performance toward continuous improvements and the pursuit of ever-advancing quantitative and qualitative achievements. There is now an extensive body of literature on sport as a cultural, social, and economic phenomenon and on the ethical rules that should govern its conduct. In this contribution, I aim to focus on a hypothesis that is no longer very far off: technologies that could lead an athlete to the "perfection" of their technical gesture through devices capable of acting directly on the brain as the seat of movement, acting on the sensory-motor system.

This idea is inspired by a recent literary citation. This consideration leads to an exploration of the interaction between philosophy, applied ethics, and works of fiction as important analyses of human behavior motives and dilemmas, as well as a brief re-examination of the debate on perfectionism and anti-perfectionism applied to sport. After this Introduction, in Section 10.2, I will provide a very brief general overview of what is called neuroenhancement,

DOI: 10.4324/9781003520290-11

to indicate the plausibility of the hypothesis to be discussed. In Section 10.3, I will offer some examples of how recent novels have effectively and persuasively addressed ethical issues related to new technologies, artificial intelligence, and the digital world in particular.

From here, in Section 10.4, I illustrate the idea of artificial perfection that could be achieved in certain sports based on the intuition of a novelist. In Section 10.5, I revisit some arguments related to the aspiration to perfection and its negative effects. In the concluding section (Section 10.6), I reconsider how the perfection that can be achieved or approached through technological aids is contrary not so much to the current explicit rules of professional sport but to the human phenomenon of sport itself. Perhaps we could think of the "perfect sport" and the "athlete who never makes a mistake" as an exhibition of beauty and human success, akin to a solo performance by a musician or a dancer (though almost robotic), but not as an example of the competitive human interaction that defines sport itself (and our everyday life).

10.2 Enhancement and Sports

The enhancement of human performance is the increase in skills (abilities, attributes or competences) by means of medical or technological methods, so as to improve a person's overall performance (see better, run faster, remember more accurately) (Rosen, 2008). Examples are an intraocular lens; chemical doping in sport; but also, a special training program that resorts to technological aids.

Neuroenhancement is a form of enhancement that acts directly on the nervous system to improve in a general sense its functioning with respect to a specific performance (Antal et al., 2022). It can also be aimed at compensating for what, from a performance point of view, may be considered a deficit but is not from a general developmental point of view (e.g., different salience of sensory stimuli, progressive decline in focusing and attention, etc.).

Neuroenhancement (neuro-doping) seems more related to control than to strength or speed. It seems oriented toward coordination, concentration, and endurance (Fisicaro et al., 2020). Currently, it is not easy to discriminate or draw a precise line between enhancement and neuroenhancement, at least for some forms of intervention available today. The most important types of neuroenhancement are related to pharmacological interventions and interventions on brain electro-chemistry (such as electrical or magnetic stimulation).

Transcranial direct current stimulation is a widely used tool in which a small constant direct current is applied through at least two electrodes positioned on the scalp, depending on the targeted brain regions, thanks to a battery-powered current stimulator (Chinzara et al., 2022). Stimulation changes the excitability of neurons in the brain by hyperpolarizing or depolarizing their membrane potential. tDCS causes cortical changes both during and after the stimulation, which usually takes from 5 to 30 minutes. Its effects on brain function can last from minutes to hours, depending on duration and intensity of the stimulation.

tDCS alters brain functioning, varying the neuronal resting membrane potential. A positive stimulation (anodal) causes a depolarization of the resting membrane potential, which can increase neuronal excitability and spontaneous cell firing. A negative stimulation (cathodal) causes a hyperpolarization of the resting membrane potential that can decrease the neuronal excitability linked to spontaneous cell firing. tDCS is a form of neurostimulation that so far has been mainly used on healthy subjects to enhance (in laboratory so far) mathematical cognition, reading, memory, mood, learning, perception, decision-making, creativity, motivation, and moral reasoning.

It seems that tDCS also enhances motor skills and can be profitably used in the field of sports, especially in professional athletes. Recent studies have shown that tDCS can both improve power and reduce perception of effort, increasing endurance.

From a general ethical point of view, the main issues of resorting to neuroenhancement are related to safety, inequalities in access, inequality in the potential individual benefits, inability to detect use, and implicit coercion (when use becomes widespread). And for sports specifically, the conditions that qualify an enhancement as doping.

Considering the rapid pace of progress in the field of nervous system intervention research (neuromodulation, optogenetics, BCIs), it seems no exaggeration to speculate that neuroenhancement may soon lead to significant improvements. Above all, it is plausible to assume that new tools will allow for extremely targeted enhancement that may have different uses and thus different ethical evaluations.

10.3 Taking Inspiration from Fiction: A Long and Recently Revived Tradition

As stated in the introduction, novels are an inexhaustible source of profound descriptions, insights, and reflections on human behavior and social scenarios (Choo, 2021). Recently, several distinguished authors in the Anglophone world have focused their works on the innovations brought by technology and how these innovations influence our choices and ultimately our lives, or at least promise to do so in the near future. Therefore, it is interesting to consider three works in particular, as exemplars of this trend and the opportunities they offer to scholars with an empirical and systematic approach to certain topics. Although, as will be seen, only one of the three cited novels presents a scenario directly relevant to sports, the following brief overview helps to better understand how an approach to applied ethics can benefit from a narrative treatment that liberates expressive possibilities and embeds ethical dilemmas more deeply into the everyday lives of people.

"Klara and the Sun," authored by Kazuo Ishiguro, is an original exploration of artificial intelligence and human emotion (Ishiguro, 2021). Set in a near-future dystopian society, the narrative follows Klara, an Artificial Friend (AF), designed to provide companionship to children. Through Klara's unique perspective, Ishiguro delves into themes of love, loneliness, and the ethical implications of AI.

Ishiguro's novel, beyond being a literary moving masterpiece, is a speculative fiction that imagines a world where AI is seamlessly integrated into everyday life. Klara, the protagonist, is an AI robot endowed with advanced observational and empathetic capabilities. Her design emphasizes the potential of AI to understand and respond to human emotions, showcasing an intricate blend of technology and psychology.

Klara's character is a testament to the advancements in robotics and artificial intelligence. Her ability to perceive and interpret human emotions with a high degree of accuracy represents a leap forward in AI development. Ishiguro's depiction suggests a future where AI can achieve a level of emotional intelligence that rivals human capability. In addition, Klara derives energy from the sun, symbolizing a sustainable approach to powering advanced technologies.

The novel raises critical ethical questions about the creation and use of AI (Sun, 2023). Klara's existence and her interactions with humans bring to light issues related to AI consciousness, rights, and the moral responsibilities of creators and users. In this vein, Ishiguro's imaginative portrayal of AI in "Klara and the Sun" can serve as a valuable source of inspiration for real-world research and technological development. In particular, the idea of an AI-managed humanoid robot as a successor of a specific human being is both fascinating and disturbing.

So, the novel emphasizes the importance of creating AI that can understand and respond to human emotions. This can inspire researchers to focus on developing AI systems with enhanced emotional intelligence, capable of providing better companionship and support. Above all, the ethical dilemmas presented in the novel can guide discussions and policies regarding AI development. Ensuring that AI systems are designed with ethical considerations in mind is crucial for their integration into society (cf. Lavazza & Vilaça, 2024).

Ian McEwan's "Machines Like Me" is a thought-provoking novel set in an alternative 1980s London, where technological advancements have far outpaced those of our historical timeline (McEwan, 2019). The story revolves around Charlie, a man who purchases one of the first synthetic humans, Adam, and his partner, Miranda. Through the interactions between these characters, McEwan explores the complexities of artificial intelligence, human emotions, and ethical dilemmas.

McEwan's novel is a portrayal of a world where artificial intelligence and robotics have reached unprecedented levels of sophistication (Patra, 2020). The character of Adam, a synthetic human, serves as a central figure in illustrating the potential and challenges of advanced AI. Adam represents a pinnacle of AI and robotic engineering, possessing advanced cognitive abilities, emotional depth, and physical resilience. This portrayal suggests a future where robots can not only mimic but also surpass human capabilities in various domains. Adam's design includes sophisticated algorithms that allow him to learn, reason, and make ethical decisions. McEwan imagines an AI that can engage in complex moral reasoning, challenging the boundaries between human and machine ethics. Thus, the novel delves into the intricacies of human-robot interactions, exploring themes of companionship, trust, and emotional bonds. Adam's presence in Charlie and Miranda's life raises questions about the nature of relationships and the possibility of genuine emotional connections with AI.

The novel emphasizes the importance of incorporating ethical reasoning into AI systems. Researchers can draw inspiration from Adam's capabilities to develop AI that can navigate complex moral landscapes, making decisions that align with ethical principles and societal values. McEwan's exploration of human-robot relationships highlights the potential for AI to enhance human life through companionship and emotional support. This can inspire further research into improving the social and emotional intelligence of AI, making them more adept at understanding and responding to human needs (cf. Colombino, 2022).

The ethical dilemmas presented in the novel can inform policy-making and regulatory frameworks for AI (. Ensuring that AI systems are designed and deployed with ethical considerations in mind is crucial for their acceptance and integration into society. McEwan's portrayal of Adam's cognitive and emotional capabilities encourages the development of AI that can process and understand human emotions. This can lead to advancements in creating more empathetic and responsive AI systems.

Dave Eggers's novel "The Every" serves as an examination of the growing influence of technology and social media in contemporary society (Eggers, 2021). As a sequel to his earlier work, "The Circle" (Eggers, 2013), the novel delves deeper into the implications of pervasive digital surveillance, data privacy, and the ethical dimensions of technology. Set in a near-future world, the narrative follows Delaney Wells, a former forest ranger, who infiltrates the tech giant known as The Every with the intention of exposing and undermining its power.

Eggers's portrayal of The Every, a conglomerate formed from the merger of the world's largest search engine and social media company, presents a dystopian vision of technological advancement (Terentowicz-Fotyga, 2025). "The Every" epitomizes a society where every aspect of human life is monitored and analyzed. The company's vast array of apps and devices collects data on users' behaviors, preferences, and even emotions, highlighting the potential dangers of unchecked data accumulation. The Every develops numerous apps designed to optimize and control human behavior. These apps, ranging from mood regulators to social scoring systems, raise critical ethical questions about autonomy, consent, and the manipulation of human behavior.

The Every's algorithms not only anticipate users' needs and desires but also shape their decisions, underscoring the potential loss of individuality and free will. In this sense, the Every envisions a corporate-controlled scenario where technology tries to solve all societal problems. This vision, however, is deeply flawed, as it overlooks the nuanced ethical and social issues that arise from such pervasive control.

Eggers's imaginative depiction of technology in "The Every" provides a rich source of inspiration and caution for real-world research and technological development, particularly concerning the ethical aspects of social media and new apps. The novel highlights the urgent need for robust ethical frameworks to govern the development and deployment of social media platforms and applications. Researchers and developers must consider the implications of data privacy, user autonomy, and consent in their work.

In addition, Eggers's portrayal of algorithmic control encourages further research into the impact of predictive analytics on human behavior. Understanding the psychological and social effects of algorithmic interventions can inform the development of more ethical and transparent AI systems. Indeed, the novel illustrates the complex interplay between technology, society, and ethics, highlighting the need for collaboration between technologists, ethicists, sociologists, and policymakers can lead to more holistic approaches to technology development.

Eggers's narrative emphasizes the importance of public awareness and digital literacy. Educating users about the ethical implications of technology and empowering them to make informed choices can mitigate some of the risks associated with digital surveillance and control. The novel's technological imagination serves here as both a cautionary tale and a source of inspiration for real-world research, guiding the development of ethical, transparent, and user-centric technological solutions.

10.4 The (Artificial) Perfection in Sports

As explained above, *The Every* is a novel plenty of insights into future scenarios, described with extensive detail. Eggers excels at hypothesizing unsettling technological developments and their personal and social consequences, particularly in the realms of relationships, control, and commerce.

But in just a few lines, referring to a research program that is only hinted at and plays no particular role in the story, he opens up a very interesting glimpse into the future of neuroenhancement concerning some sports and consequently neuro-doping.

"Did he mention MPOs?" Delaney asked. "I thought they banned that." Muscle precision optimization was a catch-all term for nanotechnology that improved—perfected, really—eye-brain-muscle coordination. A tennis player

using it could place a ball in the exact same spot a hundred times out of a hundred. Errors were virtually impossible.

They say, "Professional sports banned it" (The Every, ch. XIII).

We know that recent forms of training and higher performance equipment can increase performance to the highest level in some sports (shooting, archery, golf, gymnastics, diving, etc.). These are sports where coordination and precision are crucial, and you do not directly challenge an opponent but try to achieve the highest score. MPOs is just a name of a hypothetical neurotechnology, but we cannot exclude that we will have something similar, capable of enabling perfect performance in the sports mentioned.

A device like MPO could be implanted with minimal risk and through a standardized procedure, as demonstrated by the recent experiment conducted by Neuralink (Drew, 2024). Once a brain-computer interface is effectively integrated with the sensorimotor areas of the athlete, neuroenhancement could indeed enable coordination suitable for achieving near-perfect performance in the individual disciplines mentioned above. In tennis, however, the quality of a shot depends on the quality of the opponent's previous shot, so placing "a ball in the exact same spot a hundred times out of a hundred" would not be as straightforward as executing a gymnastic routine or a complex dive, where one can autonomously choose the starting conditions.

In any case, the use of a device similar to MPO by a single athlete, notwithstanding the safety issues (which are very complex and delicate but will not be analyzed here as they are not the focus of my interest), would provide an enormous competitive advantage over opponents. However, one might think that such an opportunity to enhance performance would soon be seized by many athletes, willing to integrate their sensorimotor capabilities with technological assistance to reach levels of performance otherwise unattainable.

It should not be thought that a device like MPO acts like the software of a precision machine. Technical skill, concentration, determination—in other words, many of the physical and psychological qualities necessary to be a champion—would still be required to excel in their respective sports. This makes the scenario of enhancement toward perfection in sports performance more realistic and interesting. In this sense, it is possible to analyze how it can and should be framed within the existing rules and the conception of sport that most people seem to implicitly share.

First, let's consider the current World Anti-Doping Agency's (WADA) Spirit of Sports. The spirit of sport is the celebration of the human spirit, body and mind. It is the essence of Olympism and is reflected in the values we find in and through sport, including health; ethics, fair play, and honesty; athletes' rights as set forth in the Code; excellence in performance; character and education; fun and joy; teamwork; dedication and commitment; respect for rules and laws; respect for self and other participants; courage; community; and solidarity. The spirit of sport is expressed in how we play truthfully. So, doping is fundamentally contrary to the spirit of sport.

All those who use the MPO can achieve a perfect performance, reach the maximum expected score. The intuition many would have is that it's not good, we don't like it, it's not right, it's not fair. However, it does not seem that this intuition is based on the principles of the spirit of sport that we usually consider. Let us imagine that the MPO is a perfectly safe technique. As a neuroenhancement, it is fantastic for surgeons, pilots, artists, craftsmen, who always aspire to repeat their maximum capacity for visual-muscle coordination and precision of movement.

But let's think of sports as well. A sort of perfection from athletes is what fascinates us and makes us go crazy for a champion. David Foster Wallace's essay "Federer Both Flesh and Not" (2012; first published in 2006) is a very good example that provides deep insights into the nature of excellence and beauty in sports. Wallace describes Federer's gameplay with an almost poetic reverence, emphasizing the elegance and fluidity that characterize his movements. This theme is central to understanding why Federer stands out not just as a winner but as an artist on the tennis court.

Wallace meticulously details Federer's technical skills, from his fluid backhand to his powerful serve. Federer's ability to combine power and finesse, making challenging shots look effortless, is a focal point of Wallace's admiration. Wallace likens watching Federer to witnessing a ballet, where every movement is a blend of strength and grace. This comparison underscores the beauty inherent in Federer's style of play, which transcends mere athleticism.

Wallace captures the almost mystical experience of watching Federer play live, a sensation that resonates deeply with tennis fans and casual viewers alike. Wallace describes moments during Federer's matches where time seems to stand still, and the audience is collectively mesmerized by his performance. These moments of transcendence highlight the unique emotional impact Federer has on those who watch him.

Federer's ability to engage and captivate his audience is a testament to his charisma and the spectacle of his matches. Wallace's vivid descriptions help readers understand why Federer is beloved worldwide. In this sense, Wallace's essay is not just a sports commentary but also a philosophical exploration of human excellence and the nature of genius. Wallace reflects on the concept of excellence, using Federer as a case study to explore how talent, hard work, and mental fortitude combine to create a phenomenon.

The essay "Federer Both Flesh and Not" delves into the idea of the sublime, where Federer's performances are seen as moments of pure beauty that elevate the spirit. Wallace's philosophical musings on these moments invite readers to consider the deeper meaning of sports and performance. Wallace's reflections on Federer provide valuable insights that extend beyond the realm of tennis, offering lessons for various fields of study and professional practices.

But what if it turned out that outstanding performance is just due to an implant in Federer's brain, for instance, the Muscle Precision Optimization device imagined by Eggers? It is true that Wallace stresses Federer's psychological resilience and mental toughness (cf. Weinberg & Gould, 2019), in combination with a reflection on human excellence and on what it means to be truly great, a genius. However, the essay's exploration of the aesthetic dimensions of Federer's game highlights the importance of beauty in sports (cf. Gumbrecht, 2006). In this sense, beauty is a quality associated with perfection and diverges from the idea of sport as competition, transforming it into a pure exhibition that could align with the perspective of an enhancement that approaches the perfection of gesture and performance. However, as will be seen, this stands in opposition to the fundamentals of sport as we generally experience and like it.

10.5 Perfection in Sports: Pros and Cons

At this point, we can ask ourselves whether multiplying the number of Federers on the tennis courts—Federers who are even more performant and closer to perfection, understood as beauty and excellence—is what athletes should strive for and what sports enthusiasts should desire to see realized.

Aristotle's concept of arete, or excellence, can be a classical guide to understanding the pursuit of perfection in sports. In Aristotelian ethics, achieving excellence involves fulfilling one's potential through virtuous actions and habitual practice. According to Aristotle, excellence is not merely about winning but about realizing one's full potential and achieving balance and harmony in one's actions. This philosophy can be applied to sports, where true perfection is seen as the harmonious integration of physical skill, mental acuity, and moral character (cf. MacIntyre, 1981). Aristotle also emphasized the importance of practice and habit in achieving excellence. In sports, this translates to rigorous training and consistent effort, which are essential for athletes striving for perfection (Austin, 2013).

On the other hand, Platonic ideals suggest that perfection is an abstract, unattainable form that athletes strive toward. This perspective views perfect performance as an ideal that motivates continuous improvement. In sports, the perfect performance is a goal that athletes aim to approximate, even if it can never be fully realized (Reid, 2011). The pursuit of this ideal form drives athletes to constantly refine their skills and push their boundaries. This continuous striving for improvement is a key element in the philosophical discussion of perfection in sports (Vallerand, 2007).

Contemporary psychological research makes a distinction between adaptive and maladaptive perfectionism in athletes. Adaptive Perfectionism is characterized by high standards and a positive striving for excellence. It is associated with greater motivation, better performance, and higher satisfaction (Stoeber & Otto, 2006). Maladaptive Perfectionism involves excessive concern over mistakes, fear of negative evaluation, and a tendency toward self-criticism. Maladaptive perfectionism can lead to anxiety, burnout, and decreased performance, highlighting the dark side of the quest for perfection (Flett & Hewitt, 2002).

The well-known Csikszentmihalyi's concept of flow describes a state of complete absorption and optimal performance. Athletes in flow experience deep focus, a sense of control, and a loss of self-consciousness. Flow is often perceived as moments of perfection in sports where athletes perform at their peak. Achieving flow requires a balance between skill and challenge, clear goals, and immediate feedback. Understanding these pathways can help athletes and coaches create conditions conducive to peak performance (Csikszentmihalyi, 1990).

Very recently, as is well-known, technological advancements play a significant role in enhancing athletic performance and approaching perfection. For instance, technologies like motion capture and biomechanical modeling allow for detailed analysis of athletic movements, helping athletes optimize their techniques and reduce injury risks (Lees, 2002). Other innovations such as high-altitude training, cryotherapy, and resistance training are used to improve physical capabilities and recovery times, pushing athletes closer to their peak performance levels (Hoffman, 2014). Wearables track metrics such as heart rate, speed, and movement efficiency, offering immediate feedback to athletes and coaches. This data can be used to make informed adjustments to training regimens (Seçkin et al., 2023).

The use of performance-enhancing drugs (PEDs) is a very effective way to improve performances, but it raises significant ethical questions about fairness and the integrity of sports. The entire history of sport, since ancient Greece, is interwoven with attempts to enhance performance through the targeted intake of substances, starting with special dietary regimes. More recently, various types of molecules, products of medical research, have been ingested by athletes and subsequently banned by national and international sports authorities (Rosen, 2008). What is of interest here is a different form of "doping" that allows for a qualitative leap not previously achievable with any type of drug.

In the context of the vibrant ethical debate on chemical doping, some scholars argue that PEDs level the playing field or enhance the spectacle of sports, making competitions more interesting (Savulescu, Foddy & Clayton, 2004). But the main argument, beyond safety issues, is that each athlete has the right to the maximum of autonomy in their choice, and that is impossible to assure equality among athletes even though we should ban any external aids.

However, critics contend that PEDs undermine fair competition, pose health risks, and contradict the spirit of sport, which values natural talent and hard work (Møller, 2009). The intense pressure to achieve perfection can negatively impact athletes' mental health. Indeed, the pursuit of perfection can lead to stress, anxiety, and depression, especially when athletes face unrealistic expectations from themselves, coaches, and the public (Hughes & Leavey, 2012).

10.6 The Importance of Imperfection in Sports

There is a general idea that imperfection plays a crucial role in the richness and authenticity of the sporting experience. Some scholars argue that imperfections highlight the human element in sports, making it more relatable and authentic. Imperfections and fallibility remind us that athletes are human beings with flaws, making their achievements more meaningful and inspiring. Novak (1976), for instance, discusses how the imperfections and unpredictability in sports make the achievements of athletes more authentic and relatable to the human experience.

Imperfections contribute to the narrative and drama of sports, making it more compelling and engaging for spectators. The unpredictability resulting from human error or unexpected events creates memorable and emotionally charged moments. In this vein, the unpredictability and imperfections in sports contribute to its dramatic appeal, keeping audiences engaged and invested. Embracing imperfection can also be seen as a rejection of the unethical pursuit of perfection through means such as doping or other forms of cheating. It advocates for fair play and the true spirit of competition. Møller (2010) argues that the pursuit of perfection through performance-enhancing drugs undermines the ethical integrity of sports. Imperfections, on the other hand, preserve the fairness and spirit of sport.

Simon and colleagues (2014) maintain that striving for an unattainable perfection can lead to a dehumanizing experience, where athletes are seen more as machines than as humans. Embracing imperfection acknowledges the limitations and inherent value of human experience. In addition, mistakes and imperfections are essential for learning and growth. Athletes learn from their errors, which is a critical part of their development and improvement over time. Dweck's (2006) research on growth mindset shows how viewing mistakes as opportunities for learning rather than failures fosters resilience and continuous improvement in athletes.

As already stated, the relentless pursuit of perfection can lead to negative psychological effects such as anxiety, burnout, and decreased enjoyment. Embracing imperfection can promote a healthier and more sustainable approach to sports. Studies by Gould and Whitley (2009) show that the pressure to achieve perfection can lead to significant mental health issues in athletes, suggesting that a focus on imperfection and process over flawless outcomes can benefit mental well-being.

Imperfections in sports often reflect broader cultural values and narratives. They contribute to the diversity and richness of sports traditions around the world. Gumbrecht (2006) discusses how different cultures appreciate various aspects of sports, including imperfections, as they resonate with local values and traditions. Also, imperfections can enhance the sense of community and connection among fans, as they often rally around athletes in moments of failure as well as success. This shared experience fosters a deeper emotional bond and communal identity. Giulianotti and Robertson (2007) stress how the communal experience of sports, including the collective support during imperfect moments, strengthens social bonds and community identity.

Thus, scholars advocating for the general idea of imperfection in sports present a quite compelling case that imperfections contribute significantly to the authenticity, drama, ethical integrity, learning, mental health, cultural value, and community aspects of sports. Embracing imperfection allows for a richer, more humanistic approach to sports, highlighting the importance of the journey, growth, and ethical considerations over an unattainable pursuit of perfection.

But one can ask what's special about MPO as depicted in *The Every*. An implantable device capable of assuring a real perfect (or quasi-perfect) performance seems to be a more direct challenge to the debate among perfectionists and anti-perfectionists, which is basically based on aspirations, values, and principles. MPO is the first potential realization of a perfect single performance (a tennis shot). As seen, many people agree that sport needs imperfection, a brain (and a body) that is not a deterministic and infallible machine. But what kind of imperfection?

So far, I have focused on certain aspects of neuro-doping, but a human improvement such as the MPO that is first and foremost a useful improvement for all can end up killing sport in a new way. In the face of this thought experiment, we see that error, lack of perfection, which athletes and coaches (and fans) fight and hate, but which we never quite overcome, are necessary for sport. After all, error and imperfection are what allow for surprise, the outsider who beats the champion, the hope that can be rekindled at every opportunity.

In particular, total predictability is something that sports cannot accommodate. The possibility of maintaining a consistently high-level performance, verging on perfection within the boundaries of the given discipline, removes any element of surprise from the competition. The contestability of victory and the open-ended future of the event are the conditions that make sport what it is and what makes it so engaging and instructive.

Perfection achieved through some form of enhancement is not only questionable according to classical anti-perfectionist criteria. These criteria emphasize that imperfections add authenticity, richness, and depth to human experiences. They are considered to contribute to personal growth, creativity, and ethical behavior. Embracing imperfection can also enhance mental health, reduce anxiety, and promote ethical integrity, leading to a more fulfilling and balanced life. This nuanced understanding encourages individuals to appreciate the beauty and learning opportunities in their imperfections while continuing to strive for their personal best.

The issue with new forms of enhancement is that they risk annihilating precisely what sport proposes as its most significant element for both participants and spectators. The personal factor that each individual can bring to the competition—through talent, training, dedication, and the capacity to endure—allows for a chance of success or at least achieving results that are not predetermined. An element of randomness, potential surprise, and overturning of predictions are aspects that captivate the audience and make competition in sports unique.

Obviously, not all sports would be transformed in the same way by this form of neuroenhancement. For example, team sports or the challenges of one athlete against another (such as tennis) could not be completely enhanced by excellent individual performances. Indeed, victory would go to the one who adopts the best tactics. But even in these cases, something that is the hallmark of sport would be lost. The ability to bear the psychological burden of shooting the last decisive penalty, the fact that a celebrated champion unexpectedly misses a free throw or commits a double fault on serve, etc.

If we could achieve fail-safe coordination by means of a technological training technique, so that the result of perfect performance could be achieved without any real form of doping, would we not be making progress in principle but transforming sport and making it less appealing?

This opens up the question of how to continue to seek legitimate improvement (think of swimming costumes for natatory sports, shoes for marathon running, nutrition for any sport) and at the same time preserve that imperfection that seems to be a fundamental characteristic of sport. At the level of athletes, perhaps the effort to improve cannot have a limit if it is pursued with safety and awareness. At the overall level, regulators may be concerned to maintain that component of imperfection that characterizes sport as much as our lives, and that is why sport is so loved and so useful to those who play it.

In conclusion, the fictional example of Muscle Precision Optimization demonstrates how the evolution of sport in symbiosis with technology can lead to advancements that would be welcomed in other human activities, but in the realm of competitive athletic performance, these advancements have the potential to completely undermine the spirit that governs the competitions, at least in certain disciplines. Therefore, there is a rationale beyond those presented so far for limiting or even banning implantable devices like the MOP to safeguard the concept and spirit of sport as we know it today.

While the MOP is not likely a technological development that will be available soon, its theoretical consideration can help us better understand how to preserve sport in all its most positive aspects. This is evident when we analyze a human activity that strives for perfection (like any other) but knows it cannot achieve it; it is precisely in this impossibility of achieving perfection that the secret of its success and relevance lies.[12]

Notes

1 After singling out the core, original ideas of the chapter (namely, the MPO hypothesis), in conducting the preliminary research, I utilized a chatbot to assist in gathering and reviewing initial literature relevant to the subject matter. This AI tool facilitated the identification of key sources, which were subsequently explored in greater depth through traditional research methodologies.

2 I thank Alberto Carrio for promoting and organizing a very relevant research project culminated in this book.

References

Antal, A., Luber, B., Brem, A. K., Bikson, M., Brunoni, A. R., Kadosh, R. C., ... & Paulus, W. (2022). Non-invasive brain stimulation and neuroenhancement. *Clinical Neurophysiology Practice, 7*, 146–165.

Austin, M. W. (2013). Sport as a moral practice: An Aristotelian approach. *Royal Institute of Philosophy Supplements, 73*, 29–43.

Bellamy, R. V. (2009). Sports media: A modern institution. In A. A. Raney & J. Bryant (Eds.), *Handbook of sports and media* (pp. 66–79). Routledge.

Chinzara, T. T., Buckingham, G., & Harris, D. J. (2022). Transcranial direct current stimulation and sporting performance: A systematic review and meta-analysis of transcranial direct current stimulation effects on physical endurance, muscular strength and visuomotor skills. *European Journal of Neuroscience, 55*(2), 468–486.

Choo, S. S. (2021). *Teaching ethics through literature: The significance of ethical criticism in a global age*. Routledge.

Colombino, L. (2022). Consciousness and the nonhuman: The imaginary of the new brain sciences in Ian McEwan's *Nutshell* and *Machines like me*. *Textual Practice, 36*(3), 382–403.

Csikszentmihalyi, M. (1990). *Flow: The psychology of optimal experience*. Harper & Row.

Drew, L. (2024). Elon Musk's Neuralink brain chip: What scientists think of first human trial. *Nature*. https://nature.proxyucr.elogim.com/articles/d41586-024-00304-4

Dweck, C. S. (2006). *Mindset: The new psychology of success*. Random House.

Eggers, D. (2013). *The circle*. Knopf.

Eggers, D. (2021). *The every*. Vintage.

Fisicaro, F., Lanza, G., Bella, R., & Pennisi, M. (2020). "Self-neuroenhancement": The last frontier of noninvasive brain stimulation? *Journal of Clinical Neurology, 16*(1), 158–159.

Flett, G. L., & Hewitt, P. L. (Eds.). (2002). *Perfectionism: Theory, research, and treatment*. American Psychological Association.

Giulianotti, R., & Robertson, R. (2007). Sport and globalization: Transnational dimensions. *Global Networks, 7*(2), 107–112.

Gould, D., & Whitley, M. A. (2009). Sources and consequences of athletic burnout among college athletes. *Journal of Intercollegiate Sport, 2*(1), 16–30.

Gumbrecht, H. U. (2006). *In praise of athletic beauty*. Harvard University Press.

Hoffman, J. (2014). *Physiological aspects of sport training and performance*. Human Kinetics.

Hughes, L., & Leavey, G. (2012). Setting the bar: Athletes and vulnerability to mental illness. *The British Journal of Psychiatry, 200*(2), 95–96.

Ishiguro, K. (2021). *Klara and the sun.* Faber and Faber.
Lavazza, A., & Vilaça, M. (2024). Human extinction and AI: What we can learn from the ultimate threat. *Philosophy & Technology, 37*(1), 16.
Lees, A. (2002). Technique analysis in sports: A critical review. *Journal of Sports Sciences, 20*(10), 813–828.
MacIntyre, A. (1981). *After virtue: A study in moral theory.* University of Notre Dame Press.
McEwan, I. (2019). *Machines like me.* Jonathan Cape.
Møller, V. (2009). *The ethics of doping and anti-doping: Redeeming the soul of sport?* Routledge.
Novak, M. (1976). *The joy of sports: End zones, bases, baskets, balls, and the consecration of the American spirit.* Basic Books.
Patra, I. (2020). Man with the machine: Analyzing the role of autopoietic machinic agency in Ian McEwan's *Machines like me. Psychology and Education, 57*(9), 610–620.
Reid, H. L. (2011). *Athletics and philosophy in the ancient world: Contests of virtue.* Routledge.
Rosen, D. M. (2008). *Dope: A history of performance enhancement in sports from the nineteenth century to today.* Greenwood Publishing Group.
Savulescu, J., Foddy, B., & Clayton, M. (2004). Why we should allow performance enhancing drugs in sport. *British Journal of Sports Medicine, 38*(6), 666–670.
Seçkin, A. Ç., Ateş, B., & Seçkin, M. (2023). Review on wearable technology in sports: Concepts, challenges and opportunities. *Applied Sciences, 13*(18), 10399.
Shang, B. (2020). From Alan Turing to Ian McEwan: Artificial intelligence, lies and ethics in *Machines like me. Comparative Literature Studies, 57*(3), 443–453.
Simon, R. L., Torres, C. R., & Hager, P. F. (2014). *Fair play: The ethics of sport.* Westview Press.
Stoeber, J., & Otto, K. (2006). Positive conceptions of perfectionism: Approaches, evidence, challenges. *Personality and Social Psychology Review, 10*(4), 295–319.
Sun, Y. (2023). Post/human perfectibility and the technological other in Kazuo Ishiguro's *Klara and the Sun. Critique: Studies in Contemporary Fiction, 64*(3), 504–511.
Terentowicz-Fotyga, U. (2025). Do it yourself dystopia: The digital future in Dave Eggers's *The Every. Critique: Studies in Contemporary Fiction*, 6(2), 382–393.
Vallerand, R. J. (2007). Intrinsic and extrinsic motivation in sport and physical activity: A review and a look at the future. In G. Tenenbaum & R. C. Eklund (Eds.), *Handbook of sport psychology* (pp. 59–83). Wiley.
Vamplew, W. (2021). *Games people played: A global history of sport.* Reaktion Books.
Wallace, D. F. (2006). Federer as religious experience. *The New York Times.* https://www.nytimes.com/2006/08/20/sports/playmagazine/20federer.html
Wallace, D. F. (2012). *Both flesh and not: Essays.* Little, Brown and Company.
Weinberg, R. S., & Gould, D. (2019). *Foundations of sport and exercise psychology.* Human Kinetics.

Index

Note: 'n' denotes footnote numbers

FSC
www.fsc.org
MIX
Papier | Fördert
gute Waldnutzung
FSC® C083411

Kolibri 360 GmbH
Ferdinand-Jühlke-Straße 7
99095 Erfurt, Deutschland
produktsicherheit@kolibri360.de